HOME-BASED SERVICES
FOR CHILDREN
AND FAMILIES

Nat'l symposium on

HOME-BASED SERVICES
FOR CHILDREN
AND FAMILIES

Policy, Practice, and Research

Edited by

SHEILA MAYBANKS, M.S.W.

National Clearinghouse for Home-Based Service to Children
The University of Iowa
Iowa City, Iowa

and

MARVIN BRYCE, Ph.D.

National Clearinghouse for Home-Based Service to Children
The University of Iowa
Iowa City, Iowa

CHARLES C THOMAS • PUBLISHER
Springfield • Illinois • U.S.A.

Published and Distributed Throughout the World by
CHARLES C THOMAS • PUBLISHER
Bannerstone House
301-327 East Lawrence Avenue, Springfield, Illinois, U.S.A.

With THOMAS BOOKS *careful attention is given to all details of manufacturing and design. It is the Publisher's desire to present books that are satisfactory as to their physical qualities and artistic possibilities and appropriate for their particular use.* THOMAS BOOKS *will be true to those laws of quality that assure a good name and good will.*

Printed in the United States of America
V-OO-2

Library of Congress Cataloging in Publication Data

Maybanks, S. & Bryce, M.
National Symposium on Home-Based Services, 1st, University of Iowa, 1978.
Home-based services for children and families.

Sponsored by the National Clearinghouse for Home-Based Services to Children.
Bibliography: p.
Includes index.
1. Social work with children--United States--Congresses. 2. Youth services--United States--Congresses. I. Maybanks, Sheila. II. Bryce, Marvin. III. National Clearinghouse for Home-Based Services to Children. IV. Title.
HV741.N37   1978   362.7'1'0973   78-23598
ISBN 0-398-03880-5

CONTRIBUTORS

Marvin Bryce, Director, National Clearinghouse for Home-Based Services to Children, The University of Iowa, Iowa City, Iowa.

Patricia Cautley, Director, Project OPT, Division of Community Services, Wisconsin Department of Health and Social Services, Madison, Wisconsin.

Alice Collins, Lecturer, School of Social Work, Portland State University, Portland, Oregon.

James Dowd, Assistant Director, Family Life Center, Family Service Association, West Atlantic City, New Jersey.

Marylee Dunu, Team Leader, Lower East Side Family Union, New York, New York.

Judith Evans, Director, Parent-Infant Department, High/Scope Educational Research Foundation, Ypsilanti, Michigan.

Mary Ann Fahl, Social Service Supervisor, Home-Community Treatment, Mendota Mental Health Institute, Madison, Wisconsin.

Lawrence Gary, Director, Institute for Urban Affairs and Research, Howard University, Washington, D.C.

Ludwig Geismar, Professor, Social Work and Sociology, Director of Social Work Research Center, Rutgers University, New Brunswick, New Jersey.

David Gil, Professor, Florence Heller Graduate School for Advanced Studies in Social Welfare, Brandeis University, Waltham, Massachusetts.

Harriet Goldstein, Associate Director, Association for Jewish Children of Philadelphia, Philadelphia, Pennsylvania.

David Haapala, Director of Training, Homebuilders, Catholic Community Services, Tacoma, Washington.

Ray Hawkins, Consultant, Comprehensive Emergency Services, The Urban Observatory of Metropolitan Nashville, Nashville, Tennessee.

Gertrude Hoffman, Acting Branch Chief, Child and Family Services, Division of Program Development, Department of Health, Education and Welfare, Washington, D.C.

James Hyde, Jr., Director, Division of Preventive Medicine, Massa-

v

chusetts Department of Public Health, Boston, Massachusetts.

Betty Kaplan, Coordinator, Lay Health Visitor Program, University of Colorado Medical Center, Denver, Colorado.

Jill Kinney, Director, Homebuilders, Catholic Community Services, Tacoma, Washington.

Gratia Koch, Coordinator, FACT, Systems Unlimited, Iowa City, Iowa.

Theodore Levine, Executive Director, Youth Service, Inc., Philadelphia, Pennsylvania.

Dorothy Manrow, Counselor, FIND, Inland Counties Regional Center, San Bernardino, California.

Elizabeth McDaid, Director, Extension Services, Youth Service, Inc., Philadelphia, Pennsylvania.

Phyllis Moen, Department of Human Development and Family Studies, Cornell University, Ithaca, New York.

Marcia Moore, Assistant Program Manager, FIND, Inland Counties Regional Center, San Bernardino, California.

Donna Morrissey, Psychologist, Home-Community Treatment, Mendota Mental Health Institute, Madison, Wisconsin.

Abraham Morse, Administrator, Family Development Study, Children's Hospital, Boston, Massachusetts.

Eli Newberger, Assistant Professor, Pediatrics, Harvard Medical School, Children's Hospital, Boston, Massachusetts.

Ann O'Keefe, Home Start Program Director, Administration on Children, Youth and Families, Department of Health, Education and Welfare, Washington, D.C.

Robert Reed, Professor of Biostatistics, Harvard School of Public Health, Cambridge, Massachusetts.

LaVesta Reeves, Program Manager, FIND, Inland Counties Regional Center, San Bernardino, California.

Lou Roach, Home Training Consultant, Developmental Disabilities of Crawford County, Prairie du Chien, Wisconsin.

Michael Ryan, Director, FAMILIES, West Branch, Iowa.

David Shearer, Director, Portage Project, Portage, Wisconsin.

Edward Skarnulis, Assistant Professor, Department of Family Practice, University of Nebraska Medical Center, Omaha, Nebraska.

Richard Small, Doctoral Candidate, School of Social Work, University of Washington, Seattle, Washington.

Douglas Stephens, Supervisor, In-Home Family Service, Iowa Children and Family Services, Des Moines, Iowa.

William Theisen, Associate Professor, School of Social Work, University of Iowa, Iowa City, Iowa.

Ann Tuszynski, Director, Family Life Center, Family Service Association, West Atlantic City, New Jersey.

Joseph Weber, Graduate Research Assistant, Oklahoma State University, Stillwater, Oklahoma.

James Whittaker, Professor, School of Social Work, University of Washington, Seattle, Washington.

Marion Wilson, Director, Early Education, Ferguson-Florissant School, Ferguson, Missouri.

INTRODUCTION

THE National Clearinghouse for Home-Based Services to Children was established to facilitate interest, inquiry, and experimentation into home-based models of social, educational, and health services to children and their families. One major way in which the Clearinghouse accomplished these goals was the sponsoring of the National Symposium on Home-Based Services, held on April 24, 25, and 26, 1978.

The Symposium involved persons familiar with the social policies underlying the concept of home-based care, persons experienced in the design and delivery of such services, and researchers familiar with the potential and the problems of evaluating home-based programs. These persons, and many enthusiastic and committed participants, made the Symposium a truly exciting milestone in the development of home-based services.

This publication of the proceedings of the First National Symposium on Home-Based Services, *Home-Based Services for Children and Families: Policy, Practice, and Research,* will contribute much to what we know about the delivery of services to families in their own homes. This book is intended to provide theoretical background of sufficient depth to encourage broader public and professional support of home-based services. Because the book includes many descriptions of successful home-based programs, readers wishing to implement or improve similar programs in their own areas will find much helpful information and inspiration. The authors speak to the knotty questions of research and program evaluation, and they provide evidence of the efficacy and cost benefits of home-based care, thus giving direction to ongoing research needs.

The Clearinghouse staff edited the presentations, which stand as chapters, organized by categories of policy, practice, and research. These are artifical categories, to be sure, as there is much overlapping between program design and evaluation, and between underlying policy and program operation.

Remarks by Gertrude Hoffman, Division of Program Development, Department of Health, Education and Welfare serve as the introductory chapter to this volume. Ms. Hoffman provides the entire home-based service movement with a value orientation and a review of society's formal involvement with children and families. She calls for advocacy for families on the part of human service professionals.

While it assumes a clear position favoring home-based services, the chapter by Marvin Bryce, Director of the National Clearinghouse, is more than a polemic. It traces the history of social services to families and places in historical, economic, and theoretical perspectives the trend back to home-based care.

Section II, Policy, examines many of the assumptions regarding service delivery to families. More importantly, the authors in this section offer alternative approaches and interpretations which utilize family and community *strengths,* rather than emphasizing family limitations and family pathology. The range of issues dealt with in this section is great, including a critique of the economic system, an analysis of allocation of funding in home-based research, and a delineation of the principle of normalization. This section challenges us to rethink our values and our images of ourselves, of families, and of our professional roles.

Section III consists of nineteen program descriptions organized by social, education, and health services, and services for the developmentally disabled. As readers will note, these programs provide a great variety in scope and intensity. The concept of home-based care is broad enough and flexible enough to embrace a breadth of needs. Ideas and advice for the practitioner are here on such practical program considerations as staff training, building research into program design, using volunteers, locating funding, and enlisting community support.

The final section deals with evaluation of home-based social and educational service programs. Research outcomes on the efficacy and cost-effectiveness of home-based services have been positive and encouraging. Much remains to be done in the area of research, and if there is a central message in this section it is that clear communication between those who do research and those who provide service is a necessity.

The Clearinghouse staff is proud to assist in the publication of this useful volume. The contributors, coming from diverse backgrounds and disciplines, offer a range of styles, from informal to scholarly. The editors have attempted to retain these individual styles, convinced that differences contribute to greater utility.

The National Clearinghouse on Home-Based Services to Children is sponsored by the Institute of Child Behavior and Development, The University of Iowa School of Social Work, and FAMILIES of West Branch, Iowa. Support of the Clearinghouse and preparation of this volume is provided by Community Services Training Grant #84-P-09556/7-01, Social and Rehabilitative Service, of the Department of Health, Education and Welfare.

The Clearinghouse gratefully acknowledges the contribution of the persons whose works follow, and the support of Pauline Godwin, Stephen Clark, and Bernice Kennedy of the Department of Health, Education and Welfare.

S.M.
M.B.

CONTENTS

Page

Introduction ix

SECTION I: INTRODUCTION TO HOME-BASED SERVICES

Chapter
1. TURNING OURSELVES AROUND: A CHALLENGE TO THE
   PROFESSIONAL COMMUNITY — *Gertrude Hoffman* 5
2. HOME-BASED CARE: DEVELOPMENT AND RATIONALE —
   Marvin Bryce 13

SECTION II: POLICY

3. THE POLITICS OF RESEARCH FUNDING: WHO GETS IT,
   HOW, AND WHY? — *Lawrence Gary* 29
4. PARENTS' WAGES IN THE CONTEXT OF MEANINGFUL WORK
   AND ADEQUATE INCOME POLICIES — *David Gil* 40
5. SINGLE PARENT FAMILIES: IMPLICATIONS FOR
   SOCIAL POLICY — *Phyllis Moen* 51
6. SUPPORT, NOT SUPPLANT, THE NATURAL HOME:
   SERVING HANDICAPPED CHILDREN AND ADULTS —
   Edward Skarnulis 64
7. RESIDENTIAL GROUP CARE AND HOME-BASED CARE:
   TOWARD A CONTINUITY OF FAMILY SERVICES—
   Richard Small and James Whittaker 77

SECTION III: PRACTICE
NETWORKS

8. THE ESTABLISHMENT AND MAINTENANCE OF A FAMILY

xiii

Chapter   *Page*
DAY CARE NETWORK — *Alice Collins* 91
9. DEVELOPING COMPREHENSIVE EMERGENCY SERVICES —
   Ray Hawkins 103

EDUCATIONAL SERVICES

10. THE HIGH/SCOPE PARENT-TO-PARENT MODEL —
    Judith Evans 115
11. PARENTS AS EDUCATORS: THE PORTAGE
    PROJECT — *David Shearer* 125
12. FAMILY CENTERED UNIT FOR HELPING CHILDREN
    BECOME AWARE OF DEATH — *Joseph Weber* 136
13. HOME AND SCHOOL: PARTNERS IN LEARNING —
    Marion Wilson 145

SERVICES FOR THE DEVELOPMENTALLY DISABLED

14. HOME-BASED SUPPORT SERVICES: AN ALTERNATIVE TO
    RESIDENTIAL PLACEMENT FOR THE DEVELOPMENTALLY
    DISABLED — *Gratia Koch* 157
15. THE IMPACT OF HOME TRAINING CONSULTANTS ON THE
    LIVES OF DEVELOPMENTALLY DISABLED PERSONS AND
    THEIR FAMILIES: A STUDY OF HOME SERVICE IN
    RURAL AND URBAN WISCONSIN — *Lou Roach* 165

HEALTH SERVICES

16. FAMILY ADVOCACY: IMPLICATIONS FOR TREATMENT AND
    POLICY — *James Hyde, Jr., Abraham Morse,*
    Eli Newberger, and Robert Reed 177
17. PREVENTION OF ABNORMAL PARENTING PRACTICES WITH
    LAY HEALTH VISITORS — *Betty Kaplan* 186
18. FIND: A MODEL FOR HOME-BASED INTERVENTION FOR
    AT-RISK INFANTS — *LaVesta Reeves,*
    Marcia Moore, and Dorothy Manrow 194

Chapter   Page
                   SOCIAL SERVICES

19. THE LOWER EAST SIDE FAMILY UNION: ASSURING
    COMMUNITY SERVICES FOR MINORITY FAMILIES —
    Marylee Dunu 211
20. THE MENDOTA MODEL: HOME-COMMUNITY TREATMENT —
    Mary Ann Fahl and Donna Morrissey 225
21. THE EFFECTIVE USE OF VOLUNTEERS IN HOME-BASED
    CARE — Harriet Goldstein........................... 237
22. HOMEBUILDERS' APPROACH TO THE TRAINING OF
    IN-HOME THERAPISTS — David Haapala and
    Jill Kinney 248
23. SERVICES TO CHILDREN IN THEIR OWN HOMES:
    A FAMILY-BASED APPROACH — Theodore Levine and
    Elizabeth McDaid 160
24. FAMILIES PROGRAM DESIGN: GIVING FAMILIES
    RELEVANCE IN TREATMENT — Michael Ryan 272
25. IN-HOME FAMILY SUPPORT SERVICES: AN ECOLOGICAL
    SYSTEMS APPROACH — Douglas Stephens.............. 283
26. HOME-BASED SERVICES TO PROTECTIVE SERVICE
    FAMILIES — Ann Tuszynski and James Dowd......... 296

                SECTION IV: RESEARCH

27. RESEARCH OBJECTIVES OF IN-HOME INTERVENTION —
    Patricia Cautley 311
28. HOME-BASED CARE TO CHILDREN: HARMONIZING THE
    APPROACHES OF RESEARCH AND PRACTICE —
    Ludwig Geismar.................................... 325
29. HOME START WITHIN HEAD START —
    Ann O'Keefe 333
30. WARM BODIES AND COLD CASH: ESSENTIAL INGREDIENTS
    FOR HOME-BASED RESEARCH —
    William Theisen.................................... 343

    Index... 353

HOME-BASED SERVICES
FOR CHILDREN
AND FAMILIES

SECTION I
Introduction to
Home-Based Services

Chapter 1

TURNING OURSELVES AROUND: A CHALLENGE TO THE PROFESSIONAL COMMUNITY ON BEHALF OF CHILDREN AND FAMILIES

GERTRUDE HOFFMAN

THIS chapter will attempt to provide sub-
stance to an often reiterated statement, that of commitment to
the preservation of the family as the primary means of assuring
the healthy growth and development of children.

The Administration for Public Services is pleased to be col-
laborating in support of the National Clearinghouse for Home-
Based Services to Children and looks forward to the momentum
this project will provide to this Administration's long-range
plans to sustain and strengthen family life throughout the
country.

President Carter plans to convene a White House Conference
on Families in 1979, the main purpose of which is to examine
the strengths of American families, the difficulties they face,
and the ways in which family life is affected by public policies.
This public forum can offer an opportunity to exchange the
hollow rhetoric of the past for fundamental, dynamic, social
policies that support families as the primary caregivers to
children. This will be true only if all of us do our homework —
which will be discussed later.

Recently, Arabella Martinez, the Assistant Secretary for
Human Development Services, submitted preliminary proposals for our agency's 1980 budget. At that time, she stated
that legislative proposals in the Congress are pressing child
welfare programs to focus on the family and on in-home services to avoid the institutionalization of children, for foster care
to many children is often no more than that. The current

5

system, according to the Assistant Secretary, seems to neglect children in many ways: we permit some to languish their entire childhoods in an average of two to three foster homes; we do not prepare them either for return to their own homes or for adoption; and we do not prepare them for entry into adulthood. The system itself, she said, may be a social problem. The legislative directives, the Assistant Secretary concluded, clearly aim toward more family-oriented services in the child's own home.

For those of us on the firing line, no longer is it enough to deliver services geared to dealing solely with the problem of an individual child. We must begin to focus on *full* family living in the current cultural and social milieu.

Of course, we cannot turn the clock back and pretend to reestablish family life as it used to be. The traditional family, consisting of two parents who were legally married and who lived in a community with extended family members, with the mother at home providing care for the children, is no longer the only concept of "family." Today's public policies must reflect the changes in family life that have been evolving since the end of the Victorian era and particularly since the end of World War II. Our social, economic, and political policies *must* mirror the changing role of community and public supports geared to helping families maintain their primary care responsibilities.

Every vital society, in solving some of its problems, creates new ones. For example, new health measures have assured longer life; this blessing for some has been a bane for others, creating many of the current physical, social, and economic problems that face our aging population. The result is an increased need on the part of society to support, in numerous ways, the elderly and their families.

The increase in education for women, in the emancipation of women, in the mobility of families to pursue new and different job opportunities, in communications system — all have solved many problems for families; all offer increased chances for expanding opportunities. But, and it is a big "but," they have also created new problems — in carrying out childrearing responsibilities, in maintaining family ties, and in establishing roots and a sense of belonging.

The human organism does not change in its basic, common, human needs. Children born in 1978 have the same basic needs for love and nurture, for a sense of stability, self-esteem, and importance as those born in 1900. Meeting these basic needs, however, is the challenge we all face. Accepting nontraditional family constellations must also be faced. The changing roles of women and men are here to stay. Men and women now share in the production of income, in household tasks, in parenting and childrearing. The changing life-styles in families should not be seen as iniquities to wish away, but as challenges to us all — challenges to find ways to meet the needs of children and to help nontraditional families preserve the essential ingredients of stable family life.

Up to now, too much of our energy has been spent bewailing the divorce rate, births out of wedlock, single parent households, etc., with too little energy and too few resources expended on finding out more about the stresses on the family in the present day world that contribute to these conditions. What we need to do is examine families who *do* cope and who *are* successful, thereby gaining the knowledge and insights that can enable us to create new, sustaining mechanisms to help *all* families function better. Far more research and experimentation than are being carried out today are necessary if we are to uncover and provide these strengthening measures.

In our search for new measures, new services, and new delivery systems, care must be taken not to dispose of those that have proven effective. This book will discuss, on the positive side, such old "friends" as homemaker services, day care, emergency services, and the highlighting of training of competent personnel, with emphasis on increasing their quality and potency as well as availability. On the negative is, for example, the decrease in homemaker service as a child welfare support system for families in stress. The potential of this service for improvement of family life is great, yet some people say the cost of homemaker service is prohibitive as a child care sustaining program. Whatever that cost is, however, it cannot match the dollar cost of long-term institutional care, to say nothing about the cost in broken homes and spirits.

Another negative is in the area of day care services, which is certainly one of the most effective home-based services for children and families. Although such services have been around since 1854, only 10 percent of the children of working mothers have access to regulated day care services. Of these children, the most neglected are of school age. Many are ten to fourteen, the ages most vulnerable to social hazards.

Rising rates of births out of wedlock to ten- and twelve-year-olds and of alcoholism and drug abuse among children of these ages support the need for a hard appraisal of child care resources for the children of working parents and of the need to reassess this country's work ethic. For example, the *Washington Post* recently carried a series of articles on the increased requests from parents in upper-middle-class families for the courts to take custody of their young adolescent and preteenage children. In each case, the mother was employed.

When day care is provided, too often it is not the kind that offers the stability that grows out of a continuum of care. Now, if we accept the premise that day care is a supplement to family care, then the child's relationship to the caregiver must serve as the key to quality care. Thus, we must find ways to achieve and maintain ongoing, long-term, nurturing day care for children.

Today, hundreds of thousands of children, from infants to adolescents, live away from their families in foster homes, group homes, and large institutions. Some are in such care under the auspices of child welfare services; some, under juvenile systems; and some, under mental health and mental retardation systems. Far too many of these children are in out-of-home care because of society's failure to work with families to prevent their placement.

In the past, a family began to receive services only when one or more family members could no longer cope with his or her problems. Under these circumstances, child welfare services encouraged placement of the children. Today, this need not be the case: the dysfunctioning of a family can often be avoided or minimized if comprehensive services within the community are provided to the family in the home.

To this end, the Department of Health, Education and Welfare has myriad proposals and shifts in program emphasis to support home-based service programs. Head Start, parent-child development centers, youth programs, services to the handicapped — all are geared toward full family functioning. In addition, training for better parenting, which is an increasing concern of educators as well as of health and welfare officials, is reflected in the Department's recent legislative and fiscal efforts.

HEW's Office of Human Development Services, the agency responsible for social and rehabilitative services to children, youth, families, the aging, the handicapped, and Native Americans, is designing major changes in most of its programs. The agency, for instance, envisions comprehensive services delivered to whole families from a single source.

Also in the plans are the provision of services to prevent the placement of youths in inappropriate institutions and the development of centers for programs that will offer services for the specific problems of young people. Youth, instead of being seen as a problem that will not go away, will be prized as a national resource that needs positive outlets for its skills and energies.

For some years, the area of preventive youth services has been largely neglected. Therefore, the agency's first initiative will be to give priority to the establishment of a planning and advocacy capability in urban areas and in community agencies concerned with the problems of young people.

Currently, the Children's Bureau of the Office of Human Development Services has seven projects dealing with preventive services. These projects focus on reaching families at risk before a decision is made to place the children. Because of the strong research component in these projects, some new directions for child welfare services are expected in three years. In addition, the Bureau, now responsible for the Section 426 training grants, has set as its priority for these grants the reduction of family breakdown and the provision of supports to prevent the separation of parents and children.

The Administration for Public Services has four projects to enhance home-based services. One is the development of a statement that will increase understanding of the effects of public policies on families. Two projects, designed to provide temporary residential living arrangements for mothers and their small children, seek to increase the mothers' parenting capabilities. The fourth, designed by American Indians for Indians, will develop day care services and teach parenting skills.

At this time, the Office of Human Development Services does not intend to redirect or change Title XX. While this is largely a state-directed program, designed to give flexibility to states and to be responsive to state and local needs, the Assistant Secretary believes more time should be given to the three-year-old program before major changes in or more federal direction related to the program take place. Therefore, although the federal government does not intend to redirect Title XX as of this time, states *can* change their state plans to assure that more home-based services are provided to the very large number of recipients of Title XX services. As professionals and as citizens of our own states, we need to seek change in the Title XX administration so that more home-based services are provided to prevent family breakdown. We must also plant "the mustard seed" for change in state policies.

Services to handicapped children and their families are of serious concern, especially since it is often in desperation that the institutionalization of these children takes place. It is because of the great dearth of home-based services that these children are deprived of families who could meet their basic needs.

Recently, the author talked with a researcher who had completed a two-year study in the United Kingdom on the implications of the rising expenditures for institutional care of children, youth, and the aged. The hypothesis posed was that modern families did not choose to care for their own family members, preferring the State to shoulder the responsibility. At the completion of the research project, the findings and conclusions were unequivocal: modern families *do* want to care for their own families. Without extended families, with mothers working, with the economic factors involved, etc., they cannot find the means to do so, and it is with great sadness that they relinquish their responsibilities. The project also showed that all of the Western democracies, and particularly the industrial nations, were willing to pay for and assume responsibility for institutionalized or out-of-home care. Precious little, in comparison, was expended on home-based supports, in spite of the relative cost-effectiveness of home-based programs.

Our approach to the problem of our times has been fragmented and of the "band aid" variety. At best, our current efforts can be described as small. True, the task is nearly overwhelming, but somehow, in some way, we must turn ourselves around from our parochial way of operating.

Professionals must take the lead. We need to find more effective ways to associate with and influence the policy makers. As long as providers of services remain isolated from those who establish public social policy, we will continue to construct barriers to accomplishing major change. Social policy making must rise from the bottom to the top. Thus, across the length and breadth of the country, voluntary agencies, organizations, individuals, and groups need to develop a dialogue; on the eternal and unchallenged importance of the family to a child. This dialogue must articulate the benefits our nation will realize from the preservation and appreciation of all our children.

The inherent integrity of the family as the primary care system must be at the core of any kind of social policy development, and there must be built-in safeguards against harm to that system. That we are dangerously close to aiding in the destruction of family life, because of archaic ideas about family responsibility, individual ability to be self-sustaining, and family relationships, gives rise to the question: How do we strike down the barriers to comprehensive service delivery where and when they are needed?

Conferences with emphasis on facilitating interest, inquiry, and experimentation into home-based social, health, and educational services to children and their families, where the child's home is the primary service setting, are one important means of finding ways to coordinate services. The array and variety of home-based programs described in this volume indicate the depth of concern and the knowledge abroad in the land.

We know so much better than we do. How then do we translate the knowledge and conviction into social policy which will support all families and all communities? The only answer this author has was offered before: increasing the dialogue among people.

Much more needs to be done in disseminating knowledge and materials, and the effort of the Clearinghouse at The University of Iowa is a major thrust in doing just that.

The majority of people share the belief that childhood is the time for building for the future, that nothing takes the place in our lives of the oldest institution known to man: the family. In the life of each of us, to touch home base is a recurring necessity. Only the times have changed. For a child, a home base with firm roots still provides the cornerstone from which that child can go forth with the inner strengths necessary to cope with the outside world. To help guarantee these strengths for all children, we must somehow pursue a policy that will compel this country to offer universal services that will sustain and undergird all families.

In closing, I want to paraphrase a vignette written by Emily Kimbrough which illustrates graphically the most important need of a child:

A family took their four-year-old to the circus for the first time. In the middle of the show, with the elephants trumpeting, the lions roaring, the band playing, and all the rings swirling, the boy was sitting on the edge of his seat, hands clasped, eyes flashing from left to right and sparkling with excitement. Suddenly he leaned over and whispered in his mother's ear, "Mummie, sing 'Three Blind Mice'." His mother put her lips to his ear and sang "Three Blind Mice." He returned to the edge of his seat and again entered the great, big, wonderful world of the circus. He had touched home base; his sense of trust had been renewed — and he could now take another step out and up.

We all need to renew with fervor our commitment to a family and to a home base for all children.

Chapter 2

HOME-BASED CARE:
DEVELOPMENT AND RATIONALE

MARVIN BRYCE

THE lag in the evolvement of home-based social, health, and educational services for children and their families has many ramifications. It may be understood from several perspectives: political, economic, social, historical, and professional. As Queen points out, such authorities as Dewey, Small, and Marshall long ago proved the impossibility of dealing with one social problem without affecting many phases of the common life.[1] The purpose of this introduction is not to treat these various influences on family and child welfare services in this country, although that would be a worthwhile task. The intent here is to place the development of home-based care in historical perspective and review the factors which cannot be ignored by those who are interested in the general welfare of children and families.

Historical Perspective

DeToqueville, the French traveler who made so many observations about American life, noted 150 years ago that Americans were placing unusual emphasis on the creation of institutions as a method of managing social problems. He was aware that Americans expect institutions to rehabilitate residents of all ages and circumstances.[2] William Hammond, a neurologist, insisted in 1879 that the effects of institutional living on most patients were detrimental and that "The violent rupture of social and family ties is especially injurious."[3] Rothman suggests that the penitentiary, asylums for the insane, orphanages, and reformatories for delinquents were widely utilized before 1900 as a tool for social control. Punishment and

13

cure were thought to be related. He points out that the institution did not fulfill either the modest or the grandiose hopes of the founders; yet, today we still live with many of these institutions, accepting their existence as inevitable:

> Despite a personal revulsion, we think of them as always having been with us, and therefore as always to be with us. We tend to forget that they were the invention of one generation to serve very special needs, not the only possible reaction to social problems. In fact, since the progressive era, we have been gradually escaping from institutional responses, and one can foresee the period when incarceration will be used still more rarely than it is today.[2]

Indeed, institutions have contributed greatly to the needs of the blind, the deaf, the retarded, delinquent, and disturbed. The residential institution has been the only developed alternative to many families. We imported the concept of the residential institution from abroad and made it a big business, true to the American way. According to one estimate, the involuntary institutional care industry alone may approach a cost of 50 billion dollars.[4]

As early as 1850, an increasing number of Americans began to doubt the wisdom of bringing large numbers of children together in institutions; yet, in 1909, when the entire population was only 92 million, 100,000 children were in institutions.[1] In that year, the White House Conference on Children and Youth took the position that "Home life is the highest and finest product of civilization . . . Children should not be deprived of it except for urgent and compelling reasons."[5] In 1941, the Child Welfare League of America restated this position and emphasized the value of having children remain in their own homes if at all possible. The League expanded on the damaging effects of separation: "Every child who must leave his own family suffers profound emotional and social disturbance which can never be altogether compensated."[6] Two decades later, Turitz addressed the continued delay in the development of home-based services. She wrote:

> We cannot substitute platitudes about strengthening family life, preventing delinquency, or promoting mental health, for

action. It is not enough to utter pious sentiments about our obligation to maintain children in their own homes, if those serve only to ease our conscience and relieve us of responsibility to do anything further.[7]

Turitz appealed to us to "free ourselves of traditional approaches and existing patterns of community and agency structure." Meanwhile, foster care placements have mushroomed and institutions now house 300,000 more children than in 1910. The increase in institutional placements has outstripped population growth by a margin of two to one.

Economic Perspective

Kahn has observed that in-home services can be provided at less financial and human cost than out-of-home care.[8] The cost of intensive in-home care appears to be less than half that of institutional care, about twice that of foster care, and about the same as group care. The cost varies depending on intensity of service and geographical location. In Iowa, the cost of institutional care for a child approaches 20,000 dollars annually. This does not include much of the administrative overhead costs or the approximately 8,000 dollar capital investment per child in residence. Foster care is also more costly than reported figures suggest, since administrative costs are not included in the reported data.

The cost for one year of in-home service provided by the more intensive programs ranges from 5,000 to 17,000 dollars. Data from Cotter and Ferleger indicates that a family in New York City can receive comprehensive home-based services for 17,000 dollars a year, which is considerably less than the average annual cost for substitute care in that state.[9] Two intensive home-based programs in Iowa report annual costs of 4,000 and 9,000 dollars per family (Iowa Children's and Family Services, Des Moines, and FAMILIES, West Branch). Homebuilders of Tacoma, another intensive home-based program, reports a cost of 2,507 dollars per client family less than substitute care in Washington.[10]

Substitute care in the United States has been reported to

range from a low of 780 dollars for a child in foster care in New Mexico to more than 50,000 dollars for a child in a secure detention center or a treatment facility for emotionally disturbed. Using these funds to provide special services to a family in its own home seems far more reasonable. Recent legislation, especially Title XX and the more recent HR 7200 effort, favors home-based care. The bill HR 7200 is an attempt to mandate home-based placement prevention services.

Theoretical Perspective

The reasons most often given for placement reflect our cultural and professional predisposition. A few of the more familiar ones are listed here, along with a counter rationale for each:

1. Separation of the youngster from a detrimental peer group: but institutions are not famous for their positive peer models.
2. Protection of the placed family member from a dysfunctional family system: but usually little is done to alter the family system, and the child is returned to, or kept out of, the family permanently. Other children in the family often take their turns for placement as they grow up.
3. Some children are placed to take advantage of special education resources in institutions: but recent legislation requires school systems to make provision for education of all children in some way.
4. A growing number of youngsters are placed for several weeks on "guest status" or for evaluation only: this action is most often taken by courts or clinicians who do not know what else to do. In most instances, there have already been numerous evaluations. Also, observations of a child's behavior outside their familiar habitat may not be valid beyond that setting.
5. The subjection of one family member to treatment by a group of professionals: but children treated outside their natural environment present serious prognostic problems.
6. Protection of the community from destructive behavior:

but the youngster will be returning to the community.

There are other, more subtle, reasons why so many children are placed away from home. Workers underestimate the family's capacity and tend to identify with the child. Motivated by good intentions, social workers, judges, clinicians, and others try to rescue the child, believing they do him or her a service by removal from the home. Some conditions witnessed by human services personnel encourage rescue. Placement as an attempt to avoid pain or treat for a "cure" is not the first line of defense. Teaching survival and demonstrating caring through investment in the family should come first. It has been demonstrated that placement occurs despite the belief that the placement system is inadequate and even harmful.[11]

Habit is not to be taken lightly as a reason for proceeding in a fixed manner. There is an old saying that we are more comfortable with the devil we know than the devil we do not know. We do what we know how to do best.

> Paradoxically, our most highly developed child welfare services are those provided at the point of complete family breakdown, where separation of the child from his family must take place, and where emotional crippling of the child has already occurred. The distinctive skills in child welfare are those developed in the *placement* of children; and the distinctive body of knowledge is that pertaining to *separation* of the child from his family.[7]

Workers are more inclined to place when the parents request placement. A request for placement may be the parent's way of asking for help, an expression of grave concern, a wish to be relieved of responsibility, a release of guilt, or the conveyance of any number of other possible messages. Even if the request is an expression of the parent's desire to discontinue the role of parenting at that point in time, it would still seem that everything possible should be done to avoid placement.

The shortage of professionals who know how to work with families in the home, and who are willing to work the hours involved and in the conditions often present, encourages placement. Schools of social work, public health nursing, and early childhood education programs need to review their curricula in this area. A well-integrated body of knowledge, theory, and practice skills is needed for the development of curriculum in home-based care.

The common practice of child placement has serious economic and political ramifications. Who would be bold enough to invest 40,000 or 20,000 dollars a year in a family of five, arranging for decent housing, medical and dental care, transportation, a psychiatrist, food and clothing, recreation — anything needed. We do not hesitate to spend that much on a single institutionalized family member. Who gets the money is indeed an important factor in determining who gets service, where the service is provided, and the nature of the service.

It is a curious phenomenon that we have continued decade after decade to place a large number of children in institutions when we have so little systematic research to support the effectiveness of the institutional method. As recently as one year ago, the Office of Child Development noted:

> A major criterion for determining the quality or effectiveness of the institutional experience has been the incidence of discharge from the institution. If a child is released and returns to the community, it is generally assumed that the institutional experience was effective. Thus, meeting of standards and discharge from the institution have comprised the major research thrusts.[12]

In recent years there has been evidence of the high psychological, social, and economic costs of placement. Spitz, Bowlby, and others have addressed the practice of placement of very young children and raised serious questions about institutional care.[13] Rosenham, Goffman, and Hobbs are included among those who have documented the negative effects of separation and institutionalization of both children and adults.[14,15,16]

The failure of foster care as it has been used has been substantially documented. Geiser has outlined reasons for foster placements. It appears that most placements could be avoided;[17] as one group of authors states, "We know that the relative use of institutions and foster homes in different communities has more to do with historical accident that with the needs of children."[18] Recent research on home-based programs designed to reduce placement show dramatic results, [7,19,20] yet there has been minimal development of those placement prevention programs.

Rationale for Home-Based Care

When viewed from a health and preventive frame of reference, rather than a deviant or pathological one, home-based care refers to all those supportive and supplemental services to a family in or near the family home. Such services are, or may be, found in that network of established, sanctioned institutions, such as the educational and legal systems, health and welfare systems, political and industrial institutions, and religious and recreational complexes. In addition, the informal services of volunteers and neighbors are included. Special services should be offered as a matter of course to children and their families, in keeping with the recognition that the family is the primary social institution and our nation's most valuable natural resource. We seem to become aware of this only after the family has made it known that it is in serious trouble. It has been repeatedly demonstrated that emergency use of out-of-home care is likely to lead to long-term or permanent family breakup. The Comprehensive Emergency Service program in Nashville is an outstanding example of service to prevent such breakups; still, the need for home helps as a family and child welfare preventive measure has not been sufficiently developed in America. The homemaker working with families and children becomes a symbol of dependency, neglect, poverty, and disorganization and her assistance is not seen as a right similar to medical and nursing care. In fact, the bulk of homemaker service is now being channeled to the medical patient.[8]

In America, the tendency is to withhold services until someone in the family, through some type of coping behavior manifested outside the family system, asks for help and is then defined as a patient, client, probationer, or special student. A definition of home-based care must take into account this unpleasant reality. A functional definition, external to the family and that may encompass the participating public, will define the family and not just the child as the service unit. In addition, the characteristics of the service delivery method must be included in the definition of home-based care. The following are characteristics of home-based care programs which have been developed in the past decade:

1. Home-based care is provided primarily in the home.
2. The parents remain in charge and are counted on to participate.
3. The family system and natural habitat are utilized and the family is related to as a unit.
4. The program will help, or arrange for help, with any problem area presented by the family or observed to be a problem by the service providers.
5. The program makes a commitment of contractual substance to the family. Some home-based health and educational programs with a primary prevention or developmental emphasis are less intense in nature.
6. Extensive use is made of the natural resources of extended family, neighborhood, and the community.

At this early period in the development of in-home care, the service extended to the family has most likely been previously available outside the family setting.

The Family as Service Unit

We have long given lip service to the influence of the family on the development and shaping of behavioral patterns of individuals and to the importance of working with individuals. We know it is essential to focus on the family as the service unit, but practical application of this knowledge has been hampered by a number of factors. Professional social work was born at a time when medicine was concerned with newly discovered internal organisms. Psychoanalytic thought was preoccupied with internal psyche. The pattern of the religious confessional had long been with us. Jane Addams was forgotten in our search for identity as a profession. It was left to John Dewey and his disciples in education to stress the importance of the relationship between the internal and the external. There is evidence that Jane Addams influenced Dewey, but the Depression and World War II were the major factors which helped professional social work begin to view the individual in context of the whole environment. The problem, however, remained of how to implement in practice what was accepted in theory. In 1959, Spiegel and Bell could still write: "In the context of the habitual lip-service (theory) paid to the importance of family as a whole, isolated groups or individuals have attempted to maintain a focus on family in formulations and treatment procedures, but attempts to bring the family to the forefront have not been established."[21]

Fifteen years later, Minuchin, a leading authority on work with families, notes:

> The importance of the individual's context is recognized, but there has been a curious dearth of therapeutic attempts to modify that context. This is particularly striking in the case of children who can be assumed to be deeply involved with some form of family group . . . . the general therapeutic response has been to separate him from those influences, either by individual psychotherapy, or by behavioral therapy, or "parentectomy."[23]

Bell, Satir, Jackson, Ackerman, Bowen, and a host of others have urged and directed the reorientation from the individual to the family system. However, their focus has been limited primarily to family interaction and work in the hospital or office. The foster home syndrome and institutional experience attest to the futility of trying to work with youngsters removed from their natural habitat. Hobbs notes that the most functional definition of an emotionally disturbed child "requires attention to both individual and social variables, with extensive weighing to the latter."[19]

To use the description of a group of family researchers writing about the family as the unit of service, the home-based approach truly "recognizes the family (and natural community) as an arena or school for life and interpersonal relationships."[23] One psychiatrist notes that as the family becomes the center of the service delivery system, it is more difficult to maintain the usual (and perhaps unnecessary) distinctions between preventive measures, acute care, after care, and training.[24] These distinctions have nothing to do with family needs and serve only to help the service agency set priorities. Essentially, psychiatry continues to exclude the child from his family and vice versa, polarizing adult and child in practice; yet, few in any discipline will deny the importance and soundness of giving greater attention to persons in their natural context. The home-based programs developed during the last decade give priority to this concept.

In addition to these primary arguments for home-based care, there are other advantages. For instance, entry and reentry problems are eliminated. Opportunities abound for modeling, teaching, nurturing, and directing. In fact, a major advantage is the opportunity to work on the family's own turf, on anything presented as a problem. One social worker notes that "the nonverbal communication packed into a one-hour session seems to telescope weeks or even months of effort in a private office."[25] Working with families in their homes conveys far more regard for the family's integrity, honor, and rights than placement of one of its members.

Lessons From Other Nations

Other developed nations have universal, publicly financed, social and health service systems. These benefits provide a family policy framework in which the well-being of children and their families is given high priority. As a result, there is no need for special programs to intervene in situations of child abuse and neglect. Statistics show that a high standard of living has not been sacrificed in order to provide universal services.

Among the benefits to French children and families are paid maternity benefits, maternal and child health programs, single wage earners allowances, and special cash benefits for low-income parents to pay for day care. Also provided are comprehensive and universal preschool services for children aged three and older. These services have not affected the birth rate.

Canada, France, and Germany all maintain high levels of

personal income but provide health care coverage for virtually all their people. This contrasts with the United States, which provides health care services for only 10 percent of its population.

In the United Kingdom, health visitors, who are registered nurses with special training, visit every newborn infant at least once. Sweden employs 1 percent of its population as home helpers; mail carriers are trained and subsidized to provide special assistance to isolated families. Clients of these services are referred to as *customers*. Begun in 1920 by the Red Cross, the home-helps services have been administered and financed by the Swedish government.

The various supportive and supplemental health, educational, and social services provide for continuity of care beginning before birth. It is no accident that these countries do not separate families in order to provide services as often as we do in the United States.

Summary and Discussion

Houghton writes that the Victorian home was a peaceful, sacred place. Even for agnostics, the home was a temple. Within the family, one learned the sentiments of attachment, comradeship, reverence for others, and love. Recalling John Stuart Mill, Houghton describes the family as the foundation for the religion of humanity.[26]

It is not unusual today to hear or read about the decline of the family as an institution; the family in crisis; or the changes brought about by the industrial revolution, the depression, or government intervention. The family as an institution is not weak or fragile as some suggest. What is often mistaken for family decadence is nothing more than efforts to cope and to adapt to a changing society. The functions of reproduction, childrearing, and people-making prosper. The continuity of the human race seems assured. Perhaps these concerns are nothing more than increased awareness of what family life is all about. The Spring 1977 *Daedalus*, in an entire issue devoted to the family, states that serious and substantial inquiry into the family is of relatively recent origins. It now involves numerous academic disciplines and professions and is the center of many political debates. Demythologizing the family is only in its earliest state. We are among those privileged to participate in this exciting process.

Family members and community people could be used more in strengthening and supporting family life. Use of foster grandparents and senior citizens as special friends and helpers to young parents, as demonstrated by the Barrio Comprehensive Child Care Center in San Antonio, is an example. This task could be facilitated by shifting our focus from treatment, which implies a professional "cure," to coping or managing, which is an ongoing process.

The home-based approach must be committed to a principle of making the first and greatest resource investment in caring for children and their families within their own homes before more radical substitute care approaches are used. For this to become a matter of general practice, social policy makers must focus on policy as it affects the family. A new approach to funding is required which accepts the family as the basic unit of service. Policy designed to serve the individual, the provider institutions, special interest groups, and the politician, does not necessarily benefit families. Rather, such policies encourage those institutions intended to serve the family to become antithetical to families and family life. The public then becomes wary of utilizing those institutions, and parents are often disenfranchised and overwhelmed. We must then ask: Do health, educational, and social institutions exist for the benefit and perpetuation of the institutions? Are they primarily self-serving and are families and individuals alike servants of the institutions?

The time has come for a closer look at the impact of social policy on our basic institution, the family. It is not enough to excuse the fact that we have no family social policy in the United States on the basis that it might lead to too much government intervention and invasion of privacy. All government policy affects family life; it is more a question of whether we will have family policy by drift or by design. Without a

planned national family policy it is unlikely that we will progress beyond the present minimal approach to home-based care
for children and families. It is our hope that the First National
Symposium on Home-Based Services will contribute measur-
ably to the continued growth and promotion of home-based
social, health, and educational services.

REFERENCES

1. Queen, Stuart: *Social Work in the Light of History.* Philadelphia,
   Lippincott, 1972.
2. Rothman, David: *The Discovery of the Asylum: Social Order and
   Disorder in the New Republic.* Boston, Little, 1971.
3. Hammond, William: *The Non-Asylum Treatment of the Insane.* New
   York, Putnam, 1879.
4. *Child Protection Report,* 26 September 1977.
5. U. S. Senate. 60th Congress, 2nd Session: *Proceedings of the Conference
   on the Care of Dependent Children.* Sen. Document No. 721, 1909.
6. Burt, Marvin and Balyeat, Ralph: A new system to improving the care of
   neglected and abused children. *Child Welfare, 53:*167-179, 1974.
7. Turitz, Zitha: Obstacles to services for children in their own homes. *Child
   Welfare, 40:*1-6, 27, 1961.
8. Kahn, Alfred and Kamerman, Sheila: *Not for the Poor Alone.*
   Philadelphia, Temple Pr, 1975.
9. Ferleger, Beatrice and Cotter, Mary (Eds.): *Children, Families and Foster
   Care.* New York, Community Council of New York, 1976.
10. Kinney, Jill; Madren, Barbara; Fleming, Thomas; and Haapala, David:
    Homebuilders: keeping families together. *J Consult Clin Psychol,
    45:*667-673, 1977.
11. Shapiro, Deborah: *Agencies and Foster Children.* New York, Columbia U
    Pr, 1976.
12. U. S. Department of Health, Education, and Welfare. Office of Child
    Development: *Statement of Priorities for Research and Demonstration
    Activities in the Area of Children At Risk and the Child Welfare
    System.* Washington, Government Printing Office, 1976, pp. 1-2.
13. Spitz, Rene: *The First Year of Life.* New York, World Health, 1952.
14. Rosenham, David: On being sane in insane places. *Science, 179:*150-158,
    1973.
15. Goffman, Erving: *Asylums.* New York, Doubleday, 1961.
16. Hobbs, Nicholas: *The Future of Children: Categories, Labels, and Their
    Consequences.* San Francisco, Jossey-Bass, 1975.
17. Geiser, Robert: *The Illusion of Caring.* Boston, Beacon Pr, 1973.
18. Shyne, Anne; Sherman, Edmund; and Phillips, Michael: Filling the gap

in child welfare research: services for children in their own homes. *Child Welfare, 51*:562-573, 1972.

19. Jones, Mary Ann: *A Second Chance for Families.* New York, Child Welfare, 1976.

20. Goldstein, Harriet: Providing services to children in their own homes: an approach that can reduce foster placement. *Children Today, 2*:2-7, 1973.

21. Spiegel, John and Bell, Norman: The family of the psychiatric patient. In Arieti, Silvano (Ed.): *American Handbook of Psychiatry, I.* New York, Basic, 1959.

22. Minuchin, Salvador: A conceptual model of psychosomatic illness in children. *Arch Gen Psychiatry, 32*:1032, 1974.

23. Bates, Josephine, et al.: *Family as a Unit of Study and Treatment.* Seattle, Regional Rehabilitation Research Institute, 1969.

24. Spiegel, John: The family: The channel of primary care. *Hosp Community Psychiatry, 25*:787, 1974.

25. Schlater, Ray: Home counseling of adolescents and parents. *Social Work, 20*:428, 1975.

26. Houghton, Walter: *The Victorian Frame of Mind.* New Haven, Yale Pr, 1957.

SECTION II
Policy

Chapter 3

THE POLITICS OF RESEARCH FUNDING: WHO GETS IT, HOW, AND WHY?

Lawrence Gary

Introduction

IN order to narrow the focus of this section, some definitions of politics, research, and family are necessary. Let us accept Amidei and Ooms' definition of *family*, which is, "A family is any group of persons with a legal or biological relationship."[1] This definition has serious limitations, but it is adequate for the purpose of this chapter. Applying this meaning, one can imagine the range of programs and issues which impact on the family.

Research is basically a systematic process of seeking answers to problems. Hence, family research is concerned with seeking answers to problems confronting families. The book *Politics, Who Gets What, When and How,*[2] provides a perspective for relating politics to research. In any meaningful definition of *politics,* the elements of conflict, power, and policy are crucial. In reviewing the concept of politics, Theodorson and Theodorson state: "Politics is the process of creating public policy through influencing or controlling the sources of power and authority. The process involves competition and usually conflict."[3] In other words, there is a struggle over values and claims to a perceived scarcity of resources, in this case, funds to support a given strategy for solving a particular problem.

There are many actors and agencies which have an interest in the family and they are very much in competition and in conflict. The following objectives should help to further limit this

29

presentation. The relative significance of family research and services as a major industry will be documented, and the structure of the funding process in one major government agency will be discussed and analyzed.

Research as a Major Industry

In 1977, the federal government supported 53 percent of the 40.8 billion dollar research and development (R and D) effort of the United States, although two-thirds of this support was for defense and space programs. It should be noted that when the expenditures for R and D are analyzed, 68 percent went to industry, 16 percent to the federal government, 10 percent to universities and colleges, and 6 percent to other nonprofit institutions and federally funded research and development centers administered by universities and colleges.[4]

Although all of the federal agencies do not submit program data on R and D efforts according to area of science, we do have some estimates on the amount of federal funds spent on social science research. This information is important, since much of the family research is conducted by social and behavioral scientists. In 1966, it was estimated that 356 million dollars was spent by the federal government on social sciences, representing a significant increase from 166 million dollars in 1966. Moreover, in this ten-year period, the social science share of all federal support had risen from 3.1 percent to 4.3 percent. During the 1966-1976 decade, the average annual growth rate for federally funded social research was 7.9 percent. While federal support for social science research has increased, it is rising at a slower rate. Contrary to what is thought, universities and colleges did not get most of the federal funds for social science research. In 1976, they received only 27 percent of the social science research sponsored by federal agencies.[5]

Family Research and Services

Federal support for social science research varies according to the discipline and the agency. Also, federal family programs are scattered throughout the government. In a preliminary review of federal programs which involve families, Amidei and Ooms identified 178 programs from fifteen federal departments and administrations, less than half of them found in the Department of Health, Education and Welfare,[1] with a combined 1976 budget of 100 million dollars (see Table 3-I). In another analysis of child and maternal health programs sponsored by the federal government, 106 such programs was identified. It concluded:

TABLE 3-I

NUMBER OF FEDERAL PROGRAMS
WHICH HAVE DIRECT IMPACT ON FAMILIES — 1976

	No. of Programs	Family Mentioned in Objectives in Catalog	Over $100M For Fiscal Year 1976
DHEW	129	19	24
Health	(27)	(5)	(5)
Education	(67)	(3)	(7)
Welfare	(27)	(7)	(9)
Office of Secretary	(8)	(4)	(3)
Veterans Administration	29	-	14
Housing and Urban Development	25	18	7
Department of Labor	21	1	5
Department of Agriculture	19	6	7
Department of Justice	15	-	2
Department of Interior/Bureau of Indian Affairs	13	2	1
ACTION	9	-	-
Civil Service Commission	6	-	-
Community Services Administration	6	2	1
Department of Treasury	1	-	-
Department of Transportation	1	-	-
Railway Retirement Board	1	7	1
President's Commission on Employment of Handicapped	1	-	-
National Labor Relations Board	1	-	-
Total	278	49	64

Note: Several departments were omitted, including Departments of State and Commerce, Environmental Protection Agency, Energy Research and Development Administration, Postal Service, Customs, and various regulatory agencies.

Source: Nancy Amidei and Theodora Ooms: *Inventory of Federal Programs.* Washington, George Washington University, 1977, p. 3.

32   *Home-Based Services for Children and Families*

These (programs) are found within five distinct executive departments. Within these departments, the programs are scattered over 15 agencies, 45 offices, bureaus or institutes . . . These 106 programs expend at least 32 billion dollars a year of which only 2.2 billion are specifically involved in actual health services for children and their mothers. The 106 programs are based on 58 pieces of legislation. These pieces of legislation have passed through almost 30 congressional committees and subcommittees.[6]

With such diversity and range of programs, one can get the impression that there is no public family policy,[7] and that there are massive overlaps, lack of coordination, and perhaps resistance to change on the part of the federal government in dealing with child and family activities. The data in Table 3-I suggest that monetary resources are substantial for family-related projects. In this chapter we are concerned with the ways in which these federal funds are distributed and allocated for family research.

Because the Department of Health, Education and Welfare is the major resource for family research and service projects, we will limit our remarks to one agency within it, the National Institute of Mental Health (NIMH).

According to the most recent data, NIMH has increased its total resources spent for children and youth (the family) from 9.2 percent of the 1970 budget to 17.1 percent of the 1976 budget.[6] This increase is significant, given the assaults on the agency during the Nixon and Ford administrations.[8] However, the Carter Administration has shown interest in both mental health and family issues. Out of the budget of 418.6 million dollars, only 71.9 million, or 17.1 percent of the total budget, was spent on child and family mental health. It should be noted that of the 74.7 million dollars spent by NIMH for extramural research, 21 million, or 28.1 percent of the total, was spent for child mental health. This, however, was only 4.8 percent of the NIMH budget. Also, the same amount of funds, 20.1 million dollars, was spent for training and child mental health. Again, the data point to the fact that there are significant research services and training funds for family projects.

Funding Process

In general, the major elements in the research funding process for NIMH include the administrator, the review committee, and the principal investigators. Each element makes important decisions which are distinctly related to the politics of funding family research.

Although many NIMH administrators will say they have little influence over policy, program, or who gets grants, this is not the case. In fact, the administrators write up program statements, prepare forward plans, solicit proposals, give technical assistance, recommend people for review committees, and have personal and professional relationships with committee members. These administrators represent a range of academic disciplines and specialized skills. We have identified twenty-four top NIMH administrators who had significant influence over the funding of research projects in 1976. Of these, five or 20.8 percent were females, and nineteen or 79.1 percent were males. So far, only two minorities have been identified — one black and one Spanish-surnamed male.[9] Unfortunately, we were not able to obtain additional information on the training, interest, and skills of these administrators. Preliminary observations suggest, however, that the administrative set at NIMH is essentially a white, male-dominated group.

After a proposal has been submitted and assigned to a program unit, the administrator sends the proposal to a member of the Executive Review Committee. According to an NIMH publication: "Initial Review Groups are panels of the best qualified, primarily non-government consultants chosen for their expertise in a given field . . . Initial Review Groups review, evaluate, and rate research grant applications. Each committee has between 10 and 15 members."[9]

In an essay on research grants, Greenberg reached a different assessment of this peer group process:

> Peer review, a process virtually unknown outside the scientific community, is the sacrosanct ritual of the grant business, involving, as it does, panels of specialists, mainly from universities, to grade the applicants and their proposed research

projects. Sensible on the face of it, and routinely touted as
instilling a competitive spirit into research, the system, however, is frequently assailed as an invitation to backscratching
and a boon to scientific conversation. Critics contend, for
example, that reviewers with their own scientific regulations
to protect are not likely to be sympathetic to mavericks pro-
posing research that does not harmonize with their own
scientific perceptions; peer review is too inbred. . . .[10]

This is an excellent commentary on the federal research
funding system. However, several recent reports on the peer
review systems at the National Science Foundation and the
National Institutes of Health have challenged the assumptions
of the "old boy" networks in regards to who gets government
grants.[11] These research reports concluded that the peer review
system is relatively free of cronyism; scientists generally believe
the system is equitable; there is no evidence of bias in favor of
established investigators; and there is little bias against the
young scientists. Women's groups and minority groups of
scientists have questioned these conclusions, primarily because
these studies did not deal in any meaningful way with sexual
and racial biases in the peer review systems.

Twenty-eight initial review committees were identified, fourteen in research and fourteen in training, not including the
National Advisory Mental Health Council. The latter is a
group of twelve distinguished lay and professional persons who
review the recommendations of the Initial Review Group. Since
this Council seldom reverses the decisions of the Initial Review
Group, the latter committee will be the focus of our analysis.

As of July 1, 1977, there were 310 persons on the NIMH
review committees, although the number authorized was 363.[12]
Of these, 34.8 percent were psychologists, 26 percent were psychiatrists, and 12 percent were sociologists (see Table 3-II).
These committees were dominated by white males: 71 percent,
or 220, were men, and 29 percent, or 90, were women. It was
estimated that there were 32 blacks on these committees, representing 10.3 percent of the total. These data suggest that the
NIMH review committees are dominated by white male psychologists and psychiatrists.

TABLE 3-II

THE DISCIPLINES OF PERSONS ON
NIMH REVIEW COMMITTEES — 1977

Discipline	Number	Percentage
Psychology	108	34.8
Psychiatry	79	25.5
Sociology	38	12.2
Social Sciences	25	8.1
Medical Sciences	20	6.4
Nursing	20	6.4
Social Work	20	6.4
Total	310	99.8

Source: U. S. Department of Health, Education and Welfare:
HRA, HSA, CDC, ADAMHA, Public Advisory
Committee: Authority, Structure, Function and
Members. Washington, Government Printing Office,
1977, pp. 52-83.

The regional representation on these committees is uneven;
the East Coast is overrepresented with 29 percent of the
members. In fact, almost half of the members reside on either
the East or West Coasts (see Table 3-III). The data show that 50
percent of the committee members live in the following six
states: New York, California, Massachusetts, Illinois, Pennsylvania, and Maryland. It should be noted that members on these
committees were affiliated with a range of colleges and universities. The five universities with the highest number of staff on
review committees are UCLA, Boston University, Michigan,
Minnesota, and Texas. Among black colleges and universities,
Howard University had the highest number of representatives.
Very few representatives were associated with black schools.
Overall, 81.3 percent of the members of NIMH review committees were associated with colleges and universities.

Since July 1977, new members have been added and others
dropped from the Initial Review Committee. Apparent outside
pressures have forced NIMH to include more women and minorities, especially blacks, on these committees. For example, as

TABLE 3-III

REGIONAL REPRESENTATION ON
NIMH REVIEW COMMITTEES — 1977

	Number	Percentage
South	51	17
East Coast	89	29
West Coast	48	16
Midwest	60	19
Mountain	26	8
New England	32	10
Others*	4	1
Total	310	100

* Others refers to Canada, Puerto Rico, Etc.

Source: U. S. Department of Health, Education and Welfare: HRA, HSA, CDC, ADAMHA, Public Advisory Committees: Authority, Structure, Function, and Members. Washington, Government Printing Office, 1977, pp. 52-83.

of November 30, 1977, 117 women (35%) were on these committees, compared to 90 (29%) in July 1977. Since July 1977, twelve blacks have been added. Both females and minorities have better representation on the training committee than on research committees. Looking specifically at who gets the funds, one begins to see the relationship between committee structure and who is funded. In 1975, NIMH awarded 1,064 research grants, and psychologists received 50 percent of the awards and 42 percent of the funds (see Table 3-IV). Psychologists and psychiatrists together received 50 percent of the research awards and 66 percent of the funds, and constituted 60 percent of the NIMH review committees in July 1977 (see Table 3-II). Moreover, colleges and universities and other schools accounted for 81 percent of the awards and 73 percent of research funds in the mental health fields. Earlier, it was stated that 81.3 percent of the members on NIMH review committees were affiliated with universities and colleges.

It is very difficult to collect additional information on prin-

TABLE 3-IV

NIMH RESEARCH AWARDS BY DISCIPLINE OF
PRINCIPAL INVESTIGATORS – FY 1975

Discipline	Number of Awards		Value of Awards (In Millions)	
	N	%	Amount	%
Psychology	526	50	$62.7	42
Psychiatry	164	15	14.8	24
Biological and Medical Sciences	153	14	7.8	12
Social Sciences	159	15	9.1	14
Others	62	6	4.7	8
Total	1,064	100	$99.1	100

Source: U. S. Department of Health, Education and Welfare: National Institute of Mental Health Research Support Programs and Activities. Rockville, 1976, p. 1.

cipal investigators such as sex, race, age, publication record, organizational affiliation, and so forth. Recently, however, NIMH did present some data on known minority principal investigators. Out of a total of 1,148 active research grants as of July 18, 1977, there were only 83 known minority principal investigators.[13] The data would suggest that minority scholars did not have meaningful access to federal research funds. Black scholars, especially those at black colleges and universities, are particularly disadvantaged. The most recent data, from fiscal year 1974, shows that the federal government only spent 21.3 million dollars on research and demonstration efforts at black institutions, although federal obligations to non-black institutions were 21 billion dollars for the same period.[14] For 1974, the Alcohol, Drug Abuse, and Mental Health Administration, which includes NIMH, spent 80.6 million dollars for research and development at colleges and universities, but only 719,000 dollars went to black schools. The author of "The Significance of Research for the Survival of Black Colleges,"[15] states that the federal government, including NIMH, has not supported research at black colleges and universities even though the institutions have the capabilities for developing quality research programs.

Conclusion

In this chapter, consideration was given to social research as a major industry and the structure of the funding process at NIMH. There are several emerging issues which are of particular concern to many black scholars and practitioners.

In general, blacks and others have been used as "guinea pigs" in both biomedical and social and behavioral sciences research. What comes to mind is the now famous Tuskegee Syphilis Study, the testing and experimentation of birth control on poor and black women, experimentation with various drugs on blacks in mental hospitals and prisons, and social surveys which label whole communities. The list is incomplete. We must insist that the rights of human subjects be protected even when it makes our research more difficult.

Too many scientists have tended to view black communities as well as black families from a monolithic perspective. There is diversity within black communities like any other community.[16] Since many researchers assume a uniform black experience, they are caught in a situation where they tend to compare blacks and whites, that is, using a comparative research paradigm.[17] Often, the researcher ends up comparing middle-class white families with low-income blacks and draws all kinds of erroneous conclusions.[18] We must devote more effort to helping destroy the assumed superiority of the comparative research model in social and behavioral sciences research in this country where blacks are always compared to whites. Black scientists and their white colleagues must build comparative research paradigms within black communities. As suggested earlier, blacks are a diversified people. More research emphasis should be placed on understanding these differences within black communities so that more appropriate treatment strategies can be developed for improving the quality of life in black communites.

REFERENCES

1. Amidei, Nancy and Ooms, Theodore: *Toward An Inventory of Federal Programs With Direct Impacts on Families.* Washington, George Washington U, 1977.
2. Lasswell, H. D.: *Politics, Who Gets What, When and How?* New York, McGraw, 1936.
3. Theodorson, George and Theodorson, Achilles: *A Modern Dictionary of Sociology.* New York, T Y Crowell, 1969.
4. National Science Foundation: *National Patterns of R & D Resources: Funds and Manpower in the United States 1953-1977.* Washington, Government Printing Office, 1977.
5. Federal support of social science research rising at slower pace. *Mosaic,* 6:38, 1975.
6. Hersh, S. P.: *Child and Youth Activities of National Institute of Mental Health 1976.* Presented at National Advisory Mental Health Council, 7 December 1976.
7. Kamerman, Sheila and Kahn, Alfred: Explorations in family policy. *Social Work, 21:*181-186, 1976.
8. Brown, Bertram: *The Crisis in Mental Health Research.* Presented at American Psychiatric Association Annual Meeting, Miami Beach, 13 May 1976.
9. U. S. Department of Health, Education, and Welfare, NIMH: *National Institute of Mental Health Research Support Programs and Activities.* Washington, Government Printing Office, 1976.
10. Greenberg, Daniel: The edgy competitive world of research grants. *Washington Post,* p. A18, 18 October 1977.
11. Roark, Ann: How much cronyism in federal peer review? *Chronicle of Higher Education, 16:*5, 1978.
12. U. S. Department of Health, Education, and Welfare: *HRA, HSA, CDC, ADAMHA, Public Advisory Committee: Authority, Structure, Function, and Members.* Washington, Government Printing Office, 1977.
13. Data from Program Analysis and Evaluation Section, Division of Extramural Research Programs, NIMH, November 1977.
14. U. S. Federal Interagency Committee on Education: *FICA Report, 3:*8, 1976.
15. Gary, Lawrence: The significance of research for the survival of black colleges. *J Black Studies, 6:*35-54, 1975.
16. Green, Vera: The confrontation of diversity within the black community. *Human Organizations, 29:*267-272, 1970.
17. Banks, Curtis: White preference in blacks: A paradigm in search of a phenomenon. *Psychological Bulletin, 83:*1179-1186, 1976.
18. Gary, Lawrence: Mental health research agenda for the black community. *J Afro Am Issues, 4:*50-60, 1976.

Chapter 4

PARENTS' WAGES IN THE CONTEXT OF MEANINGFUL WORK AND ADEQUATE INCOME POLICIES

DAVID GIL

Introduction

THIS chapter discusses a cluster of social policies designed to assure adequate incomes, meaningful work, and social recognition to all individuals and families. These ingredients seem to be a necessity for harmonious family life and healthy child development. It is therefore unrealistic to expect social services alone to prevent breakdown of families and placement of children in foster care as long as the normal workings of social and economic forces deprive families of adequate income, work, and prestige, and thus undermine family life and child development. Significant improvements in the quality of family life can be attained only through political processes directed at fundamental changes of established social and economic values and institutions; they can simply not be attained through professional and administrative processes directed merely at marginal modifications of social service patterns.

Conventional Approaches to Social Policy Development

In spite of the political nature of policy issues, public and scholarly discussions of social policy in our society often pretend to be politically neutral, value-free, objective, and scientific. However, a review of social policy literature in the United States reveals that these analyses and recommendations of many authors reflect open or tacit acceptance of the central features of

40

the prevailing social, economic, and political order. The policies and institutions of this order are shaped by, and in turn reinforce, the values of social inequality, competition, selfishness, domination, and exploitation. Commitment to, or at least acceptance of, this societal order and its underlying values and dynamics permeates not only the writings of "conservative" thinkers, but all those of "liberal" and "progressive" ones, even though the latter authors tend to advocate expansions of welfare state programs.

It is important to note that welfare state measures and their precursors have consistently been used as *balance wheels* to promote political stability in inegalitarian societies and to control dispossessed and deprived segments of their populations. This has been so since land enclosure, in fourteenth century England, pauperized former feudal serfs and tenant farmers by separating them from their means of existence and driving them into towns as "free" wage laborers for an emerging capitalist economy. Illustrations of welfare state measures are the English Statute of Laborers (1350), the English Act on Vagabondage (1388), the English Poor Law (1601) and its later revisions, and nineteenth and twentieth century social security, public welfare, Great Society, and War on Poverty measures in Europe and the United States. The costs of welfare programs were not assumed by business enterprises and by privileged segments of the population who benefited from the availability of a dispossessed, active labor force and unemployed labor reserve, but were always transferred to the State, which means to the entire population, with a larger proportional tax burden usually borne by those less able to do so in terms of distributions of wealth and income. In other words, indirect costs of business were socialized, while benefits were privately appropriated. These outcomes of welfare state policies and practices were due mainly to the fact that economically powerful groups tended to dominate the political institutions of the State, its legislative and executive branches, and its consciousness and ideology-shaping institutions, including schools, universities, churches, the arts, and the mass media.

An Egalitarian Approach to Social Policy Development

An alternative approach to social policy development is neither objective nor value-free but is committed openly to human development, social equality, individual liberty, self-direction, freedom from domination and exploitation, cooperation, and collectivity-orientation. Such an approach is also committed to social, economic, and political institutions shaped by these values. Transformations of prevailing values and institutions require extended political processes aimed at bringing about significant changes in perceptions of self-interest, in values, in consciousness, in human nature and human possibilities, as well as corresponding transformations in policies and institutions by collective actions of people whose perceptions and values have already changed. Critiques of prevailing social policies and the interpretation and advocacy of alternative ones could be integral aspects of such a comprehensive political strategy. Other aspects include specifying alternative values and goals, advocating policies which involve significant changes in the distribution of existential resources, social status, power, and rights, and the quality of human relations. In Andre Gorz's terms, social policy development can be compatible with a political struggle for radical transformations, when instead of pursuing *reformist reforms,* which pacify and stabilize the status quo of power and rights, one demands *revolutionary reforms* which criticize and challenge that status quo.[1]

The Prevailing Societal Context

What are the major elements of the prevailing societal context which revolutionary reforms challenge? The central feature of the established social order is that most people have been effectively separated from material and symbolic means of existence. As a result of historic processes of expropriation, most people now lack opportunities to be self-reliant and self-directing in their lives; they are forced instead to depend on a minority who have gained effective control over society's material and symbolic resources, and who use and exploit everything and everyone as factors of production, rather than for meeting the needs of all people. To fit into this system and its dehumanizing division of labor, the self-directing capacities of people are destroyed selectively through a process referred to euphemistically as "public education" and their creativity and human essence are wasted.[2,3]

Furthermore, over five hundred years of capitalist development indicate that availability of an unemployed labor reserve will keep wages down and will increase profits. Conventional economic theory, taught in our universities and followed by our government, lend a scientific aura to this exploitive practice by declaring certain levels and unemployment as full employment and by reinforcing the myth that reductions in unemployment will inevitably stimulate inflation. Fear of unemployment and its consequences (poverty, shame, and a sense of failure) is a potent incentive for people to participate willingly in dehumanizing and exploitative work and to compete for employment and for promotions in the hierarchical structures of the work system. Competitive and capitalist economic and political institutions have produced a selfish, acquisitive, exploitative, and antagonistic mentality. Everyone is now practically alone and is everyone else's potential adversary. Discriminatory practices, such as racism and sexism, are direct or indirect consequences of competitive values, structures, and dynamics. Perhaps the saddest aspect of this entire context is that people tend to blame themselves when they fail in this system in which there are always more losers than winners and that people tend to feel powerless to change the established system and regain control over their lives.

Solutions to the Prevailing Societal Context

There are rational and comprehensive solutions to the dehumanizing societal context sketched above. Essential elements of such comprehensive solutions seem to be —

a. elimination of the results of historic processes of expropriation, domination, and exploitation through liberation and socialization of privately controlled means of existence;

b. establishment of an unconditional right to material and nonmaterial productive resources for all humans on equal terms, which would allow them to sustain their and their kin's existence; satisfy their biological, social, and psychological needs; realize their innate potential; and enhance the quality of their lives through productive, creative, meaningful, self-initiated and self-directed work, and through voluntary cooperation with other free and equally entitled humans;

c. establishment of decentralized, local and translocal, genuinely democratic, libertarian, and egalitarian institutions for management of resources; for organization of work and production; for coordination and distribution of goods, services, rights, and responsibilities; and for governance.

Initial Steps: Meaningful Work and Adequate Incomes

One feasible step toward eventual and comprehensive transformation of society is the elimination of the dehumanizing welfare system which implies the legitimacy of institutionalized injustices. The existing welfare system and welfare mentality are beyond reform and should be replaced with unconditional rights to meaningful work and adequate income, to every individual and to every household. The assured income should not be less than the lower-level budget of the United States Bureau of Labor Statistics (BLS), which, in 1977, was 10,481 dollars per year for an urban household of two adults and two children.[4] Considering current costs of living, such an income is necessary for decent survival. This standard of living ought to be assured primarily through creation of meaningful work opportunities for all, fitting individual capacities and potential, geared to all age levels, and compensated for at wages based at least on the lower-level BLS budget. Child care work undertaken by parents and the care of sick and incapacitated relatives ought to be options within such a general work and income policy.

Persons unable to work because of health, youth, advanced age, or involvement in educational programs should receive incomes out of general revenues of the federal government, at lower-level BLS budget levels, and should be subject to random audits rather than to demeaning case-by-case investigations.

These policies would require modifying prevailing tax policies, and reallocating societal resources. Incomes up to the lower-level BLS budget, less the tax component of that budget, would be tax-exempt. Earned and unearned incomes above that level, regardless of source, would have to be subject to a truly progressive tax. Sales tax, other indirect taxes, and the Social Security system would have to be phased out because of their regressive impact on after-tax income, and progressive taxes on all forms of productive wealth would have to be instituted. Prevailing state and local taxes should be replaced by an appropriate surtax on the federal income tax. The practice of deficit budgeting, which benefits mainly owners of wealth from whom governments borrow at high interest to cover deficits, would be terminated and budgets would have to be balanced through adequate taxation of high incomes and wealth. Activities destructive to human well-being, such as the war establishment, which are liberally supported by the federal budget, should be phased out, and resources now wasted on these activities transferred to the work and income policy. There is no doubt that our aggregate productive resources and human capacities could assure to every individual and household a decent standard of living at and beyond the lower-level BLS budget, provided we manage our resources in a rational manner geared to meeting the needs of our people. The issue is, therefore, one of social choice and commitment rather than one of administrative and technical expertise.

Parents' Wages in the Context of Meaningful Work and Adequate Income Policy

Parents' wages, a social policy proposed about ten years ago,[5,6] fits into the cluster of work, income, and tax policies sketched here. Such a policy could be an important step toward a humanistic-egalitarian society and should, therefore, be pursued as a revolutionary reform. Because a watered-down version of such a policy could fit into the conventional status quo welfare state model, the entire policy context and value system within which policies are conceived, interpreted, and pursued must be changed.

The premises of the parents' wages concept are that child-rearing and child care are essential contributions to society. Because individuals who rear children usually cannot do other productive work, their contributions should be defined as valued components of the aggregate social product (Gross National Product) and should entitle them to appropriate shares of goods and services.

Administration of a parents' wages policy can be simple. Expectant mothers and parents choosing to undertake child care on a regular, full-time or part-time basis would notify a local United States Treasury disbursement office of the circumstances entitling them to wage payments. Such notifications would be the basis for wage payments until a claimant notified the office of changes in, or termination of, his or her child care responsibilities. The disbursement office would not be concerned with qualitative aspects of child care, but solely with the implementation of wage payments and with random checks of the validity and accuracy of claims. Recipients of parents' wages would be responsible for notifying the disbursement office of any changes in their child care arrangements and corresponding entitlements. Such notifications could be administered through a set of questions on the back of wage checks or on separate return coupons.

Parents' wages would be adjusted annually to reflect changes in the lower-level BLS budget. The entire program would be financed out of general revenues of the federal government. Wages would be considered part of household income and would be subject to income taxes in the same manner as all other earned income. Considering parents' wages as taxable income is necessary, as all qualifying parents should be entitled to the wages regardless of other income and source. Taxation would assure that households with incomes other than parents' wages would retain only a declining portion of the wages as other income increased.

Since the BLS budget is affected by family size, the number of children cared for by a parent would be reflected in the wages. Parents engaged in full-time employment or self-employed should receive a fraction of parents' wages since child care involves 24-hour-a-day, 365-day-a-year responsibilities. As the time spent on regular employment decreases because of child care, the fraction of parents' wages would increase. One further source of variation in wage levels could be the stage of development of children. When children are old enough to attend day care facilities and schools, and when such settings are provided publically and parents make use of them for parts of a day, some reduction in parents' wages may be appropriate.

In two-parent households, parents would be free to share child care responsibilities under the proposed policy. Either parent could pursue employment or education for part of their time and take on child care responsibilities for another part. Parents' wages would be divided among them in accordance with their respective time allocation to child care. The combined wages of two parents would not exceed the amount of one appropriate full-time wage.

Parents' wages as proposed here, in the context of meaningful work, adequate income, and progressive tax policies, would result in many changes in the allocation of societal resources; in the division of labor and organization of production; in symbolic goods and services; in human relations and the quality of life; and in societal values and consciousness. Only a brief summary of these changes are presented here; a more detailed analysis may be found in *Unraveling Social Policy*.[7]

Social Policy

A major focus of the parents' wages policy is a redefinition of work, which challenges the prevailing notion that work is only those activities included in the GNP, involving monetary rewards, and contributing directly or indirectly to profits and accumulation of capital. Instead, the policy defines work as activities by parents concerned with meeting human needs of their children, and contributing to individual and societal development.

Another focus of the policy is a redefinition of rights to shares of the social product and to social recognition, or prestige. No longer would concrete and symbolic rewards be restricted only to individuals engaged in activities leading to profits. Parents, engaged in life-sustaining and enhancing activities on behalf of their children, would be entitled to social recognition and to appropriate shares of available goods and services. Furthermore, men and women would have real options to care for their children (part- or full-time) or to engage in educational activities, employment, and self-employment. Regardless of their choices, they would be assured social recognition and an adequate income.

Once people have a genuine right to make choices and the assurance of social prestige and adequate income, power relationships would change. People would no longer be motivated by insecurity and by fear of unemployment and poverty; they would no longer have to compete with one another for alienating, poorly rewarded positions. Their self-image, sense of self, and their entire existential milieu will thus gradually begin to change. The quality of work will also undergo significant changes in order to attract workers with genuine options.

Assuring every individual and household a decent income through meaningful and respected work including child care, and when appropriate, through government transfers, would also result in a significant redistribution of after-tax incomes and in significant changes in income-related allocation and development of resources. The range between high and low incomes would be reduced significantly, as incomes would cluster closely around the mean. Absolute poverty would be eliminated, and relative poverty with its psychological, social, and political correlates would be significantly reduced. The results of the social policy cluster suggested here would not be simply a new variation on the conventional theme of privilege and deprivation, but an entirely new theme: the elimination of derivation and a challenge to privilege in every sphere — psy-

chological, social, economic, and political — the essence of
revolutionary reforms.

The comprehensive institutional changes attained by these
revolutionary reforms would be reflected in corresponding
changes in the overall quality of the existential milieu, and
hence in new human experiences involving a rehumanized context of work and living and more fulfilling human relations.
These new experiences would gradually lead to changes in
consciousness, perceptions of interests, and values; changes
which in turn would tend to reinforce the foregoing institutional transformations.

Epilogue

Structural and symbolic changes, as sketched here, will not
be attained without extended political education and struggle.
Such changes will be resisted by individuals and groups who
are currently dominant in economic, political, and cultural
spheres and who see the changes as against their best interests.
Resistance to the policies advocated here is likely to be effective
until growing segments of the population unite in political
movements working for the dissemination of egalitarian and
humanistic values.

The crucial question posed by this analysis is how to bring
such movements into being. There is no simple answer, but
one thing seems certain: whatever else is necessary for an effective political strategy, people must be helped to transcend the
myths and the false perceptions of self-interest which now reinforce their commitments to the prevailing order, even though
this order tends to frustrate their intrinsic human needs and
their underlying, genuine human interest.[8] One effective approach to debunk prevailing myths and to correct false perceptions of self-interest is to bring out the truth about the constant
frustration of people's need in the context of prevailing social,
economic, and political realities.

Everyday struggles over work, income, and tax policies could
become an arena for political education in reality and in enhancing critical consciousness.

Rather than building broad coalitions to secure reformist reforms which merely rescue the established, inegalitarian social order, one needs to struggle for meaningful revolutionary reforms such as the work, income, parents' wages, and tax policies discussed here. Such struggles, if pursued forcefully yet without violence and hostility, should spread critical consciousness among constantly growing segments of society, a prerequisite for overcoming the prevailing, powerful resistance to egalitarian-humanistic values and social policies.

REFERENCES

1. Gorz, Andre: *Strategy for Labor*. Boston, Beacon Pr, 1967.
2. Braverman, Harry: *Labor and Monopoly Capital*. New York, Monthly Rev, 1974.
3. Bowles, Samuel and Gintis, Herbert: *Schooling in Capitalist America*. New York, Basic, 1976.
4. *New York Times*, p. 32, 30 April 1978.
5. Gil, David: Mothers' wages — One way to attack poverty. *Children, 15*:229-230, November-December 1968.
6. Gil, David: Mothers' wages — An alternative attack on poverty. In National Conference of Social Workers: *Social Work Practice 1969*. New York, Columbia U Pr, 1969.
7. Gil, David: *Unravelling Social Policy*. Cambridge, Schenkman, 1973, 1976.
8. Gil, David: unpublished, 1978.

Chapter 5

SINGLE PARENT FAMILIES: IMPLICATIONS FOR SOCIAL POLICY

PHYLLIS MOEN

SINGLE parent families are increasingly prevalent in the United States today. Nearly 90 percent of these one parent families are headed by women. While female-headed families result from a number of conditions, such as death of a spouse, illegitimacy, and marital separation, the greatest increase has resulted from divorce. Between 1970 and 1975 the number of divorced women heading families nearly tripled. These changes in marital status have great impact on the living arrangements of vast numbers of children. Between 1960 and 1970, for example, the number of children living in one-parent families increased by 60 percent.[1]

A number of factors contribute to this large-scale social change in family structure, including the ideological, such as the Women's Liberation Movement; the structural, such as no-fault divorce; and the economic, the woman's increased participation in the labor force. Public policy also contributes, as transfer payments have been shown to affect the number of women heading families who set up their own households rather than moving in with relatives.[2]

The purpose here is to examine the relationship between policy and the single parent family. In order to do this we must cast a wide net over a range of social concerns. Few policies deal explicitly with the single parent family, but many have unintended consequences which touch the lives of women and men raising children alone.

Public images concerning the family in the United States establish the milieu in which public decisions are made. A major assumption is that the discrepancies between the realities of single parenthood and the public image of this family form

51

contribute to the inconsistencies and inadequacies of policies for this emerging structure. Implications of these public images for interpreting present policies and suggesting policy alternatives need to be discussed. We will explore three dimensions of the single parent issue: the sociocultural images of the family; the single parent family itself; and current policy orientations.

The Sociocultural Context

Looking at families from a broad, sociocultural level of analysis requires examining both structural and normative images. They are intimately connected; what is believed to be the dominant family form is also believed to be the "best" family form. Public images have both a belief component (the way families really are) and a value component (the way families really should be).

For most Americans, the term *family* means a two-parent family with children, usually two or three, and possibly a dog. This white, middle-class, idealized version of the family is so instilled in our imagery that scholars and lay persons alike label other family forms in a pejorative way, as "deviant," "broken," or "unstable."[3] Unfortunately, this image is also a component of the identity systems of single parents. Few escape the societal stigma of being different; they therefore label themselves and their families as abnormal as well as unique.[4,5]

The reality of the situation is that in the United States today one out of every three adults is single, widowed, or divorced, and this number is growing.[6] One out of every six children in the United States is being raised in a single-parent household. While the number of single-parent families is increasing, the number of husband-wife families has begun to decline.

Has the idealized traditional family form ever really been the norm? Retrospective analysis has shown that there was considerable variation in the ¸past; there have always been single-parent families.[7] Across societies, it has been estimated that at one time only 65 percent of the women in the world over the age of fifteen are married.[8] There are and have been a range of family types, from the single parent family to the three-generation family and the communal family. If one defines the traditional family as a husband, a wife who is not in the labor force, and two children, only 6 percent of American families fit this model in 1976.[9] While it is true that most children at any one time are living in husband-wife families, it is estimated that between 20 percent and 30 percent of the children growing up in the 1970s will have parents who are divorced and that an additional 9 percent will lose one or both parents by death.[10] Yet our image of the family is such that anything not resembling the traditional nuclear family is labeled as deviant.

This distorted perspective concerning the structure of American families has tremendous consequences, not only in the realm of policy but in the patterning of daily events. Institutions and organizations operate on the assumption that there are two parents, one of which is available to carry on transactions during the day. Schools hold parent-teacher conferences, concerts, and registration during the day. Doctors and dentists have parents, i.e. mothers, bring their children at a convenient time for the doctor and dentist, not at a convenient time for the parent. An indicator of the relative worth of the parent's, i.e. mother's, time is the hours spent in waiting rooms in a variety of clinics waiting for children to receive medical services. Public and private service agencies take for granted the availability of an adult family member to transact the family's business during the day. An even greater constraint on the single parent is the structuring and scheduling of gainful employment, which denies that employees have family responsibilities.

Even as schools, medical clinics, and the entire volunteer network function on the assumption of the traditional two-parent family form, so does the absence of a comprehensive child care system.[11]

Allied with the assumption of the mythical traditional family as both the ideal and the norm are assumptions concerning the "pathology" of the single-parent form[12] and the transitional quality of that form. While it is true that four out of five divorced and widowed persons remarry, a greater proportion past the age of thirty remain single.[13,14] But the myth of the single parents as being between husbands removes the responsibility of public agencies to face the particular needs of this growing group.

The Family Context

Major issues in moving from a two-parent to a single-parent household involve the redistribution of tasks. Functions that were once performed by the missing spouse must either be taken over, modified, or dropped altogether by the single parent. Two major family activities that have public as well as private consequences are providing for the economic well-being of family members and caring for and socializing of the children. Each of these tasks will be appraised within the contexts of the single-parent family form and policy. As 90 percent of the single-parent families are headed by women, the issues here are formulated from their perspective.

The ability of the female head to succeed in the provider role is contingent, to a large extent, on her own resource of education, skills, and work experience, *and* the constraints of also fulfilling the child care role. Because men have traditionally been the family providers, women are viewed as essentially marginal workers and are given marginal jobs that pay poorly, are low status, and insecure.[15] Much of the discrimination against women in the marketplace results from this ideological imagery of the man as provider.[16,17]

Jobs are structured to require a great deal of both time and commitment, leaving little time for family responsibilities. The same job constraints that prevent husbands from participating more in family tasks also operate against single parents who try to combine provider and homemaker roles.[18] Market work is almost always a series of obstacles for the single parent because there is rarely an adequate, reliable, inexpensive form of child care.[19] Hours are inflexible and long, and few part-time jobs pay enough to support a family. In short, jobs are structured for the male provider, who has a helpmate to smooth the domestic details of living.

Women earn less than 60 percent of what men do in every occupational category.[20] They are the last hired and the first fired;[21] because of the traditional division of labor, women are often not equipped either with the training or the experiences to make a decent living.[22]

The economic straits in which most single-parent families find themselves result both from the discrimination against women and family structure. The two-parent family has more resources, with the cushion of an extra adult to meet changing economic needs; much of the income differential between families headed by women and those headed by men is a consequence of the number of earners in the family. In 1973, the average single male parent earned over 12,000 dollars, while the female single parent earned 6,000 dollars. Two-parent families earned an average of 15,000 dollars in 1973. Over 60 percent of 3.2 million children living in families below the poverty level are in single-parent families.[23]

Coping with both provider and parenting functions, the single parent operates under special constraints with respect to time for child care and other domestic functions. The fact that single parents are raising children in families with one less adult has certain repercussions. For the parent, it means no respite from the twenty-four-hour responsibility for parenting. As Brandwein and others have noted, one of the assets of the two-parent family form is the presence of another adult to provide consultation and support as well as a replacement or back-up in the care and socialization of children.[3] In fact, a study of single-parent families in Great Britain found that social isolation and loneliness were the main personal problems of single-parent family heads.[24]

For the children, being raised in a single-parent environment means access to fewer adults and a corresponding emphasis on peer relationships.[25] Public images of children in single-parent families depict them as more likely to "get into trouble" than are children from two-parent families. Children in homes without fathers are assumed to have problems in sex role socialization and adjustment. Research suggests that family structure per se makes little difference in the socialization of children.[26]

It seems that negative impacts on children stem from economic causes rather than the absence of a parent. The Finer

Report on single-parent families in Great Britain found that the most detrimental effects on school attainment and social adjustment of children resulted not from their single-parent family status, but from the economic hardships these families faced.[27,28]

The Policy Context

The single parent form, with either a male or a female head, is obviously poorly equipped to fulfill both the provider and child care functions. Except for the minimal supports provided by Aid to Families With Dependent Children (AFDC) and in-kind transfers, it would seem that society holds the family responsible for providing and caring for its offspring, but with little public support.[29] In fact, public policies concerning employment and wage rates and the absence of comprehensive child care operate against the single parent successfully fulfilling both of these roles.

How could services best facilitate the functioning of the single parent form? This question can best be answered by providing some alternatives to the two prevailing orientations that either implicitly or explicitly color policy formulations: the static and traditional view of families, and the single issue orientation to problems.

Most families do not fit the traditional mold, yet policy is designed for precisely that mold. Moreover, programs are formulated for families at one point in time, failing to take into account possible and probable changes in composition or structure.

What is required is the recognition that individuals pursue a number of careers, including marital and parental careers; that these can be joined or separate; and that the transition points of entering or leaving a particular career can be real crisis points.[30]

Attention has already been drawn to the shifting needs of the traditional two-parent family over its life cycle development.[31,32] Some observers suggest that greater variability in family structure will become the norm, not only across families but at different periods within the same life course of individuals.[33] If this is true, service agencies will have to be sensitive to the shifts in families' needs, depending on shifts in family form as well as changes in the life cycle. For example, by 1975 more than one in four parents under age twenty-five who was the head of a family was without a spouse.[23] The needs of the single-parent family at this stage of household establishment and the rearing of young children are probably greater than at any other period.

Policies should not discriminate against the single-parent family, but also it is necessary for agencies to be sensitive to the variations in needs across single-parent and two-parent families and the changes in these needs over time. Failing to delineate the specific needs of the single-parent family has also resulted in a failure to differentiate between variations in structure, life cycle stage, situation, and needed supports.

Social services could also assist in what the Finer Report notes as the major personal problem of single-parent families: their social isolation.[27] There is evidence that marital separation results in emotional trauma, both from the separation itself and the isolation following the separation. Goode found that over three-fifths of his respondents had experienced various kinds of personal disorganization or trauma.[5] Weiss found that participants in the seminars for separated adults reported anxiety following separation.[34] Weiss labels this and other symptoms *separation distress* and notes that it seems to fade as time passes without contact with the spouse.

Seminars such as those held by the Harvard Laboratory of Community Psychiatry could facilitate the adjustment of recently separated parents to the emotional as well as social impacts on this fundamental change in their lives. Other analysts have suggested the need for divorce centers for legal and financial assistance, as well as information concerning entitlement to social services to newly separated individuals.[35] Self-help groups, such as Parents Without Partners, are a positive step forward in dealing with the public stigmas of single parenthood and in coping with the emotional travail that accompanies this change in status.

Family needs arising from the death of a parent or from military service are treated by social agencies as somehow more legitimate than the equivalent needs arising from divorce, separation, or a child born to a single woman.[3] Movement from this *deviant* to a *variant* perspective would result in the needs of families being evaluated without regard to "respectability" of particular family structures[36] and would be a psychological support as well.

The fact that government has pursued policies aimed at traditional two-parent families has meant that programs geared specifically for the single-parent family have been fragmented, dealing with isolated issues out of context. What is required is a holistic approach that recognizes that economic concerns of the family cannot be resolved apart from parental concerns and that neither can be isolated from the psychological state of the family head. Moreover, the economic, parental, and psychological aspects of the single-parent family cannot be appraised apart from the structural constraints of the labor market and emerging policies concerning work and child care.

To improve the functioning of single-parent families will require more than the restructuring of social services. Provision of child care, for example, will facilitate the integration of the family and provider roles of the single parents, but the problems of discrimination will remain. As Sawhill notes, no amount of work effort on the part of female heads of families will go very far in reducing their poverty and dependence, as long as these women face such low wages in the market.[37]

Enabling women to be gainfully employed in spite of their child care demands is not the answer. Issues of discrimination and occupational segregation will have to be resolved before women can adequately support their families. Transformations in the scheduling and time for employment may be the ultimate solution to the role overloads resulting from being both provider and parent. The issue of parenting cannot be resolved merely by the provision of day care: it is far more complex. As Caldwell and Rossi have pointed out, child care should be seen as a supportive environment rather than as a substitute or supplement to maternal care.[38,39] Day care facilities could then take on the role of another parenting person that enhances rather than detracts from the development of the child.

The relationship between parenting and social isolation needs to be considered as well. As Pearlin and Johnson point out, marriage can be a source of emotional and concrete help in dealing with the strains of living.[40] Social supports could be provided to periodically relieve the single parent from the total burden of child care and to provide both emotional and instructional help in the raising of children. Such strategies as temporary and emergency child care, child development specialists, homemaker services, and family resource centers have been suggested for improving the parenting of all family types.

Conclusions

The issues raised here lead to two conclusions: (1) policies should provide for and consider not one but a variety of family types, and (2) policies should facilitate the economic and child care functions of all families.

What is required is a definition of the deficiencies in the single-parent family, not as the failure of individual family members, but as the failure of institutions to provide the supports required for this particular family structure. Such has been the indictment of the Finer Committee Report on single-parent families in Great Britain: "It is not being brought up by a single parent which, of itself, is damaging to the children, but rather the multiple disadvantages and hardships caused by their gross financial and social deprivation . . . It is society by its lack of provision, and not the parents themselves, which is failing these children."[28]

The Finer Committee's recommendations include comprehensive financial support without welfare stigma and such services as day care and counseling service. They also recommend encouraging part-time work, the availability of social services in the evenings and on Saturdays, and making it possible for either parent to stay home with young children if he or she so desires.[27] There is every indication that the variety in family forms is here to stay.[41,42] Indeed, it may be unusual, as

Weiss notes, for families not to experience some period of marital separation.[4] The public image of the traditional family has not only impeded the functioning of single parents, it also restricted other marital and familial options such as staying single, marrying late, and not having children.[43]

The National Academy of Science has asked the central policy question: What can be done to help families remove or lessen the constraints they face? They have also provided the answer: "the problems of children are inseparable from the problems of those who are primarily responsible for their care and nurturance."[23]

If the role of social services is to restore, maintain, and enhance the social functioning of individuals and families, then why has there been this foot-dragging concerning public supports for enhancing the functioning of single-parent families? Part of the reason can be explained in the image of the two-parent family as the ideal. In spite of evidence to the contrary,[27,28] there is a prevailing belief that being brought up by a single parent is in itself damaging to the children. There is also a question of differential power. Dealing with the single-parent family as a familial problem is far easier than resolving the work overload of the single parent through modifying the structure of employment and other institutions. Plack discusses the differences in boundary permeability between the economy and the family, saying that for the traditional provider role, the demands of work are permitted to intrude upon the family, but not vice versa: family needs are not to permeate the occupational sphere.[18]

Skolnick's discussion of the communal movement is equally applicable to the single-parent family form.[44] She states that there has always been variation in families, but that these variations have been considered deviant because no argument was made for them on principle. Increasing numbers of families with only one parent, including fathers raising children, unmarried mothers raising children, and single persons adopting children, are making the case for this variant form to be included under the umbrella of *normal*.

REFERENCES

1. Ross, Heather, and Sawhill, Isabel: *Time of Transition.* Washington, Urban Inst, 1975.
2. Cutright, Phillips: Components of change in the number of female family heads aged 15-44: United States, 1940-1970. *J Marriage and the Family, 36*:714-721, 1974.
3. Brandwein, Ruth; Brown, Carol; and Fox, Elizabeth: Women and children last: The social situation of divorced mothers and their families. *J Marriage and the Family, 36*:488-489, 1974.
4. Weiss, Robert: *Marital Separation.* New York, Basic, 1975.
5. Goode, William: *Women in Divorce.* Glencoe, Free Pr, 1956.
6. Kreps, Juanita and Clark, Robert: *Sex, Age, and Work: The Changing Composition of the Labor Force.* Baltimore, Johns Hopkins, 1975.
7. Laslett, Peter and Wall, Richard: *Household and Family in Past Time,* Cambridge, Cambridge U Pr, 1972.
8. Boulding, Elise: *Women in the Twentieth Century World.* Beverly Hills, Sage, 1977.
9. Norwood, Janet: New approaches to statistics on the family. *Monthly Labor Review, July*:31-34, 1977.
10. Bane, Mary Jo: Marital disruption and the lives of children. *J Social Issues, 32*:103-109, 1976.
11. Kamerman, Sheila and Kahn, Alfred: Explorations in family policy. *Social Work, 32*:103-109, 1976.
12. Moynihan, Daniel: *The Negro Family: The Case for National Action.* Washington, Department of Labor, 1965.
13. Carter, Hugh and Glick, Paul: *Marriage and Divorce: A Social and Economic Study.* Cambridge, Harvard U Pr, 1970.
14. Glick, Paul: A demographer looks at American families. *J Marriage and the Family, 15*:15-26, 1975.
15. Gross, Edward: Plus a change? The sexual structure of occupations over time. *Social Problems, 16*:198-208, 1968.
16. Gronseth, Erik: The breadwinner trap. In Howe, Louise (Ed.): *The Future of the Family.* New York, S & S, 1972, pp. 175-191.
17. Gronseth, Erik: The husband-provider role: a critical appraisal. In Michel, Andree (Ed.): *Family Issues of Employed Women in Europe and America.* Leiden, Brill, 1971.
18. Pleck, Joseph: The work-family role system. *Social Problems, 24*:417-427, 1977.
19. Woolsey, Suzanne: Pied piper politics and the child care debate. *Daedulus, 106*:127-146, 1977.
20. U. S. Department of Labor: *Earnings Gap Between Men and Women.* Washington, Government Printing Office, 1976.

21. Lloyd, C. B.: *Sex, Discrimination and the Division of Labor.* New York, Columbia U Pr, 1975.
22. Ross, Heather: Poverty: women and children last. In Chapman, Jane Robert, and Gates, Margaret (Eds.): *Economic Independence for Women: The Foundation for Equal Rights.* Beverly Hills, Russell Sage, 1976, pp. 137-154.
23. National Academy of Science: *Toward a National Policy for Children and Families.* Washington, National Academy of Science, 1976.
24. Finer, M. (Ed.): *Report of the Committee on One-Parent Families.* London, Her Majesty's Stationary Office, 1974.
25. Condry, J. C. and Simon, M. A.: Characteristics of peer and adult-oriented children. *J Marriage and the Family, 36:*543-554, 1974.
26. Burgess, Jane: The single-parent family: a social and sociological problem. *Family Coordinator, 9:*137-144, 1970.
27. Schlesinger, Benjamin: One parent families in Great Britain. *Family Coordinator, 26:*139-141, 1977.
28. Ferre, Elsa: Growing-up in a one-parent family. *Concern, 20:*7-10, 1976.
29. Birdwhistell, R. L.: The idealized model of the American family. *Social Casework, 50:*195-198, 1970.
30. Feldman, Harold and Feldman, Margaret: The family life cycle: some suggestions for recycling. *J Marriage and the Family, 37:*277-284, 1975.
31. Schorr, Alvin: The family cycle and income development. *Social Security Bulletin, 29:*14-25, 1966.
32. Oppenheimer, Valeri: The life-cycle squeeze: the interaction of men's occupational and family life cycles. *Demography, 11:*227-246, 1974.
33. Bernard, Jessie: *The Future of Marriage.* New York, Bantam, 1972.
34. Weiss, Robert: The emotional impact of marital separation. *J Social Issues, 32:*135-145, 1976.
35. Brown, C. A.; Feldberg, R.; Fox, E. M.; and Kahew, J.: Divorce: chance of a new lifetime. *J Social Issues, 32:*119-132, 1976.
36. Marciano, Teresa Donati: Variant family forms in a world perspective. *Family Coordinator, 24:*1975.
37. Sawhill, Isabel: Discrimination and poverty among women who head families. *Signs: Journal of Women in Culture and Society, 1-3:*201-221, 1976.
38. Caldwell, B.: Infant daycare — the outcast gains respectability. In Koby, P. (Ed.): *Child Care: Who Cares: Foreign and Domestic Infant and Early Childhood Development Policies.* New York, Basic, 1973.
39. Rossi, Alice: A biosocial perspective on parenting. *Daedulus, 106:*1-31, 1977.
40. Pearlin, Leonard and Johnson, Joyce: Marital status, life-strains, and depression. *American Sociological Review, 42:*704-715, 1977.
41. Bernard, Jessie: Changing family life styles, one role, two roles, shared roles. In Howe, Louise (Ed.): *The Future of the Family.* New York, S & S, 1972.

42. Duberman, Lucile: *Marriage and Its Alternatives.* New York, Praeger, 1974.
43. Safilios-Rothschild, Constantina: *Women and Social Policy.* Englewood Cliffs, P-H, 1974, p. 106.
44. Skolnick, Arlene and Skolnick, Jerome: *Family in Transition,* Boston, Little, 1971.

Chapter 6

SUPPORT, NOT SUPPLANT, THE NATURAL HOME: SERVING HANDICAPPED CHILDREN AND ADULTS

Edward Skarnulis

EACH year, thousands of families are broken by unnecessary placements of handicapped children and adults into group homes, institutions, foster homes, and other residential facilities. The costs of such placements are high: family members are emotionally drained; society assumes a one million dollar debt for an individual's lifetime care; and the handicapped person, who is the pawn in the game, suffers the loss of loved ones as well as the loss of opportunities for normal development. While this chapter focuses on mentally retarded persons, the human service principles discussed can apply to all disability groups and *normal* populations as well.

The Developmental Principle

Educators like Itard and Seguin in France and Howe in the United States were showing us alternative solutions to this practice as far back as the nineteenth century. Their attitudes epitomized what we today call the Developmental Principle. That is, they believed a mentally handicapped person would grow and develop if given the right environment, and that such an environment requires a profound belief in the handicapped person as one worthy of the same dignity given to nonhandicapped people. Certainly, then, the person is not an inanimate object without feelings or understanding. Tied into the Developmental Principle is belief in the Dignity of Risk.[1] Simply put, this means that just as you and I must learn through experience and risk-taking, it is vitally important not to encap-

64

sulate a handicapped person in an overprotective, artificial world where he or she can never know the experiences that go with living and learning. Robert Smithdas put it well:

> I think that I was very fortunate, because while I was growing up I was not inhibited by my family or teachers in doing the things I wanted to do. If I felt like wandering around my home or the neighborhood, my family permitted it. At the first deaf school I attended, all of the teachers were concerned that I would wander away from the premises, but that didn't keep me from wandering about the grounds as much as I pleased. Later, when I went to the Perkins School for the Blind, where I attended high school, all of the deaf-blind children were protected by their teachers and carefully guarded against anything that might cause injury. I rebelled against having a constant companion, because I felt that I was capable of taking care of myself and I didn't want a companion when I wanted to do certain things. I feel that this type of supervision has changed to a great degree in many of the schools that have special departments for deaf-blind children. Today, teachers are beginning to realize that the way to help a child to grow is to encourage his curiosity and help him experience as many things as he possibly can by touching them, tasting and smelling them, or by exploring them in any other way that seems feasible.[2]

The Principle of Normalization

In 1959, Bank-Mikkelson of Denmark formulated a principle called Normalization, which was translated into English in 1969 by a Swede, Bengt Nirje. It is a most eloquent statement of what parents want for their children. Throughout the 1950s and 1960s, parents were upset about the failure of the government to help their retarded sons and daughters. They were frustrated in trying to explain their needs to professionals and government functionaries. Then they discovered the Principle of Normalization, which means ". . . making available to the mentally retarded patterns and conditions of everyday life which are as close as possible to the norms and patterns of the mainstream of society."[3] These were not naive parents who wanted to believe their children were not mentally retarded, or that the condition could be cured. They just felt that if their children could live with normal people, in their home towns, they could have more stimulation, more developmental growth experiences, and could come as close as possible to achieving their maximum potential. For example, normalization means not having to go to bed at the same time as younger brothers and sisters just because you're retarded; celebrating holidays like everybody else and not on a different day because the institution does not have full staff levels on July 4 or December 25. It means being treated like an adult if you are one, enjoying the company of members of the opposite sex, living in a normal rhythm of life so that when you get old and want to stay in surroundings that are familiar to you someone does not cart you off to a nursing home. Normalization means self-sufficiency; making it on your own in your home with a little help from a friendly visitor or Meals on Wheels.

Normalization is deceptively simple. It forces us to reexamine our terminology and our traditional ways of providing services. If I am *Mr.* Skarnulis, then why should my mentally retarded adult friend not be called *Mr.* Smith? Does an isolated institution called Hope Haven really provide hope? How are people likely to be served in such an environment? Are state hospital-schools truly either hospitals or schools? Someone has asked if special education in schools is either special or education. Is *special* a euphemism for *deviant*? Is *education* a euphemism for *segregation*?

Certainly there are times when we cannot treat people with handicaps as though those handicaps do not exist. Remember that Normalization means making available conditions as *nearly* normal as possible, and Dignity of Risk means *reasonable* risk. Accepting these principles requires using good judgment. We should neither smother people with protection nor should we push them into water over their heads. Somehow we must develop the ability to differentiate between limits that we set for handicapped people and the limits that they or their handicaps or environments set for themselves.

The Residential Assumption

Have we lost our rationale for residential systems in this country? Parents rarely say "We need our son out of the house seven days a week." What they say is "How can I keep him from scratching his sister?" or "We haven't had a chance to join a bowling league or spend a weekend alone together since Jimmy was born." Their first pleas to social service agencies are for ordinary relief like babysitting, which other parents take for granted. Too often, unimaginative professionals and rigid service structures make simple, inexpensive, creative options more difficult to provide than expensive extremes like group homes, institutions, and foster care. Solutions to human problems are defined in terms of available resources rather than human needs.

Somewhere on the path to developing residential systems, we have stumbled onto a nineteenth century mindset, the Residential Assumption. This Residential Assumption means a person is assumed to need residential facilities simply because he or she is mentally retarded. For years that assumption went unquestioned. We all grew up hearing things like "The Scott girl is going to an institution." "Why?" "Oh, she is retarded, you know." It always seemed like a reasonable answer. Now, if parents of a child with normal intelligence had the audacity to approach a social worker and demand removal of their child to a residential facility, the caseworker would be duly outraged. However, it has been common for parents to expel their handicapped sons and daughters without censure simply because they are often given no less drastic solutions to their stress. Teachers, doctors, social workers, and psychologists have sometimes been the catalyst in encouraging such action on highly questionable grounds, such as a belief that the mere presence of a handicapped child in a family will be detrimental to the siblings; or a knee-jerk conclusion that the child is the problem when the real problems are lack of school programs, respite care, or vocational opportunities. There is a rather lazy presumption that family pathology is brought on by stress, which is probably true, and the stress would not have existed if the child were not handicapped, which may or may not be true.

The Residential Assumption persists in spite of our knowledge that about 97 percent of mentally retarded persons are *not* in residential systems and despite the fact that neither *mentally retarded* nor *residential services* refer to easily defined, homogeneous categories. The term *mentally retarded* may describe a profoundly retarded, medically fragile, nonambulatory child; it may describe a mildly retarded adult who is married and employed in a well-paying job. It includes people who are literate and those who are not; people who are emotionally disturbed, and those who are healthy; people who live alone and others who live with family or friends.

Another characteristic of the Residential Assumption is that having entered a residential continuum, a person must remain there indefinitely. This is the basis for a number of court actions which allege that some residential systems are engaging in extralegal incarceration with no assurance the residents will ever be released. Unfortunately, the prevalent view in the minds of many parents, private citizens, and professionals is that mental retardation alone is sufficient justification to remove people from a normal environment into an artificial one. Everyone knows mentally retarded people should be with their own kind; everyone knows they cannot care for themselves. Everyone, that is, except mentally retarded people and their families.

Support, Not Supplant, the Natural Home

What are residential services? Are they needed and, if so, why?

Certainly residential services are needed, at least sometimes. They exist to meet the needs of all of us when we cannot be served in our own homes. Some examples follow: a college student who lives in a dormitory is a consumer of residential services; hospitalization for severe physical or emotional problems is a form of residential services; homes disrupted by divorce or death, or homes where a child is abused or neglected, cannot support these children, and alternatives such as care by extended family members or foster families may be necessary. Rural communities that have limited vocational or educational opportunities may require inhabitants to work or go to school elsewhere during the week. Indian reservations may have boarding schools, and traveling salesmen stay at Holiday Inns.

In all cases, the reason for admission into the residential setting is clear.

What Is Needed

In 1968, a frank director of a service for mentally retarded persons in San Francisco said to a naive student, "Look, mothers need diagnosis and assessment of their retarded children as much as they need a hole in the head; they have been told many times what is wrong; what they need is services . . . It is services that are required, not surveys, committees of inquiry, or other expensive excuses for inaction."[4]

Imagine the plight of a tired mother of six children, all under ten years of age, when a physical therapist tells her she must exercise her handicapped three-year-old's legs an hour a day. It is not surprising that we see evidence of stress in that family nor should we be puzzled when she tearfully requests removal of the handicapped child from the home.

Parents need generalists, not specialists. They need housekeepers who can dust, scrub floors, or wash dishes and are also willing to help with the handicapped child. They need ramps built for the child's wheelchair, support bars in the bathroom, hard-of-hearing handsets on the telephone, multitextured toys to stimulate tactile perception, financial assistance with medical bills, and transportation to hospitals and community agencies. In-home teachers and classes on child development are great, but only after survival needs are met.

The following are some ways a service system could operate. A child has just been born and parents have been told that she has a serious physical or mental problem. A nurse, doctor, or social worker at the hospital may refer the family to a local association for retarded citizens or another agency which serves handicapped people. The agency sends someone to the hospital or the home, preferably another parent who has shared the same experience. Going to the family rather than requiring them to come to the agency is a symbolic departure from the traditional superior relationship that service agencies assume. All people feel more comfortable talking about personal crises on their own turf. Home visits clarify that the family is the client whom agency personnel exist to serve. The family is encouraged to explain what they want, in their own words. They may need prompting to admit a need for money, transportation, or medical equipment. In some cases, the parents have less difficulty accepting their child's handicap than do members of the extended family. Perhaps the grandmother or uncle or aunt is the one who needs education or counseling.

It should be made clear at the outset that the family calls the shots and the agency is the family's partner. "What do you think you need to help your son or daughter grow and develop?" It is what the parents perceive to be important, and the agency's ability to be their interpreter, that will yield the best results for the child. Most people cannot use technical jargon and may require help to translate those needs into suitable requests. A creative and knowledgeable counselor can understand a parent's general concern about money and costs of medical care, and translate those concerns into specific funding sources.

When families come to service agencies with specific problems that need specific solutions, it should be kept simple. The mother is exhausted? Give her some help in the home so she can have some time for rest. The parents have no time for recreation and social life? Then provide them with babysitters or weekend helpers who can not only take care of the handicapped child but the other siblings as well. The neighbors are giving the family a rough time? Send a staff member to meet with the neighbors. If that does not work, contact local authorities to prevent harassment. Too often we give people well-intentioned advice when they do not have the emotional resources to act on it. In such cases we must do for them until they can do for themselves. Some examples of possible agency response follow:

a. Dad is out of work: The agency can help him find a job.
b. The child has a physical handicap: Thousands of prosthetic appliances and educational toys are available in special schools or hospitals; all could be loaned to families. A carpenter working with a physical therapist, speech therapist, or teacher can work miracles with scraps of wood.
c. Parents wonder who will help their child if they should die unexpectedly: The agency can help locate an attorney, and perhaps a trustworthy insurance agent or banker.
d. Toilet training is a problem: Simple bells, buzzers, and lights have been used successfully in alerting parents. Combined with behavioral modification, this problem can be resolved with the agency helping the parents.
e. Mother does not have enough time for the other children: The agency could help obtain a washer, a dryer, a second car, or even bus tokens.

Families of handicapped persons should be seen as first-class citizens who are doing their best to keep the rest of us from having to pay the costs of their child's problems. If all of these families demanded residential services, or society could not possibly absorb the costs. They are not asking for charity; they understand the problem of some solutions. What they need is concrete help.

Principle of the Least Restrictive Alternative

Sometimes, no matter what is done for them, people must leave their homes. It is done when there is a need that cannot possibly be met otherwise, a need that exists in the person, the family, or in the community.

A need in the person includes physical or emotional illnesses. For example, appendicitis requires hospitalization while surgery is performed. It constitutes a special need and therefore a special environment. Psychotic behavior which threatens the individual or others requires treatment outside the home.

A need in the family is often confused with a need in the person. Mental retardation in a family member is not a cause of family dysfunction; however, lack of support services is. Skill deficits of a handicapped family member, left unattended, create a situation of extraordinary dependency on parents or other siblings. Illness and death may also result in temporary breakdown of the family unit. When the environment is poor due to parent educational or intellectual deficits, or low social or economic status, all family members suffer. By removing the mentally retarded member, society deludes itself into thinking the problem is solved. The family condition worsens and any hope of reunion fades.

A need in the community has many faces. If one must commute from a small town to a larger city to work it is because the home community has failed to provide the right vocational opportunities. Similarly, a student who attends a university located some distance from home is no different from a mentally retarded person leaving a rural area to get job training. Put simply, the community cannot sustain its members.

Before anyone is admitted into residential service systems, the reason for placement and the objectives must be defined. If we do not know why someone is being admitted, we will never know when they are ready to return home. Without a clearly defined reason for placement, a predictable cycle of conflict develops between the service system and the family. The family is displaced, previously agreed upon arrangements become blurred by time, and roles become confused. The family wonders why their suggestions are ignored and perhaps they become more insistent. The residential staff resent such intrusions into their world, and cannot understand the causes of the friction. They perform family functions for the natural family and appropriate more and more parental authority.

Ideally, agency personnel should tailor each residence to fit the person needing services. If that is not possible, before removing a child or adult from his or her home, we must ask ourselves "What would be the most normal, least restrictive environment which will maximize continued family contact?"

In measuring degrees of restrictiveness, three measures are useful: the size of the residence, the distance from the home, and the time of residence.

Considering the size of the residence, the more unrelated people living together, the more difficult it is to personalize services to meet individual needs. Military barracks or college dormitories are good examples of this phenomenon.

A person with special needs sometimes requires much extra attention and hard work. Even in a typical household, if parents must care for both their severely handicapped child as well as normal siblings without help, someone somewhere will have to sacrifice. Either the parents burn the candle at both ends, jeopardizing their own physical and mental health, or the handicapped child may lack necessary educational or medical help, or the normal brothers and sisters may not receive proper nurture from the parents. They too may fail to develop appropriately or may become jealous of the attention paid to the handicapped sibling.

It is important to remember, however, that in the natural home the parents are invested in the outcome of their work with the handicapped child. They care what happens. The most dedicated staff members in the smallest residential facilities are never quite able to replicate that total commitment. It is far different to be awakened at 2 AM by the crying of your own child than by someone else's. The likelihood is far greater that a parent will be a stronger advocate with doctors, teachers, and social workers for his own child.

In a segregated residential facility, where demands for staff time are heavy, handicapped children have to compete for attention with other handicapped children. Only the children who are the most aggressive, cutest, or whose parents wield the greatest influence reap rewards from such an environment.

In looking at the distance of the facility from the family home, it is important to remember the saying "Out of sight, out of mind." It is not uncommon to see close family groups slowly deteriorate when a handicapped member is placed. At first the visits to the facility are frequent and warm, but interests change and loyalties wither. Economics and logistics intervene. When parents and brothers and sisters have to spend many hours traveling to distant residential facilities and must absorb the expense of such trips, it is no wonder that ties get broken. The decreasing frequency of visits becomes a source of guilt for family members who begin to devise rationalizations, such as the staff are better trained, the handicapped person is happier, or the placement will only be short-term. There is a modicum of truth in such rationalizations. It may be true that some staff have special training. But skills required to serve handicapped persons are not magical; they can be learned by parents. While it is true that families usually intended to have the handicapped child returned home in a short time, more often than not the child stays in the facility indefinitely. There are rarely contracts which require that developmental progress be made in a reasonable time. While it is true that some training occurs in residential settings, the bulk of education and training takes place during the school day. Furthermore, residential staff are seldom highly skilled individuals whose primary purpose is to provide treatment and training. They are usually ordinary people who live with the handicapped individual and relate well to that individual.

The longer a person is kept out of his or her home the more difficult it is to get back in again. Things change; neighbors move away; buildings vanish. The familiar sights, sounds, and smells can be altered dramatically in a short time. It is difficult enough for nonhandicapped persons to cope with such constant changes. But for a mentally handicapped person removed from the community for many years, the difficulty of reintegration is magnified. Paradoxically, the claims of most residential systems are that they exist to prepare people for reentry into their own homes and families. How can artificial learning environments be generalized to the real world?

The whole process of selecting from among existing alternative residences is so important that it bears repetition. Three parameters of the degree of restrictiveness which help test the appropriateness of a placement are size, distance, and time. Is the residence as small as possible? Is it as close as possible to the community where the person will ultimately live? Is the placement as short as possible? If partial services will fill the need, then it would be foolish to provide twenty-four-hour service. If a parent needs an operation, serve the child in the family home rather than a residential facility. If an adult can get along living alone, with a few support services, then he should not be placed in a nursing home. If a local hospital can perform a medical procedure, do not send the handicapped person to an institutional hospital many miles away.

Do not fabricate reasons for admission to residential facilities. Too often the word *handicapped* stimulates our helper glands. If the family has a problem and the person must enter a residence, attend to the family's problem and provide the client with reasonable living conditions. It does not make sense to establish elaborate training programs for the handicapped person when the family is in turmoil. After the family's problem has been dealt with, training needs can be focused on. We, as service providers, should enlist the parents' aid in identifying skill development programs for the child, since their willingness to continue such programs in the home is in direct proportion to their investment in such programs.

Summary

The term *exit criteria* has been used to describe the goals a person must achieve before he or she is allowed to move to more normal residences. The burden of proof is theirs. Does everyone not deserve a small, homelike environment? Is such a home a privilege or a right? The accident of fate which decreed a person severely handicapped should never be the excuse for denying them the warmth and comfort of a normal home.

Standards tend to be based upon "beds" and floor space, rather than more normalized criteria, and doctors still tend to be in charge of developmental concerns when their training is not in these areas of all. Most of all, this inappropriate management model threatens to spread the medical-model into the community despite its abysmal failure behind institutional walls. Powerful lobbies have convinced the government that because a person has an ongoing medical problem, that should dominate his whole life, and all living activities should revolve around this aspect of his person. Which is about the same as saying that since I sleep nearly a third of my life, the AMM (American Mattress Manufacturers) should decide where I can live, with whom, what I eat, etc.[5]

Failure of communities to provide adequate resources to their children, especially those who are handicapped, has often resulted in undue family stress and dysfunction. What will happen when community resources are fully adequate? With adequate services, will our children not need residential support as adults?

We must recognize that the Residential Assumption is both cause and end product of our failure to support the family or open the doors of existing community resources. Residential services are not, as we have proudly proclaimed, a symbol of our concern and love for handicapped children and adults, but a monument to our failure to support, not supplant, the natural home.

REFERENCES

1. Perske, Robert: The dignity of risk and the mentally retarded. *Mental Retardation, 10:*24, 1972.
2. Smithdas, Robert: Vocational education and the future of the deaf-blind. In *Proceedings: The Deaf-Blind Child and the Vocational Rehabilitation Counselor.* San Diego, California State Department of Education, 1975, pp. 2-4.
3. Nirje, Bengt: The normalization principle and its human management implications. In U. S. Department of Health, Education, and Welfare: *Changing Patterns in Residential Services for the Mentally Retarded.* Washington, Government Printing Office, 1972, pp. 179-195.
4. Crawford, Donald: Unpublished report.
5. Pieper, Elizabeth: Unpublished report.

Chapter 7

RESIDENTIAL GROUP CARE AND HOME-BASED CARE: TOWARD A CONTINUITY OF FAMILY SERVICES

RICHARD SMALL AND JAMES WHITTAKER

FOR the child welfare professional, the case for home-based service as an alternative to out-of-home intervention rests on an uneven argument. Certainly, the basic premises of the argument — family life is important to child development and all intervention should support family integrity — are difficult to dispute. Among other things, these premises stand as a constructive challenge to service providers; treatment philosophies which view the family as pathogenic, or which consider the individual child separate from family and community influences, are outmoded and need to be revised.

Yet despite such a persuasive foundation, extending the argument to promote home-based care as the most important single vehicle for child welfare service is much less defensible. The resulting rhetoric of reform overstates the case, and oversimplifies the essential issues. The National Clearinghouse for Home-Based Services states:

> Home life is the highest and finest product of civilization . . . children should not be deprived of it except for urgent and compelling reasons. This principle, stated by the White House Conference on Children in 1909, and restated in the Child Welfare League of America Standards in 1941, emphasizes the value of having children remain in their homes if at all possible. Yet 1,000,000 children are in substitute care today and 90 percent of the child welfare dollar is expended for out-of-home care. Home-based services to children and their families is committed to that principle of making the *first* and *greatest* resource investment in treating and caring for children and their families in their own homes.

77

The problem with these statements, apart from errors of fact, is not that they call for reorganization of the service delivery system, but that they do so based on a misleading dichotomy between home-based service and the substitute care industry. Such a dichotomy involves assumptions about group care and child welfare services as a whole which deserve a closer look. In the first place, lumping together all residential and foster care programs in a single category cannot be justified. Especially from the standpoint of group treatment, the suggestion is that every residential setting serves the same institutional purpose, with all the attendant negative connotations for child well-being and family life. Although the large, impersonal, and isolated institution for children unfortunately still exists, it is not the only model for residential placement. The fact is that group care in this country, while separating the family, is a diversity of programs, with significant differences regarding size, length of stay, staff competence, flexibility of programming, degree of family involvement, community relatedness, and a host of other factors.

Even more problematic, however, broadly labelling all child welfare services as either *home-based* or *substitute,* tends to confuse the form of intervention with its substantive intent. Thus, the implication in the statement quoted above is that the *locus* of any child care service determines its *focus* with regard to the family. There is no compelling reason to believe that simply "treating the family as a service unit on its own turf" is inevitably more effective in keeping families together, or even less detrimental to the quality of family life than intervention that takes place outside the home. Indeed, it is possible to think of situations in which temporary out-of-home care, such as intensive residential treatment or respite care for families with profoundly handicapped children, is a necessity for the maintenance of long-term family integration. It is equally possible to imagine unanticipated side effects of home-based interventions acting to increase, rather than diminish, divisive stress within a family. If one were to equate family-oriented helping *only* with home-based intervention, this would be misleading: it would deny the complex range of special needs which makes individual family integrity much more complicated than continuity to the home; and it suggests that merely avoiding placement is a desirable criterion for success in comprehensive family service.

Surely the goal of reform is not simply to relocate existing services so that they take place in the home, but to develop more effective ways of supporting family life by serving troubled children and their families in a total context. In this case, the real issue is much larger than home-based versus out-of-home intervention as competing service strategies. It is the challenge to organize all possible resources to provide a continuity of care for children whatever their needs, while at the same time maintaining a primary focus on family and community life. The objective in making a service plan for any child and family should be to build a "powerful environment" for growth, whether or not that environment includes an out-of-home placement.[1] This means adjusting our thinking and our rhetoric to a more comprehensive planning task: developing home and community interventions as creative alternatives, and redefining the boundaries between families and out-of-home settings to promote maximum interaction when placement does occur. Only when both parts of this task are emphasized can we develop an integrated network of child and family services. As we shall stress in the remainder of the chapter, the continuum of services can and should include residential group care.

Group Care as a Supportive Family Service

Establishing group care as a family support means first confronting long-standing cultural bias in the basic definition of service. Wolins and many others have pointed out that the only fully acceptable paradigm for childrearing in the United States is child care within the natural family.[1,2] Extended care outside the family, especially in group settings, is usually seen as a last resort. It may be unavoidable in catastrophic or pathological circumstances but it is always regarded with considerable suspicion. Largely as a consequence of this cultural norm, the definition of residential group placement has been a substitute for the family, providing custodial care or specialized treatment in situations in which the family is presumed incapable of caring for the child or the child is incapable of functioning in the family. As noted in the rhetoric of home-based care, the implied dichotomy in such a definition is emphatic: group care supplants rather than supports family life; children with special needs either receive help in their own homes or they are treated outside the family.

In our view, this culturally determined definition of residential placement cannot be accepted as an adequate basis for intervention. It stereotypes both parents and professional caregivers, and leads to two serious problems in the delivery of effective helping.

First, the identification of group care as an end-of-the-line family substitute implicitly isolates the residential environment outside the normative life of the community. As such, the frequent result has been dead-end placement for the children involved. It is this isolation, and not group life as a method of child care, that breeds the problems and abuses rightly deplored by advocates of deinstitutionalization and other critics of residential care.[3,4,5]

Second, the narrow definition of group care as a substitute for the family has meant the underutilization of a valuable resource in the network of services. Practitioners have largely ignored the possibility of constructive family and community involvement in residential programs. Moreover, there has been little experimentation with degrees of care in placement, or placements designed in combination with home-based services. In effect, prevailing cultural attitudes have locked group care in a limited role.

What is needed, then, is a functional definition of residential group care that is inclusive rather than exclusive of the family. Specifically, we need to reject the notion that families and residential settings are discontinuous, mutually exclusive environments for children. This is not, of course, a new insight. Constructive change based on this premise has already begun to take place within child welfare.[6] In particular, the past ten years have witnessed a slowly growing movement toward an ecological approach to group child care which emphasizes family and community involvement as crucial in the helping process.[7] In the present context, we can make good use of these ecological ideas to construct a more flexible definition of group care in relation to the family. We contend that —

residential group care is a comprehensive child welfare service. As a format for primary child care it has a unique potential for providing both a base of support and a laboratory for the development of services to children in their own homes. As a format for growth and change, it is a powerful environment in its own right. In this sense, it is a clinical intervention best understood as a total environment for teaching skills for living to children and their parents. The potential for differential family involvement is unlimited.

Obviously, this alternative definition suggests a very different picture of group care than that held by many practitioners. Yet we are convinced that it is a realistic view which is currently shaping the structure of innovative programs across the country.[8,9] Both parts of the definition are important, and both have tremendous implications for the design of child and family services.

Structural Linkages to Home-Based Care

Perhaps the most important concept contained in our definition of group care is the idea that substitute care does not have to mean the complete abdication of parental responsibility. It seems to us much more useful to consider the provision of out-of-home child care along a continuum from total substitute care for those few children whose separation from the natural family needs to be complete to traditional temporary care with varying degrees of direct parental involvement.[10] Once such a continuum is established, it becomes possible to think about the constructive integration of home-based service and differential forms of residential group care. In fact, the potential for complimentary functioning and sharing of resources is very real.

First, group care in its positive forms is a natural laboratory for the development of effective child care techniques. In this sense it can be an extremely valuable resource to home-based programs. Information garnered from specifically designed living environments with troubled and troubling children has much to offer parents, foster parents, day care providers, and other community care professionals.

Second, residential settings could be used to provide direct support in the delivery of sophisticated home-based services. This can be organizational or financial support, but it can also take the form of temporary substitute care as back up to home-based intervention in difficult situations. One example already mentioned is the possible use of periodic, temporary group care for profoundly handicapped youngsters. In this situation, respite care can be an alternative to institutionalization; in combination with intensive commitment of resources to the home, it can support the primary goal of keeping the family together. Long-term child care responsibility remains with the parents. Similarly, intensive work with families of troubled adolescents might include a partial placement where a young person is connected to a group home or other semiautonomous living arrangement as back up, while continuing work with the family unit. Here, instead of usurping family responsibility and treating the adolescent separately, group care can again be used as a temporary support. It can also be used as a positive step toward constructive integration of services. There are real possibilities for group care as a support in the selection of family-oriented services.

Parents as Partners in Helping

Aside from providing a range of substitute child care services in support of home-based programs, group care can be a powerful family intervention in its own right. In the second part of our definition, we identify residential treatment as a therapeutic environment for both children and their families. The most meaningful goal of intervention with this emphasis is to teach skills for living, not to cure an individual child nor to be an antidote to harmful influences of family and community life. There are two critical assumptions underlying this conviction:

1. Most children live with, or will return to, natural or foster families who represent their primary source of maintenance, support, and socialization. Any change that takes place must make sense in this primary context.
2. Success in treatment will vary according to our ability to involve the parents as full and equal partners in the process of helping.

With these assumptions as a point of departure, we believe that the key to including parents as partners in the therapeutic environment is differential involvement. Traditionally, many programs offer parents a single role as client, as a basis for participation in placement. The usual rationale is the belief that the parents themselves are troubled, disorganized, and in need of treatment. Yet even though this is often true to some extent,[11] limiting parents to this single vehicle for participation overlooks the numerous other possibilities for growth and change available to them such as parent education and family support groups. Further, such singlemindedness in working with families also overlooks the fact that even the most troubled families are not constantly incapacitated and may occasionally have much to contribute as volunteer parents supporters. It is the identification and utilization of these opportunities for parent involvement that lead to parents becoming full and equal partners in the helping process. The treatment program should structure family work to serve two broad purposes.

The first purpose should be to create a bridge between the group living environment and the child's own natural living milieu. Family involvement will ideally take many forms, each of which should constitute a linkage between the family culture and the culture of group life. These linkages might include conjoint family therapy, family support groups, parent education, parent involvement in life space, home visiting by the child care staff, board and volunteer participation, participation in school programs, family advocacy, educational planning, placement help in foster care or emancipation, and parents as legislative advocates.

Another purpose of family work should be to identify any natural helping networks that exist in the child's family constellation which could be called upon to support and maintain growth achieved in the group living environment. Such networks might contain extended family members, friends, clergy, natural neighbors, and other indigenous helpers. The program should be open to involving these persons actively whenever this is appropriate.

Of all the formats for parent involvement, three are especially powerful in directly including parents in their child's education for living. These are parent support groups, parent education, and parents as participants in the life space.

Parent Support Groups

In residential treatment where parent involvement has consisted mainly of work with individual families, there is a pressing need to identify ways in which families can come together and be supportive of one another. One way to achieve this is by setting up ongoing parent support groups. Many residential programs are faced with the limitations of geographical distance. When practical, however, the residential center may provide valuable expertise in staff leadership, as well as a place to meet, and other resources such as child care for siblings during group meetings. It can also encourage the idea that parents, as consumers, have an active role to play in the program and a need to know one another in order to identify common concerns. Support groups may eventually form the nucleus of a parent organization with more diverse goals and a wider reaching involvement in the program. Initially, however, the focus should be on the provision of support through shared experiences, development of informal helping networks, and the opportunity for socialization. Informal social ties and communication links should especially be encouraged, helping to overcome the true feelings of isolation that many families of troubled children experience.[12] Perhaps the most important message that can be conveyed is that someone else besides themselves and the professional staff, knows about their child, cares about his or her progress, and shares an intimate understanding of what it is like to live with and care for a troubled child. When relieved of this duty, through placement, the motivation of some families to work on problem resolution could decrease.

Parent Education

Working with parents as parents, and not as patients, should include teaching the parent survival skills, so often needed when raising a child with special needs. We pointed out earlier that the residential center can be a natural laboratory offering families much in this regard.

When physical proximity permits, the actual provision of parent education can be through a variety of teaching formats, from small group discussion to training in the home as well as in the life space.[13] However, no matter which approach is employed, the following criteria need to be kept in mind for maximum impact.

Cultural relatedness: Parent education should not only be harmonious with ethnic, class, and neighborhood values, it should fit the particular family culture. This means a sensitivity to the family's values, goals, and roles.

Situational specificity: Parents need techniques that work in the home. Thus, the ultimate test of parent education should be in the home or foster home to which the child will return. Any failure experienced there should be seen as failures of the parent educators to provide techniques that work in the real life environment of the home, rather than as failures of the parent in applying them.

Social validity:[14] Parents and foster parents need to feel that they can actively and enthusiastically support the strategies of childrearing being taught, and the choice of problem behaviors to which they are directed. This means the professional should actively seek to identify those areas of child management that are giving the parents the most pain and stress and help devise strategies to alleviate them. It further suggests that parents and child be afforded regular channels for feedback, not only on content but also on method.

Parents as Coparticipants in the Life Space

Parent involvement in the daily functioning of the residential treatment program has traditionally been minimal. Visiting days are usually ritualized, artificial, and on weekends when staff are unavailable. Two separate sets of parenting persons — child care workers and parents — come together briefly, perhaps with a social worker intermediary, to catch up on the child's progress and the family's recent history. This limited parent participation in the life space to such infrequent and uncomfortable interaction fails to exploit an opportunity for mutual learning. From the perspective of the parents, more normal involvement can mean the opportunity to see other adults managing and teaching their child. Even such events as a child care worker losing his or her temper, or failing to control misbehavior, can have benefits in demonstrating to the parent that inadequacy is not theirs alone. For the child care worker and other professional staff, greater parent involvement can mean less stereotyping of parents and more understanding of the differences that exist between the family culture and the culture of group living.

Except for geographical distance, absence of siblings, and the decreased motivation that sometimes occurs when a child is placed, the potential for parents as coparticipants is limited only by the collective imagination of staff and families. Other formats can include such simple things as frequent telephone contact, invitations to families or special friends to share in a meal, participation in special activities such as birthday parties, and regularly scheduled observation periods. Parent involvement can also truly mean shared responsibility. One way to incorporate this responsibility would be to move to a five-day model of treatment,[15] or to include parents in program and policy planning.

In all of this emphasis on parents as partners, we cannot deny that there may be difficulties. Many centers which would welcome fuller parent involvement find they cannot achieve it because of uncooperative parents, or parents who are so caught up in their own life problems that they simply do not have the energy for involvement outside their daily struggles. As noted above, many families live at a great distance from the residential center which makes frequent visits a hardship, and some programs lack the resources of space and staff to permit anything but an occasional parent visit. All of these are real issues, but they are not insurmountable. The most important first step is to move away from the tradition-bound barriers and develop a role and function for parents in the residential environment that extends beyond clinical treatment.

REFERENCES

1. Wolins, Martin (Ed.): *Successful Group Care: Explorations in the Powerful Environment.* Chicago, Aldine, 1974.
2. Wolins, Martin: Group care: Friend or foe? *Social Work, 14*:35-53, 1969.
3. Lerman, Paul: *Community Treatment and Social Control: A Critical Analysis of Juvenile Correctional Policy.* Chicago, U of Chicago Pr, 1975.
4. Wooden, Kenneth: *Weeping in the Playtime of Others.* New York, McGraw, 1976.
5. Maluccio, Anthony: Residential treatment of disturbed children: A study of service delivery. *Child Welfare, 53*:225-235, 1974.
6. Seidl, Fredrick: Community oriented residential care: The state of the art. *Child Care Quarterly, 3*:150-163, 1974.
7. Barker, Roger: *Ecological Psychology.* Stanford, Stanford U Pr, 1968.
8. Trieschman, Albert: The Walker School: An education based model. *Child Care Quarterly, 5*:123-135, 1976.
9. Simmons, Gladys; Gumpert, Joanne; and Rothman, Beulah: Natural parents as partners in child care placement. *Social Casework, 54*:224-232, 1973.
10. Schoenberg, Carl: On child welfare as a service system. *Child Welfare, 54*:5-6, 1975.
11. Fanshel, David and Shinn, E. B.: *Children in Foster Care.* New York, Columbia U Pr, 1977.
12. Garbarino, James: Unpublished paper.

13. Patterson, Gerald: *A Social Learning Approach to Family Intervention.* Eugene, Castalia Pub, 1975.
14. Wolf, Montrose: Social validity: The case for subjective measurement. *J Applied Behavior Analysis,* in press.
15. Astrachan, Myrtle: The five-day week: An alternative model in residential treatment centers. *Child Welfare, 54*:21-26, 1975.

SECTION III
Practice

NETWORKS

Chapter 8

THE ESTABLISHMENT
AND MAINTENANCE OF A
FAMILY DAY CARE NETWORK

ALICE H. COLLINS

History

SINCE family day care and natural networks play a large role in the lives of millions of families in this country, a few words about their history seem in order before describing a way in which they can increase the effectiveness of their partnership through the intervention of a consultant.

"Care given to a child, residing in his home, in the home of a non-relative for more than twenty hours a week," the usual definition of day care, has only recently become widespread custom. A hundred years ago, it was frequently cited as the only, and horrible, alternative open to poor immigrant women who had to go out to work and could not care for their own children in the normal manner. To arouse sympathy and financial support for the day nurseries they organized, upper-class men and women often cited the "drunken, ignorant neighbor" who would care for the child unless he could be placed in a nursery where he would receive proper care and training in independence. These founders were also concerned that the day nurseries be used only in this way and therefore took every precaution to prevent women who *wished* to work but did not urgently *need* to from using the facilities. In fact, one of the tasks of the first social workers was to make home visits to prevent such misuse. Later, social workers were also expected to assist families to solve the problems that had forced the child into day care so that the mother might stay home and care for him. If the mother had to work, it was seen as a symptom of serious family problems.

It is worthwhile to recall these beginnings because echoes are still heard when family day care is equated with the "drunken, neglecting neighbor" stereotype, and it is assumed that working mothers need professional help in solving their self-evident problem. These echoes are heard most when family day care for the poor is the subject of discussion.

On the whole, however, it is becoming well accepted that the majority of mothers of young children will work at some time because they need to, or want to, or are needed in business, industry, and the professions, or for all three reasons. Most young children, even before school age, will have had the experience of being cared for in the homes of others or of sharing their home with other children. Few parents today regard these exchanges as requiring professional intervention but see them simply as private arrangements between two families. Many givers and users note the difficulty of finding and keeping good arrangements as a concern, but few ask help of a social service in doing so, since it is generally assumed that social agencies are to help people who have *serious* emotional and financial problems. They do not turn to educational systems since they make some distinctions between school and babysitting.

Rather, family day care continues to be seen by participants in it as a natural continuation of an ancient way of life, common to human beings and other social animals. In times of stress such as childbirth, peak harvest, or serious family illness, young children of the extended family were cared for by relatives who expected and got similar service in their turn. In addition, there appeared to be certain individuals who not only entered into such mutual relationships but acted as catalysts for the entire family. They were well known to have certain specialized skills: the care of older family members, for example, or a way with rebellious teenagers, or with babies. They were called on, and responded, when need in their area arose; if they could not offer the necessary help at that time, they undertook to find someone else whom they would encourage to do so, while they remained as advisors and confidants to assure that the arrangement went well. Neither these *natural network cen-*

tral figures nor those who made grateful use of them considered their activity as doing anything special. Rather, this kind of matchmaking was an everyday, satisfying part of their lives.

Natural Networks

Today, although the extended family no longer functions as it once did, the central figures and the natural networks that revolve around them continue to function, with friends and neighbors replacing kin. They are usually clearly visible to those who need their help but invisible to professionals who rarely come into contact with them.

Alerted to their presence, professionals will soon begin to note natural systems and central figures all about them. There is the supermarket checker, for example, who always has a long line of older people with whom she chats, asks about absent members, and arranges for the delivery of small items between neighbors; the school secretary who listens to the problems of many working mothers when a child is ill or needs after school care and suggests arrangements with the parents of classmates; the aide at the hospital or the secretary at the office to whom others turn for advice as well as helpful practical services; the gas station operator who gives personal and mechanical help to the network of young motorcyclists who frequent his station in preference to any other. Once noted, there are many examples of individual networks which, of course, touch each other to form an overall pattern stretching almost to infinity.

Recognition of such networks is still so recent that there are many more unanswered questions than certainties about their operation. Study is being undertaken in many places to learn more about how they are similar to and different from systems of mutual support; how they are formed and for how long natural neighbors maintain their functions within the same network. Perhaps the most pressing question for professionals is how best to use them in a preventive approach to assist individuals in negotiating rough spots in their road before they stumble and fall. Family day care, where natural networks and their central figures are relatively easy to identify, offers an excellent opportunity for professionals to demonstrate how they can join these central figures (hereinafter called day care neighbors) in a productive preventive relationship.

The Consultant — Day Care Neighbor Relationship

To do so effectively, professionals need to make use of their consultant skills. This requires the formation of a partnership whereby the day care neighbor is the expert on her own network and the professional interprets behavior or gives other advice and support when the day care neighbor asks for it. It is an axiom in consultation theory that the consultee, in this case the day care neighbor, is under no obligation to accept the consultant's suggestion, a point professionals will want to keep firmly in mind as they become partners with knowledgeable nonprofessionals.

Consultants will find it relatively easy to apply the consultation principle of confidentiality to the relationship. They will find that day care neighbors have as high a regard for it as they have themselves, even having to be reassured often that discussion of a family situation told in confidence is not gossiping and will be kept entirely confidential by the consultant.

Consultation with day care neighbors differs from conventional consultation in two minor aspects: (1) the consultant, contrary to usual practice, must initiate the contact since the day care neighbor does not know that there is the possibility of making use of the service. (2) This consulting relationship is not short term but rather continues over time, with contact being made with the same day care neighbor as often as she asks for it.

In a successful partnership each partner gains, and they are more effective together than either is alone. This is indeed the case in a partnership between a day care neighbor and a consultant, though perhaps at this early stage of exploration, the consultant profits most. Through the accounts of day care neighbors, consultants can come to understand how family day care is carried on, what problems might arise when two women care for one child, what kinds of services are really wanted, and what the rewards and penalties are for both the givers and users of family day care. Consultants may, incidentally, learn a good deal about other social services; what brings people to them, and more especially, what kinds of supports help individuals solve their problems without official help; what happens when they terminate their contacts; how the agencies are viewed from inside the culture. Perhaps the greatest reward for the consultant is in finding how many strong and able allies exist in every community, well organized and offering help to others, with very little contact with professionals.

The advantages for day care neighbors are fewer, but of great significance to a truly preventive approach. Characteristically, day care neighbors offer help chiefly to their network members of friends and neighbors, and *their* relatives, friends, and neighbors. In modern society, "butting in" to offer help unasked is frowned upon. However, from their central vantage point, day care neighbors often see individuals struggling with problems they know they could help them resolve. The consultant can support the day care neighbor's wish to intervene and can encourage the widening of her network.

Inevitably, such an enlargement will lead to an increase in the number of difficult problems the day care neighbor recognizes as being outside of her competence to resolve. Here the consultant can help to provide the professional insight that may enable the day care neighbor to deal with the immediate problem and similar ones in the future. Where referral seems the best approach, the consultant can contribute her knowledge of community resources and make the referral or help the day care neighbor make it. It should be noted, however, that such situations should not be resolved by having the consultant take over and enter a direct relationship with the troubled individual. To do so would obviously unbalance the partnership.

A few other cautionary words to professionals acting as consultants may be in order. It is natural for consultants to carry into this unfamiliar relationship attitudes and practices that are comfortably familiar to them from other settings. They may tend to treat day care neighbors as though they were clients asking for a solution to a personal problem or as students or aides who need education and training in the "right" way of carrying out their work. They may expect some of the respect for their professional knowledge that they find in other consultation settings; they may feel that they must act in this kind of model with the day care neighbors, forgetting that it is precisely the day care neighbor's special knowledge of her own unique network that enables her to function as the consultant cannot hope to do. On the contrary, it is the consultant who will have the most to learn while both partners maintain their own identity. If this is not understood, the day care neighbor may think the difference implies her inferiority and incompetence in contrast to the professional's and, therefore, abdicate her role. This has frequently occurred in other situations where professional intervention and modeling destroyed natural networks without being able to replace them. It is a more difficult and time-consuming job to recruit willing individuals than to train them in a model familiar to the trainer, but the former is well worthwhile in the long run.

Establishing the Relationship

Once the consultant has, in theory, accepted the role of partner to day care neighbors, another unfamiliar task confronts her: how to find and initiate a relationship with these partners. It is not surprising that the greatest obstacle to establishing a day care neighbor service is that it requires a first long step into unfamiliar territory to find the existing natural networks and identify the central figures in them. In reality, it is not difficult to find them, although it is admittedly time-consuming and demands that the consultant adopt the new role of an anthropologist, who sets out to understand another culture and how it functions. Some preliminaries should be taken within the agency where the consultant is based. It may be assumed that many working mothers at every economic level make family day care arrangements, and that there are also young women who for various reasons want to give rather than use day care. It is necessary to make some decisions about the neighborhood to be served. Here it is useful to remember that networks are relatively small and it will be wise to start with a program to reach only a limited number. Information already in the agency files, census figures (especially school census figures), and the requests of neighborhood boards and associations may all help to pinpoint the neighborhood where a day care network might be found without the additional expense and delay of making a survey. Some information about the history of the neighborhood can be helpful; its *feel* will be different if it is one made up of the children and grandchildren of permanent residents or a new neighborhood still in the process of building first homes for young families.

Having learned what she can about the neighborhood in advance, the consultant will hopefully have now gained the courage to leave her office for firsthand observation and contacts. Neighborhood tradespeople and professionals who work in the neighborhood can provide a wealth of information. They are likely to be quite willing to discuss who gives day care in the neighborhood and volunteer their opinions about its quality. If they are not well acquainted with this field, they may refer the consultant to someone they know to be more so: the staff of the church where there is a Sunday or weekday nursery program; the school secretary who relies on certain individuals to step into an emergency with a kindergartner when his or her mother cannot be reached; the local children's services office that refers young families in need of help; the public health nurse who works with many families and knows how they function. Bulletin boards in laundromats and community centers, as well as the community newspaper, also provide the names of local babysitters.

The consultant can stop in neighborhood cafes and observe which of the staff is sought out for conversation by the regular customers. These individuals are likely to know a great deal about the local people, including who works and who gives care to the children of the working mothers. Sometimes, a waitress who is herself a working mother may prove to be a rich source of firsthand information. The more such contacts are made, the more often the consultant will hear the same names mentioned.

When she has a list of five or six names of people who give good care or who are described as knowing a good deal about child care, the consultant will be ready to take the next unfamiliar step, perhaps with a little less trepidation since the first one has convinced her that day care neighbors do exist and can be identified. Now the consultant will make personnel contact with each individual on her list, preferably by an informal telephone call rather than a letter. She will want to introduce herself as being connected with an agency and having an interest in learning more about family day care which, she understands, is also of special interest to the person she is calling. She will probably have to clarify that all she wants is a chance to talk and not to ask for day care for a particular child. The response to such a call is usually positive, even if its purpose is not clear to the prospect. Day care neighbors are so used to being asked for help that it might be taken as a mark of their position that they are always willing to accept one more demand on their time and knowledge. In fact, serious hesitation or a request for much identification or justification for the proposed visit may be a clue of unsuitability.

At the initial visit the consultant will once more make use of anthropological techniques, observing the neighborhood, how like or different the prospect's home is from those of her neighbors, who comes and goes during the interview, how they are treated, the cordiality of the prospect toward the consultant, and the degree to which she easily and naturally accepts the role of neighborhood expert assigned her by the consultant.

It will probably be best if the consultant finishes her interviews with all the prospects on her lists before making decisions about who best fits the definition of day care neighbor. Back in her office, the consultant can take the time to make a careful rating of each prospect according to dimensions which have been tested and found useful elsewhere.

Does the day care neighbor have children of her own, under high school age, and was she caring for one or more children of a working mother? Did she relate to the child and its family with friendly interest but without either sharp criticism or possessiveness? Did she talk of her own children briefly, with natural maternal pride but without request for advice about their problems? Did she volunteer some general information about the neighborhood and its children in a positive, lively, accepting manner rather than complaining about them? Was she somewhat guarded in talking about her neighbors, mentioning her aversion to gossip? Did her home seem to be a kind of neighborhood center, with people going in and out and asking her to watch their children while they kept medical appointments or went to the store?

There is one more important measure which is difficult to describe and apply because it is concerned with an intangible quality. Does the prospect have enough emotional energy to be able and willing to invest it in others without a mutual return? Experience has shown that natural neighbors in every area are likely to maintain they get as much as they give in the relationship, but in actual investment of time, thought, and action, this is not true. The relationship is much more an altruistic than a mutual one and is possible because of the freedom that the natural neighbor feels to so invest herself. Like the other measurements discussed, this vital capacity is not associated with education, age, or socioeconomic level.

Having completed the ranking, the consultant can now proceed to recruit those at the top of her list. Consultants traditionally are asked for help rather than asking others for it. Since the prospective day care neighbors do not know such help exists and is available to them, they cannot be expected to do this. However, if this first interview has been a pleasant one, a request for another will be cordially received. The consultant will be the one asking for help to assure the best possible family day care to the families in the community and will offer herself as a partner to the day care neighbor who is already informally working toward this end. The consultant may mention that although she has specialized knowledge of the dynamics of behavior and may eventually be able to make some suggestions on the management of situations that baffle the day care neighbor, she will initially have more to learn than to give since it is the day care neighbor who is central to her unique network. Hopefully, as their partnership grows into a more truly equal one, the day care neighbor will find the consultant useful in helping expand her network to include some of those who are not friends or acquaintances, but whom the day care neighbor recognizes as in need of her help.

If the day care neighbors have been well chosen they are likely to respond enthusiastically to the offer of a partnership and readily agree to add regular meetings with the consultant to their activities as part of their purely voluntary role. Professionals sometimes feel uncomfortable with this arrangement and want to set a fixed payment. To do so, however, implies that the day care neighbor is an employee of an agency; this would completely change her status in the neighborhood and in her own view. There is no way of measuring what an appropriate payment would be; to tie payments to the number of day care arrangements would destroy the natural network which it is intended to strengthen. Sometimes convincing a neighbor not to go to work is the major service. Experience suggests that day care neighbors have chosen the freedom of the volunteer role and have no interest in changing it, though a token fee for their cooperation in keeping some records of their activity has proven acceptable.

An explanation of the above fits easily into a first interview which almost invariably ends with an enthusiastic acceptance of the partnership, not necessarily based on a full understanding of this new idea. It should end with an appointment set at the convenience of and in the home of the day care neighbor. It is probable that, before that date, the day care neighbor will telephone to say she cannot undertake the partnership — she does not feel competent, her husband does not want her to, she thinks she may go to work outside the home, and other statements — she has "stage fright" at what she sees as a new task. It usually takes only a little reassurance that the consultant would not want her to take on any new roles but rather to let the consultant learn from her what she is already doing — this will settle the issue so it is hardly mentioned at the next interview.

The period of getting acquainted and establishing respective roles is usually not more than four to six weeks. The first visits will be largely occupied with the day care neighbor's descriptions of the neighborhood in response to the consultant's evident interest in learning about it. Sometimes it is helpful for the consultant to ask the day care neighbor to draw a map of the family day care arrangements known to her in her neighborhood, a device which proves to the neighbor that, indeed, she does know a great deal, and gives the consultant an introduction to a cast of characters she will hear a great deal about in the future as she attempts to understand how the network operates and where she herself can be useful.

Once the relationship is established, the consultant may want to suggest that one meeting a month be planned for, but that telephone calls or requests for visits will be welcome at any time if the day care neighbor has something she wants to talk about. Here, it is important that the consultant stress her interest in anything the day care neighbor has to say, including accounts of successes as well as requests for advice, or expressions of disappointment when things do not go well. The consultant needs to make every effort to maintain the partnership role and resist a supervisory role.

The inexperienced consultant may assume that, once the day care neighbors are widening their scope and making use of whatever help they have asked for, there is little need to maintain the relationship. In fact, it is only when these preliminaries are over that the scope of the partnership becomes valuable.

Maintaining the Relationship

The dynamic establishment of a relationship between the day care neighbor and the consultant continues to benefit both, if it is maintained over time, although there will be periods when it appears to the consultant that nothing is being accomplished and that even the few hours required to continue contact with the day care neighbor are unproductive. This may well be the result of the style in which many day care neighbors (or central figures in other kinds of networks) ask for help with a problem. Typically, instead of asking a question, they make a statement, describing their handling of a current problem or their plans for doing so in the future. The consultant, realizing that this style is very natural to individuals who are accustomed to giving, not seeking, advice, will support the day care neighbor's plan or propose possible alternatives. If these are put forward as examples of solutions described by other day care neighbors or drawn from the consultant's practice in a different field, any suggestion of supervision or direction will be avoided. The consultant will know how the suggestion has been used when, at a later interview, it is quoted back to her.

There are times, too, when the consultant will seek the advice of the day care neighbor. Once it is known that an agency is facilitating family day care arrangements, requests will be received from other professionals, and from users and givers, for help in finding and making successful matches. The consultant will direct the callers to the day care neighbor in their area. If the service does not exist there, the consultant may want the advice of a day care neighbor as to how to respond, especially in complex and disrupted family situations, where the stability of an arrangement is seriously threatened. In addition, as has been suggested above, the consultant will have gained a consumer's view of family day care and professional services of many kinds which will permit her to make recommendations and bring about more effective service delivery throughout the community.

It is not known at the present time how long a day care neighbor — consultant relationship is likely to last. Experience would suggest that it may well be five years or more. What is clear is that it is a highly productive investment of professional time, with a potential of reaching a great many presently unreached individuals with the kind of help they want in making good family day care arrangements at every preventive level.

Chapter 9

DEVELOPING COMPREHENSIVE
EMERGENCY SERVICES

RAY HAWKINS

Scope

THE National Center for Comprehensive
Emergency Services to Children was established in July, 1974,
through a contract with the Department of Health, Education
and Welfare, Children's Bureau, to disseminate information
and provide technical assistance toward the goal of establishment of Comprehensive Emergency Services in communities
throughout the United States. This effort was based on the
model program which had been operated in Nashville, Tennessee, for three years as a Department of Health, Education
and Welfare Children's Bureau Research and Demonstration
Project.

The project had the advantage of an exceptionally complete
data base and a thorough, ongoing evaluation which enabled
us to demonstrate statistically the effectiveness of the program.[1,2] In addition, through the development of broad-based
community support, the project was able to be incorporated
into the ongoing human services system. At the conclusion of
three years, the National Comprehensive Emergency Services
Center had provided direct on-site consultation and technical
assistance to 172 communities in forty-six states. Of this
number, 106 sites in thirty-nine states were and are actively
pursuing the development of a Comprehensive Emergency Services model system. This latter number includes 18 communities which have operational systems, all of which implemented
the system within the confines of existing funding through
utilization and expansion of existing services and agencies located in the respective communities. In addition, ten states have

103

made commitments to facilitate the development of this system statewide.

Development

In Nashville, Comprehensive Emergency Services (CES) evolved over a period of time as an outgrowth of the concern and action of several groups. Prior to the establishment of CES, families and children who came to the attention of the system had little in the way of services offered them, especially after 4:30 PM and on weekends and holidays. During these periods, Nashville, like vast numbers of other communities, had to depend upon law enforcement to respond to families in crisis. In too many cases, because of the lack of training and resources, the only response law enforcement could make was the removal of children and the subsequent filing of a neglect and dependence petition. As a result, Richland Village, the metro-operated shelter program, was "bursting at the seams" from overcrowding. Research showed that before the establishment of CES nearly 80 percent of those children removed from their homes would be returned home after the case was heard in court. The separation that ensued lasted as long as six to eight weeks in many cases.

Protective service workers found themselves in the very frustrating situation of having large caseloads and spending a majority of their time in court-related activities, with little time available to assist families in breaking the crisis cycle. Furthermore, because of lack of coordination and communication, the protective service unit often would not be notified for several days of the filing of a petition and placement of children in shelter care.

In early 1970, The Urban Institute, at the request of Mayor Beverly Briley, began an analysis of the most pressing social service needs in Nashville and Davidson County. Initially, this study focused on the use of Richland Village as a shelter care facility for neglected and abused children, but it was soon recognized that such a study must include the State Department of Human Services and Metropolitan Juvenile Court, as well as the other public and private agencies which are involved in the delivery of services to dependent children and their families.

To facilitate the study, a committee was formed by the mayor which was representative of this loosely defined system: the mayor's office and concerned citizen groups such as Junior League, League of Women Voters, and the Council of Jewish Women. Initially, the role of this committee was to expedite the collection of data and to share expertise and knowledge of service delivery in Nashville. For several months, this committee met regularly, providing asistance to the researchers and exploring more fully the services that were provided to children and families in crisis. Thus, the committee began to function as a cohesive group committed not only to describe the way services were provided but also to affect the quality of care provided.

The results of the study were twofold. Not only was it a valid description of how services were currently provided or not provided, but it was also a recommendation for an ongoing, coordinated comprehensive service program that would respond to families as early as possible to provide for the care of neglected and abused children. This new system would be based on expanding existing service capabilities as well as enhancing the coordination of services and agencies in meeting the needs of families and children.

The outcome was the development of a proposal. This proposal was submitted for funding as a research and demonstration project which would implement the recommendation of the initial study and evaluate program effectiveness and cost.

The Comprehensive Emergency Services system that resulted from these recommendations sought to coordinate the services offered neglected and abused children by the various public and private agencies. The existing emergency service components within the Department of Human Services were expanded to provide the service options necessary to meet the social service needs of those children and their families.

This new system incorporated several basic assumptions. *Central to the system was a belief that any system serving children and their families should seek to maintain and strengthen that family and avoid whenever possible separation of children from their parents.* To accomplish this end, it was believed that the focus should be toward the provision of supportive services directed to parents and children as early as possible. It was therefore decided the system of services would seek to respond to crisis situations involving families. A "crisis" would be defined as any situation that exposes or threatens to expose a child to situations that could lead to abuse or neglect. Another assumption was that families in crisis must be offered rescue and must be assisted in assessing the alternatives available to them so they can make decisions regarding their lives. Work by Kempe and Helfer, as well as others, has shown that probably 90 percent of the parents of neglected and abused children want to provide good care for their children. It is the system's responsibility to help strengthen these families to provide that care. Recognizing there will be situations where children and parents must be separated, the system must demand that those separations be carefully planned and time limited so children are not separated for unnecessary lengths of time nor lost in the system. The system offers immediate response and rescue in times of crisis and coordinates that response with ongoing services that seek to strengthen the families' ability to deal with the stresses they face.

The committee that had been originally formed to facilitate the research study began to function as a planning and advisory body to assist in the implementation of the new system. No one agency was expected to be responsible for all services but rather a means was sought to build on existing service capabilities and improve the coordination and interfacing of agencies so as to increase the speed and ease with which a family in crisis can receive services. The coordinating committee, as it came to be known, had four roles:

1. Assisting in the assessment of existing services that are available in a community.
2. Assisting in planning the kinds and ways services will be provided.
3. Helping facilitate the implementation of the system.
4. Evaluating and monitoring the ongoing system as to its

effectiveness.

As may be obvious, the coordinating committee's role was a political one.

To assist in the coordination of this system, written agreements were developed which outlined procedures and roles of the various agencies involved and described how the components within the system would operate in relation to one another. By resolving the bureaucratic problems, these agreements improved the flow of communication and accessibility of services so they would be available to the family in crisis. To insure the continuation of the system, the executive committee assumed a continuing role in maintaining the system and monitoring its effectiveness.

In addition to the coordination of social service agencies that provide services to neglected and abused children, the protective service unit of the Department of Human Services was reorganized and realigned into two units: one unit would handle the initial crisis situations, and the other would provide ongoing services and serve as broker to the family after the crisis was stabilized. To assist workers in the protective service units, the existing program was expanded to include an additional five program components, each of which addressed a specific service need as identified by the research report. The resulting system was composed of seven components which provide services to families in crisis. Prior to a description of these components, it is important to point out that in all seven components thorough training was and is of critical importance. Furthermore, because many areas of training overlap, it makes sense to train various components together to insure consistency in the system.

The Model

While the following components are thought to be essential to a comprehensive system, other kinds of services are not excluded. The goal is to develop a system with the widest set of options to meet the needs of the community.

Twenty-Four-Hour Emergency Intake

Intake was expanded to twenty-four-hour, seven-day-a-week service. Personnel became available after office hours and on weekends to screen calls and refer emergencies to caseworkers. Referrals were accepted for both emergency and nonemergency cases, with the former immediately referred to the regular Protective Service Unit. Integral to this twenty-four-hour capability is the ability to not only screen and refer to caseworkers, but also the ability to respond to crises with face-to-face services by a trained worker within the hour, twenty-four hours a day. The role of the intake worker is to assist the family in assessing the immediate crisis situation and explain the alternatives available to stabilize the crisis. The system has other service capabilities that the emergency intake worker can offer families to help stabilize the crisis and to reduce the stress that is overwhelming the family.

Research showed that 51 percent of the referrals were after-hours and, overall, 68 percent of all referrals required face-to-face contact. Of those referrals that were made after-hours, 78 percent required response by emergency intake staff.

Emergency Caretaker Service

Emergency caretakers are available to serve in the family's home as temporary guardians until the return of parents or until an alternative plan can be developed. Use of caretakers is time limited and provides an opportunity to explore alternatives with parents in the form of temporary in-home supervision of the children. Caretakers can be used in those emergencies where children are found alone and unsupervised. Use of caretakers in abandonment cases requires a legal base to protect the family and staff.

Emergency Homemaker Service

Emergency homemakers are available to maintain children in their own homes in crisis situations where it is impossible for parents to exercise their routine parental responsibility. Use of this service is based on agreement and desire of the parents to use services and is usually extended over a period of time. Services can be provided several hours a day for several days, or up to twenty-four hours live-in service in some cases. This service is an extension of the previously existing homemaker service which offered limited services only during the normal working day.

Emergency Foster Homes

This service provides temporary care for children who cannot be maintained in their own homes. This service is very goal-oriented and time limited in order to maintain focus on the family as a unit. Children are returned home or placed in other appropriate facilities as quickly as possible.

Emergency Shelter for Adolescents

Older children often have particular problems and needs which are not or cannot be adequately dealt with in traditional foster care. Even though they are often classed as predelinquent or beyond control, they come to the attention of the system because of neglect, abuse, or crisis in their homes. Emergency shelter is geared to meet their needs and enables the system to provide a group home or institutional setting and avoids the use of jails or juvenile detention centers for such youth.

Emergency Shelter for Families

This is a facility which can offer shelter to entire families rather than separating children from their parents. It is able to respond where the crisis involves a burned out, evicted, or transient family. Based on the needs of the community, this component can be offered in a variety of ways ranging from an agreement for the temporary use of a small apartment to a more formalized program. In Nashville, this service is provided by the Salvation Army.

Outreach and Follow-through

Outreach and follow-through provide ongoing casework assistance and services to families in their efforts to cope with problems. This service must be available in a formalized way to insure the continuation of services to families. The workers in outreach and follow-through assume case accountability as soon as the immediacy of the crisis has been resolved. In most cases, this would be the next working day. Recognizing that this one unit could not meet the service needs of a community, outreach and follow-through units also serve as service brokers to join the family with appropriate services provided in the community.

Results

The establishment of CES has led to the following changes in the child welfare spectrum in Nashville:

1. The number of neglect and dependent petitions filed was reduced from 602 in 1969-1970 to 266 in 1973-1974, a reduction of 336, or 50 percent.
2. The number of cases screened where a petition was not sworn out increased from 770 in 1969-1970 to 2,156 in 1973-1974, an increase of 1,386, or 180 percent.
3. The number of children under the age of six who were institutionalized was reduced from 180 to 0.
4. The number of children removed from their homes and placed in some type of substitute care decreased from 353 in 1969-1970 to 174 in 1973-1974, a decrease of 179, or 51 percent.
5. The number of recidivistic cases (the number of children on whom petitions were filed in given years who previously had petitions filed) was 196 in 1969-1970, but only 23 in 1973-1974, a decline of 88 percent. The recidivism rate (the percentage of children on whom petitions are initially filed who are abused or neglected again by the end of the subsequent year) declined from 16 percent in program year 1969-1970, to 9 percent in program year 1973-1974.

6. While the system served an increase of 92 percent in the number of referrals, the incremental difference in cost between the old and new system was a net savings of 68,000 dollars. A solution was achieved in which *effectiveness increased* while *cost decreased.*

Based on the results of the research and demonstration project, the program success and adaptability of the system, a national dissemination effort was made. The project led to the establishment of the National Center for Comprehensive Emergency Services to Children and Families in Crisis in July 1974.

REFERENCES

1. Burt, Marvin and Blair, Louis: *Options for Improving the Care of Neglected and Dependent Children.* Washington, Urban Inst, 1971.
2. Burt, Marvin and Balyeat, Ralph: *From Nonsystem to System: Evaluation of the Comprehensive Emergency Services System for Neglected and Abused Children — Nashville and Davidson County, Tennessee.* Nashville, Burt Associates, 1975.

SECTION III
Practice

EDUCATIONAL SERVICES

Chapter 10

THE HIGH/SCOPE
PARENT-TO-PARENT MODEL

Judith Evans

WITH rising divorce rates, an increased number of single parent households, women entering the job market and expanding their roles, and with many adults choosing to live together without a formal *marriage,* there has been increasing concern about the viability of the family unit. One of the responses to this concern was a study of the American family conducted by the Carnegie Council on Children. While cautioning that today's family is not defined in the way we traditionally think of families, the Council concludes that "in today's world, and in any future that we can imagine, families are and will continue to be the first line of support for children."

The study goes on to say that the best way to provide support to today's children is to provide support to today's parents. This same conclusion is echoed in the work of Urie Bronfenbrenner who, referring to parents as *caretakers,* asks who is caring for the caretakers. Selma Fraiberg also makes the case that *mothering* is every child's birthright and argues convincingly that the parent-child relationship should be supported by the society, not weakened.

How can parents best be supported? One of the main conclusions of both the Carnegie Council's Report and Fraiberg's analysis is that economic support has to be provided to families in a way which maintains their integrity and vitality. Our own experiences would support these recommendations. However, such social reforms are slow in coming and parents need support now. The High/Scope Parent-to-Parent Model developed over the last ten years provides a mechanism through which a community-based support system can be developed for parents of young children. The goal is to foster community competence in child development through the provision of community services by and for parents.

The model offers a framework for establishing a low-cost community-based educational program which insures that the community will assume increasing responsibility for the program's operation, requiring decreasing amounts of support from external agencies. In addition, the model features a developmentally-based curriculum, training materials, and formative and summative evaluation procedures for ongoing quality control. In this chapter, the model will be presented in terms of the program's philosophy in working with parents, the foundation of the parent-infant curriculum, a review of the implementation process, and an overview of the evaluation procedures utilized within the model.

Parents as Equals: A Program Philosophy

The creation, operation, and evaluation of a succession of programs has shown that when we work with any parent population, we are dealing with a group of interested and vital people, each of whom brings to the program a unique set of skills and varying needs. This experience has reinforced our belief in the mutuality of roles between parents and home visitor; the focus is not on *eliminating deficits* but on the challenge of supporting and expanding present skills. Rather than considering parents as an efficient means of getting through to the infant, they are seen as active, autonomous decision makers for the infant and themselves. Rather than teaching parents to use a prescribed set of activities with the child, resources are made available to support and complement parental skills and to assist parents in clarifying their childrearing goals.

Home visitors help parents realize that their views are important, that they can learn to rely on their own informed judgment in raising their infants. Parents come to understand that intuitive knowledge and a capacity to learn-by-doing is as valuable as all the child development information contained in books or in the minds of home visitors.

The High/Scope Parent-Infant Curriculum

The theoretical structure underlying the home visit program and the accompanying parent-infant curriculum is derived primarily from the child development research of Jean Piaget, who stresses that a necessary ingredient for learning is *interaction with the social and material environment*. The parent-infant curriculum is designed to facilitate this interaction process.

Piagetian theory suggests a number of conceptual areas or dimensions along which development occurs during the first years of life; in addition to language, these include causality, means to ends, and the construction of space and object permanence. These dimensions and approaches to integrating them provide the base of the parent-infant curriculum.

The curriculum does not specify adult *teaching* behaviors. Even if this were possible, such a curriculum would discourage creative problem solving by the home visitor and parent, a process which is vital to their continuing involvement with each other and the child. Curricular activities and materials are developed in the course of planning home visits, but they do not themselves constitute a curriculum. Although activities and materials are to some extent generalizable across parents and infants, they neither exhaust all possibilities nor constitute a curriculum package that can be applied uncritically in all situations.

In essence, the parent-infant curriculum is a process defined by a developmental perspective on learning. The process offers a way for adults to support the early learning of the infant by providing materials and people with whom the infant can interact and the time and freedom to do so. By focusing on the infant's actions, the home visitor supports the parent's ability to observe and interpret those actions and to provide activities which support the development of the child.

Implementation of the Parent-to-Parent Model

As individuals show an interest in implementing the model within their community, a dialogue begins between High/

Scope and community personnel. Before High/Scope staff are willing to become involved in providing the training for a full scale implementation of the model, the community needs a clear understanding of the model and a commitment to implementing the model with their families. One indication of this commitment is the community's willingness to designate an individual from the community, paid through community resources, who will be responsible locally for the implementation and maintenance of the program. A second indication is the community's development of a long-range plan for a succession of training waves to occur over a minimum of three years. Three training waves are required for a community to completely implement the model and for the model to become self-sustaining within the community. To implement the model in a community, there are essentially four steps.

Selection and Training of a Supervisor

As noted above, it is the responsibility of the community to select an individual to serve as the supervisor for the parent-to-parent program. There are certain criteria that should be considered when the choice of supervisor is made. The individual should have administrative experience, knowledge of early child development, experience working within the community, and an awareness of its resources. In addition, the individual should understand and accept the parents-as-equals philosophy of the Parent-to-Parent program. It may be difficult to meet all these criteria, since they characterize the ideal supervisor, but an effort should be made to identify an individual with the potential to develop these qualities.

In our own experience, supervisors have come from a variety of backgrounds ranging from paraprofessionals with little formal schooling experience, but whose relationship within the community provided the base for the development of the program, to professionals who have indicated their commitment to the program by volunteering to work as a supervisor for the first year, simultaneously implementing the program and seeking community funding for subsequent waves of program implementation. In selecting supervisors, communities need to be open in seeking supportive and interested personnel from a variety of sources.

Once the supervisor is selected, she or he is sent to High/-Scope, along with supervisors from other communities, for a three-week intensive training program where she or he learns about the structure of the model, its philosophy, goals, and curriculum. In addition, training focuses on the four critical areas of the supervisory role: administrative program operations; selecting, training, and supervising staff; building relationships within the community; and working with parents.

This first step in the implementation process occurs only once within a given community. However, the supervisor maintains a relationship with the High/Scope staff, using them as consultants, being kept current on new curricula, sharing ideas with supervisors in other communities, etc., throughout the program's duration within the community.

Home Visitor Selection

The recruitment and selection of home visitors is another crucial part of the program. Generally, this occurs once the supervisor has been trained and returns to the community to begin the program. The type of individuals selected to be home visitors will be different in each community. Since the program usually begins on budgets that cannot do more than support the supervisor and perhaps pay babysitting, materials, and transportation costs of the home visitors, it may be necessary to recruit volunteers. Communities should not limit themselves to volunteer staff programs, however, if there are resources to pay home visitors. Once again, the community must examine its needs and resources and make staffing decisions accordingly.

Regardless of whether staff are volunteers or paid, when the supervisor presents a description of the role of the home visitors and specifies the expectations for an individual in that role, the supervisor has to present a realistic picture of what the job entails. Home visitors, whether volunteer or paid, should have an interest in working with other adults and should be able to demonstrate a respect for parents rather than be paternalistic; they must be willing to learn new things about themselves as well as acquire child development information; and they should be able to take initiative and be persistent in sometimes frustrating circumstances.

To the degree possible, inappropriate home visitors should be weeded out of the program before home visitor training begins. In some instances, it is not possible to make an accurate assessment of an individual's potential in a short interview. Frequently, the training process itself provides the framework within which both supervisory staff and potential home visitors can more accurately assess an individual's potential.

While home visitors are recruited from a variety of community members in the first wave, subsequent waves of the program have an additional source of potential home visitors — the parents who receive home visits during previous waves of the program. Some of the strongest home visitors are those who participated in previous programs as recipients of home visits. Their participation in the program provides a strong experiential base from which their skills can be further developed through the home visitor training program.

Training Home Visitors

Once the home visitors have been selected, training can begin. Through a participatory training model that trains the home visitor in the same way they are expected to work with parents, the participants gain experience in observing, describing, and interpreting infant behavior and supporting parents' positive interactions with their child. The content of the training sessions is divided into three major topics: child development information; understanding the visitor's role; and gaining skills in supporting parents. Within the child development sessions, the theoretical framework of the parent-infant curriculum is presented. Participants learn the Piagetian-based developmental perspective on growth and development and gain skills in creating and using appropriate materials which facilitate that development.

To encourage an understanding of the role of the home visitor, participants are presented with the philosophy of the program and the rationale for the parents-as-equals approach, and they have the opportunity to examine their own values, feelings, expectations, and biases as they relate to this style of working with parents. The third area, providing parental support, includes the development of skills in building relationships with family members and designing techniques and strategies for planning, implementing, and evaluating home visits. In addition, participants work with a practice family during their training to strengthen their skills and understanding of the process of supporting parents.

Home Visiting

While training home visitors, the supervisor is also recruiting families to be visited. As was noted earlier, all families could use support in their childrearing role. However, since this is not economically feasible, choices have to be made. The criteria for a given family's participation in the program needs to be defined locally and families recruited accordingly. One community may develop the program for adolescent parents, another may implement it for the parents of handicapped children, or for families in a sparsely populated rural area, or for high risk families in large metropolitan communities. It is each community's responsibility to define its target population.

Once the target families are identified, recruited for the program, and home visitor training is complete, home visits begin. Generally, these are designed to occur weekly over a period of a year. While home visitors are responsible for planning, implementing, and evaluating the home visit, they are supported through weekly in-service training and ongoing supervision from the program supervisor.

Over succeeding waves, High/Scope staff direct involvement with the community decreases, with increasing responsibility for the program's maintenance being in the hands of the supervisor. At the same time the program is being conducted, evaluation is providing feedback to program personnel so that they can understand the current operation of the program, make training revisions where necessary, and assess program impact.

Evaluation Within the Parent-to-Parent Model

In the designing of evaluation and research instruments, High/Scope operates on the principle that *assessment is an intervention* and therefore (1) it should be educational and (2) the evaluation process should be congruent with the total program process. In other words, evaluation instruments should be constructed so that people learn something while being assessed and the instrument should have the potential to be used as a training tool as well as a part of the evaluation process. In addition, when assessment occurs in a program, it should be done in naturally occurring situations in a way which is nonthreatening and noninterfering.

Within the Parent-to-Parent Model, both formative and summative evaluation occurs with instruments which have been developed along these principles. Formative evaluation consists of a systematic documentation of the implementation process, and summative evaluation consists of an assessment of the within-program impact for parents, infants, and home visitors.

Parent assessment consists of attitudinal data and knowledge of child development, as well as demographic information which allows us to accurately describe the parent populations served and understand the ways in which the program is appropriate and inappropriate for varying communities. Since our longitudinal research on the original Ypsilanti-Carnegie Infant Education Program suggests a relationship between parent-child interactions and scores on standard achievement tests, a pre- and post-program assessment is made of parent-child interaction. We are interested in studying this relationship and looking at the ways in which the Parent-to-Parent Model impacts this interaction. Outside of the interaction situation, infants are assessed using standardized instruments for comparability with other studies, as well as on measures of verbal ability.

Home visitors' growth is assessed through two instruments developed as the model has evolved: (1) The Infant Education Interview (IEI) assesses an individual's knowledge of child development and the ways in which adults facilitate that development; and (2) the Parent-Home Visitor Interaction Instrument provides a content analysis of the verbal interaction between the home visitor and the parents during regular home visits and is designed to assess the extent to which home visitors successfully meet program goals.

While all of these formal evaluation procedures have been put into place to satisfy research needs, our day-to-day experience in working with both home visitors and families provides us with the feedback we personally need to continue our work, especially when home visitors summarize their experience in the program by saying such things as —

> Before I joined the project I had little to offer anyone besides my children. They were the only ones I felt I knew enough to teach and support. What I have gained from this program so far is hard for me to express (but) I feel I have gained a sort of respect for myself. Before entering in this project I lacked self-confidence and self-esteem. Now I feel more confident about myself.

In summary, the Parent-to-Parent Model includes a view of parents-as-equals in providing activities to facilitate infant development; it allows for the maintenance of the cultural values of the community; and it provides a low-cost quality educational program which can be implemented within the resources available to a given community. More specifically, the model provides a way to support today's parents who are the support for today's children.

REFERENCES

1. Brazelton, T. Berry: *Infants and Mothers — Differences in Development.* New York, Delta, 1969.
2. Fraiberg, Selma: *Every Child's Birthright: In Defense of Mothering.* New

York, Basic, 1977.

3. Goodson, Barbara and Hess, Robert: *Parents as Teachers of Young Children: An Evaluative Review of Some Contemporary Concepts and Programs.* Palo Alto, Stanford U Pr, 1975.

4. Hess, Robert: Parental behavior and children's school achievement, implications for Head Start. In *Critical Issues in Research Related to Disadvantaged Children.* Princeton, Educ Test Serv, 1969.

5. Jencks, Christopher: *Inequality: A Re-Assessment of the Effects of Family and Schooling in America.* New York, Basic, 1972.

6. Keniston, Kenneth and the Carnegie Council on Children: *All Our Children: The American Family Under Pressure.* New York, Har Brace J, 1977.

7. Lambie, Dolores; Bond, James; and Weikart, David: *Home Teaching With Mothers and Infants.* Ypsilanti, High/Scope Educational Research Foundation, 1974.

Chapter 11

PARENTS AS EDUCATORS: THE PORTAGE PROJECT

DAVID SHEARER

Goals and Objectives

IN the past ten years, there has been a dramatic increase in both the number of programs devoted to the early education of young children and the amount of financial and human resources dedicated to such efforts. The government has done much to permit this growth not only by providing the majority of the funding for research, development, and maintenance of such programs, but also by mandating free, public intervention in all states and for all handicapped children between the ages of three and eighteen, regardless of socioeconomic, cultural, or handicapping conditions. Together with many other model approaches, the Portage Project, in Portage, Wisconsin, is a manifestation of such interest on the part of the government and the United States educational community in general.

The target population of early childhood education includes both young children and their families. Providing an intervention program for preschool handicapped children and directly involving the parents in the educational process is an ever-increasing focus of attention. This interest is evidenced by any number of recent statements by experts in the field of early education. In a recent statement, a national commission noted:

> ... the problems of children are inseparable from the problems of those who are primarily responsible for their care and nurture. The characteristics of each child's environment are largely determined by the environment and circumstances of one or more adults ... It is therefore axiomatic that one cannot attempt to help children without influencing those

125

adults. . . . This is especially true in the case of very young
children because of the degree of their dependence and need
for close psychological attachment to a particular adult.[1]

Another report, *Preventing Mental Retardation — More Can
Be Done,* states, "Most retardation results from poor home
environment."[2] This retardation, which accounts for 75 percent
of the 100,000 new cases of mental retardation diagnosed annually in the United States, is largely found in children from
economically, socially, and educationally deprived backgrounds. Children reared in urban ghettos or impoverished
rural areas are fifteen times more likely to be diagnosed mentally retarded than middle-class youngsters.

Recognizing this critical issue, the Department of Health,
Education and Welfare (HEW), announced early in 1978 that
yet greater steps will be taken in the future to assure parental
involvement in the education of children. These steps will include support for a stronger role of parent-teacher projects,
parent advisory bodies, and development of educational materials for home use. Under consideration also are new programs
designed to teach parenting skills to young mothers, particularly teenagers whose numbers represent a growing concern.

The Portage Project has, since its beginning in 1969, recognized the importance of a strong parental role and has, in fact,
designed its program to give the *primary* responsibility for
education to the child's parents. Originally funded by the Education of the Handicapped Act, the Portage Project has developed, implemented, and demonstrated a highly successful
model educational program. The Project is a home-based
model which centers on the parents of young children, a home
teacher who helps parents become more effective teachers, and
of course, the young children in need.

The basic premises of the Portage Project as they relate to
parents are —

> Parents care about their children and want them to attain
> their maximum potential, however great or limited that po-
> tential may be.
> Parents can, with instruction, modeling, and reinforce-
> ment, learn to be more effective teachers of their children.

The socioeconomic and educational or intellectual levels of the parents do not determine either their willingness to teach their children or the extent of gains the children will attain.

The precision teaching method is the preferred model since feedback is provided daily to the parents and weekly to staff, thereby reinforcing both when goals are met. Moreover, the method provides a continual data base for curriculum modification, thus maximizing the likelihood of success for parents and children.[3]

There are many important reasons that Portage elected, nearly ten years ago, to involve parents directly in their child's education. For example:

Parents are the consumers who pay, directly or indirectly, for the program and the service their child receives. Most parents want a voice in what and how their child is taught and they want to participate in the teaching of their child.[4]

Parents, if knowledgeable about their child's program, can be the best advocates for program continuation and extension.[5,6]

Parents know their children better than anyone else ever will. Thus, parents can serve as a vital resource to center- or home-based staff in the area of functional program objectives for the child that will be useful in his or her own unique environment.

There has been an acknowledged problem of transferring learning from the classroom to the home. This occurs because there is insufficient and/or ineffective communication between parents and teaching staff. It is vitally important that there is planned consistency between the center's educational program and the educational experiences provided by the parents. Without effective parent involvement, the best possible program for the child will have little effect.[7]

Studies have shown that parent training during the preschool years is of benefit not only for the target child, but also for his or her siblings.[8] This indicates that parents are able to generalize learned skills, thus making them better parent-teachers of all their children.

Parent involvement can greatly accelerate the child's rate of learning. Fredericks has demonstrated that a systematic program by the parent in conjunction with a school program will almost double the rate of acquisition of a particular skill.[4]

The Application of the Portage Model

Administration and Target Population

The Portage Project operates administratively through a regional educational agency, the Cooperative Educational Service Agency (CESA) 12. This agency serves twenty-three school districts within its 3600 square mile boundaries and provides them with a variety of services, one of which is the early childhood program — the Portage Project. Currently, the Project provides services to 150 children and their families through its Direct Services component. The children range in chronological age from birth to six years, or older if a child cannot demonstrate readiness for a school program. All the children served have been identified as being handicapped in one or more developmental areas. Any preschool handicapped child residing in the CESA 12 area qualifies for the early intervention program regardless of type or degree of handicapping condition.

Assessment and Curriculum Planning

The assessment procedure assesses the child in each developmental area to determine his or her functioning level. Present functioning level is used as the basis for further educational planning. In the Portage Project, we use the Alpern-Boll Developmental Profile, which is administered to all the children. This instrument, administered as a parent questionnaire, is combined with direct observation of the child's behavior, when possible.

To facilitate planning for individual children, the Project staff has devised the *Portage Guide to Early Education*.[9] This curriculum guide, for use with children functioning between birth and six years, consists of a manual of instructions; a sequential checklist of behaviors, which includes five areas of development (cognitive, language, self-help, motor, and social-ization) and an infant stimulation section; and a set of curric-ulum cards to match each of the 580 behaviors stated on the checklist. The cards contain suggestions on materials and teaching procedures along with task breakdowns to assist teachers in individualized programming.

The Home Teaching Process

Following both formal and informal assessment, the home teacher often suggests three or four behaviors that are emerging and could be prescribed. The parents are given the choice of which behavior they would like to target first. The chosen goal, stated as a behavioral objective together with directions, is then written on an activity chart by the home teacher. Prescriptions are written with the goal that the parent and child will succeed on each prescribed task within one week. As parents experience success and gain confidence in their ability to teach their child and record behavior, prescriptions are gradually increased to three and four a week. These activities are often in several areas of development. For example, parents might be working on reducing tantrums, buttoning, and counting all within the same week.

The home teacher writes the activity chart incorporating the selection of targeted behaviors. Again, the most important point is for the home teacher to break tasks down and prescribe only those that can be achieved in one week. This provides the parents with rapid reinforcement since what is learned by the child is a direct result of parental teaching. The directions are written so that the parents will have no difficulty under-standing them, should they need to refer to them during the week. Recording is always uncomplicated and usually involves recording frequency of successes.

After the activity is targeted and described, the home teacher introduces the activity to the child and records baseline data of the frequency of correct responses prior to instruction. This data is recorded on the activity chart. The home teacher then follows the directions written on the chart and begins the teaching process. The home teacher thus models teaching techniques for the parents, showing them what to do and how to do it. After several opportunities, the parent takes over and works with the child, modeling for the home teacher. The home teacher then is able to offer suggestions and reinforcement which increase the likelihood that the parents will record during the week.

Throughout the visit, the home teacher stresses the importance of working with the child during the week. The home teacher leaves his or her home and office phone numbers with the parents and encourages them to call if any question or problem arises during the week. Every attempt is made to utilize materials available in the home; however, there are times when materials are brought in and left for the parents to use.

When the home teacher returns the following week, post-baseline data is collected on the previous week's activities. This helps the home teacher validate the accuracy of the parent's recording and provides the teacher with feedback concerning the degree of success achieved by the child and the child's readiness for the next sequential step. Based on this data, the home teacher alters the previous prescriptions or introduces new activities beginning with taking baseline data. And so the cycle is repeated.

Data Collection and Accountability

Evaluation is an ongoing process. The activity charts that have been left with the parents are collected at the end of each week. The home teacher is responsible for turning in these charts and a progress report each week. The progress report lists the prescribed behaviors from the previous week and whether or not the child has attained the criteria needed before success can be recorded. Prescriptions for the coming week are also recorded on the weekly progress report. A behavior log is kept for each child. All activities and the date they were prescribed are written on the log. Each success and the date the prescription was achieved is recorded according to developmental area. This log provides an ongoing record of every behavior prescribed, each success achieved, and the duration of each prescription. The log also provides a percentage of success achieved by parent, child, and home teacher. The continual input of data allows supervisory personnel and each home teacher to spot problems quickly, thus providing a continual feedback system for program monitoring and modification.[10]

Project Evaluation

The Portage Project has engaged in many types of evaluation because the questions we ask of ourselves and the questions others ask us changed as the program grew and developed. Probably, the first areas of interest were the ability of parents to teach within the model and what effect that had on the children's growth and development. To answer these questions, activity charts were analyzed and pre- and post-testing was done on the children in the Project. It was found that the overall rate of daily recording by the 75 families in the Project was 92 percent and that an average of 128 prescriptions were written per child. The children themselves were successful on 91 percent of the prescriptions. The average IQ of the children in the Project was 75, as determined by the Cattell Infant Test and the Stanford-Binet Intelligence Test. The average child gained thirteen months in mental age in an eight month time period.

Further, an experimental study was conducted involving randomly selected children attending local classroom programs for culturally and economically disadvantaged preschool children. The Stanford-Binet, the Cattell Scale, and the Alpern-Boll Developmental Skills Age Inventory were given as pre- and post-tests to both groups. In addition, the Gessell Developmental Schedule was given as a post-test to both groups. Multiple analysis of covariance was used to control for IQ, practice effect, and age. The greater gains made by the Portage Project children in the areas of mental age, IQ, language, and academic and socialization skills were statistically significant, as compared to the group receiving preschool classroom instruction.[11]

Using the children as their own controls, test results and behavioral gains were compared and measured. The mean gain in IQ scores on the Alpern-Boll Developmental Skills Age Inventory was 13.5 and was statistically significant beyond the .01 level. The mean gain in IQ scores on the Stanford-Binet was 18.3 and was statistically significant beyond the .01 level.[12]

The Joint Dissemination and Review Panel of the United States Office of Education is responsible for the review of programs which have been developed through HEW funding. This Panel then selects exemplary models for validation and refers these models to individuals or agencies wishing to start programs of their own. In November 1975, the Joint Dissemination and Review Panel unanimously recognized the Portage Project and validated it after an extensive review.

Comments on Parents as Educators

This model depends upon a structured, concentrated interaction between the home teacher, the parents, and the child. It is important to be task-oriented during the home visit. There is much teaching to do, yet there is usually some time left for having a cup of coffee and socializing. During this time a parent may talk about marital, financial, or other personal problems, and the home teacher can, and should, refer the parent to agencies or people who can help. The teacher's expertise is in teaching, not in social work, counseling, psychology, or psychiatry, but it is his or her responsibility to be aware of community resources that can serve these other needs. It then must be the parent's decision to contact or not to contact the suggested sources.

Each teacher should set up a scheduled day and time for the home visit. If there is a change, parents should be informed. Because a family may have a handicapped child or may be in need of assistance does not mean the family must forfeit their right to privacy.

The teaching staff members may see homes and family lifestyles very different from their own. Thus it is vital for the teachers to realize and accept that they are in the homes to aid parents to learn teaching skills and not to change life-styles or value systems. The teacher should remember that he or she is a guest in each home and can only maintain the child-parent-teacher relationship with the parent's assent.

Many educators have, for too long, usurped the parent's role of responsibility in education. This condition may be magnified as more states lower the age for mandatory education for handicapped children by providing early intervention as soon as a problem is identified. Parents of the children being served need guidance and support from teachers, but it is equally important to realize and accept that teachers need parental support and guidance if the children are to achieve, maintain, and increase behavioral competence. The parent-teacher relationship is one built on mutual respect and need for what each can bring to the child. This relationship with the parents and families may well be one of the most satisfying and rewarding that a teacher will ever experience.

Home-based educational service is a rapidly expanding field and as more programs are implementing a home-based service, it becomes important to identify those components that enhance the success of such programs. This places pressure on any program, but particularly those viewing themselves as model programs, to be able to define their intervention strategy in order to evaluate specific components. This must be done at the original site so that it can be tried and used by others. It must be put to the test in the field to see if it can be used effectively by others with similar results. There are far too many programs in isolated cases or studies that can define their success in terms of child growth, yet they are unable to define their intervention strategy allowing others to replicate the model. No longer does one need to be concerned with selling the home-based concept, as it is widely accepted as an effective, productive, and rewarding service. However, simply providing a home-based program is not the mysterious end in education. It simply implies that teaching is taking place in the home and not in the classroom. It is time to take a critical look at what makes a successful home-based program. It is time to state that by initiating a home-based program, one does not insure that parents will be active and effective nor does it insure that the children will benefit from such efforts.

Although there are many questions unanswered concerning home-based programs, we have learned a great deal. The Portage Project has been in the home teaching business since 1969. Let us look at what we know:

Any successful home-based program must have developed an alliance with the parents.

Parents can teach their own children and with structured sequential assistance, they can eventually plan and implement their child's educational program. By using a behavioral, systematic development approach the children can achieve in a home-based program as well as they can in a classroom program. Without direct and consistent parent involvement in any preschool setting, children will not maintain their gains.

Individualized instruction can be realized in the home.

Father, sibling, and extended family member involvement is a realistic and obtainable goal.

Differences in culture, life-styles, and value systems of parents can be incorporated into curriculum since the parents share in the planning and are the final determinants of what and how their child will be taught.

Learning is occurring in the child's natural environment, thus eliminating the problems of transferring the learning from classroom to the home.

It is more likely that the skills the child learns will generalize to other areas and be maintained if the skills have been learned in the home environment and have been taught by the child's natural reinforcer — the parent.

Through research, investigation, and practice we are learning more of the questions. Hopefully, as we continue to search, experiment, and test we will learn more of the answers. This volume (and the symposium) on home-based services exemplifies that we are on the threshold of a new era of parenting and parent education. This is a time for sharing, learning, and investigating honestly and openly. These efforts must be done responsibly and systematically. We owe it to each other and we especially owe it to the children and the parents.

REFERENCES

1. Minnesota, Department of Education, Division of Planning and Development: *Early Childhood Education in Six Midwest States: Program and Policy Development.* St. Paul, State of Minnesota, 1977.
2. U. S. General Accounting Office: *Preventing Mental Retardation — More Can Be Done.* Washington, Govt Print Office, 1977.
3. Weber, Susan et al.: *The Portage Guide to Home Teaching.* Portage, Cooperative Educational Service Agency 12, 1975.
4. Fredericks, H. D. et al.: A home-center based parent training model. In Grim, J. (Ed.): *Training Parents to Teach: Four Models.* Chapel Hill, Technical Assistance Development Systems, 1974.
5. Hayden, Alice: A center based parent training model. In Grim, J. (Ed.): *Training Parents to Teach: Four Models.* Chapel Hill, Technical Assistance Development Systems, 1974.
6. Shearer, David and Shearer, Marsha: The Portage Project: A model for early childhood intervention. In Tjossem, T. (Ed.): *Intervention Strategies for High Risk Infants and Young Children.* Baltimore, Univ Park, 1976.
7. Lillie, David: Dimensions in parent programs: an overview. In Grim, J. (Ed.): *Training Parents to Teach: Four Models.* Chapel Hill, Technical Assistance Development Systems, 1974.
8. Gilmer, B.; Miller, J.; and Gray, S.: The early training project for disadvantaged children: a report after five years. *Monographs of the Society for Research in Child Development, 33*:4, 1968.
9. Bluma, Susan et al.: *Portage Guide to Early Education,* rev. ed. Portage, Cooperative Educational Service Agency 12, 1976.
10. ABT Associates: *Exemplary Programs for the Handicapped.* Bethesda, ERIC Document Reproduction Service, 1972 (ED 079890).
11. Portage Project, unpublished data.
12. Shearer, Marsha and Shearer, David: The Portage Project: a model for early childhood education. *Exceptional Children, 36*:217, 1972.

Chapter 12

FAMILY CENTERED UNIT FOR HELPING CHILDREN BECOME AWARE OF DEATH

JOSEPH WEBER

CAN parents successfully help their children develop a positive attitude toward death which also includes a perspective of life? No human being lives in a social vacuum protected from the joys, hardships, and sorrows created by the continuing cycle of birth, life, and eventual death. Each individual continually interacts with various natural, human, and technological environments.

Unfortunately, few parents feel comfortable discussing the topic of death with their children. It has become a forbidden subject shrouded in the unknown.[1] In a study by Schneidman, it was pointed out that not only was death rarely discussed within the immediate family, but it also created emotional discomfort and anxiety among family members.[2] Even though death is as natural as birth, the family avoids facing the inescapable experience.[3] Parents rarely discuss or openly talk with their children about death. Few people ever consider death; instead, it is viewed as a personal threat to the "finiteness of human experience."[4]

A primary reason the family has difficulty discussing death is because there has been little prior experience in dealing with death.[5] Several generations ago, the management of death was a family function, which gave young and old an awareness of this natural phenomenon. It was very common for a person to die in the familiar environment of the home.[6] Because relatives and friends now die in the remote confines of hospitals and nursing homes, an awareness of death has been removed as a family function. This separation and avoidance of death has

136

caused the family to deal with the natural phenomenon by relying on myths and mysteries as a coping mechanism.[7]

Throughout history and across cultures, the family has been a key instrument in shaping and molding its members' awareness of the life cycle, which includes death. This has been accomplished through interpersonal communication within the family. The family can choose to deny or work to incorporate death into the natural process of life, rather than view death as a taboo topic.

The purpose of this family-centered unit is to help parents equip their children with a viable attitude toward life which includes an acceptance of death as well as an examination of their own fears and feelings toward death. The approach envisions the family as the center of learning for living.

The curriculum guide may be used for training sessions with parents. Information and communciation skills can help parents discuss death openly as a natural process of life. The material also lends itself to use with groups such as extension homemaker clubs, church groups, parent-teacher associations, and adult education classes.

Family Ecological Framework

The family is seen as a human system made up of subsystems of individual family members when viewed in an ecological perspective. These subsystems of family members interact with each other and outside environments. The ability of the family to interpret and process information determines how successfully the family unit copes with life. The family is viewed as a complex network of interrelated component parts which attempt to act in a stable manner over a period of time.

Using the ecological perspective, it is evident that children do not live in a world in which they interact only with their parents. Children continually interact with and receive information from the human, natural, and regulatory environments, which include friends, schoolmates, relatives formal education, church, mass media, and nature. Children turn to their parents for security in the hope of finding meaning in new events that are beyond their present and limited experience.[8] As children become aware of the surrounding environments, it is only a matter of time before they encounter events which will introduce the question of death.

Whether the event is a national disaster in which thousands of people lose their lives or the death of a family pet, parents need to be willing to answer and discuss their children's questions concerning death. Functional communication which is stated clearly and honestly has less likelihood of being confused, misinterpreted, or exaggerated. Both the sender and the receiver will be receptive to feedback as they become aware of each other's needs. If the parents are afraid to openly face the topic of death, a type of noncommunication could be experienced by the parents and child. The child may perpetuate the myths and fears passed on by his parents, looking elsewhere for answers, or try to explain death by relying on his own personal experience in the make-believe world. No matter what the situation, the child needs the parent's understanding and support, since he or she lacks experience concerning the life cycle.

World Ecological View: Cycle of Birth and Death

Individuals must view death in a very broad perspective. Not only must parents and children envision the life cycle taking place within the confines of the human environment, but they must also see its implications in the natural and regulatory environment. The natural environment includes the land, air, space, water, plants, wildlife, animals, sun, and those natural resources which support life. It is easy to envision the natural cycle of birth and death within the natural environment. An example of the cycle of birth and death is the tree as it goes through the seasons. During the spring the trees begin to sprout new leaves. As spring moves into summer, the leaves grow to their full size. In autumn, the leaves begin to lose their color and finally fall off the tree. During the winter, when the ground is covered with snow, the trees lie dormant waiting for spring to give new life.

The regulatory environment includes those educational, political, judicial, religious, and economic systems created by man to maintain and give order to the human and natural environment. An example of the birth-death cycle in this environment is the creation, discussion, and acceptance or rejection of a bill in Congress.

The ecological framework helps parents discuss the birth-life cycle with greater understanding. There are several things they can do. These include a series of family-centered activities as follows:

  a. Family field trips exploring fields, timber, and forests which could be in conjunction with a family picnic.
  b. Family projects of growing plants from seeds, or having the child take care of an aquarium where the balance of life and death may be observed.
  c. Reading with the child or suggesting different books which give a perspective of the birth-death cycle.

Process of Life: Everyone Views Death Differently

Every child is unique. Each grows and develops both mentally and physically at different rates. The child's maturity cannot always be gauged by their physical age. As the child's sphere of awareness expands, individual experiences broaden. Not every child reacts similarly to a particular event. Children interpret and react to events in their own unique fashion.

As Jackson mentions, "when a crisis like death comes along in life, the interpretation of it has to be geared to the special characteristics of the child."[8] Parents should try to cope with their child's reactions on the child's own level. A child cannot develop a healthy mental attitude toward death if significant adults depend on the denial of tragedy. It is preferable that they show an honest and open acknowledgement of the life cycle. Since the many fears of death a child may have are learned from the parents, gaining an understanding of the life cycle within an ecological perspective can help serve to reduce fears and misunderstandings about death.

Knowing that each child will interpret and view an event or happening differently, it is important to help the child understand his own feelings toward the life cycle. The child's ability to cope with a particular aspect or event concerning death may be facilitated if prior parent-child communication on the topic takes place. Mills emphasizes that such discussions should introduce the subject generally and in terms the child can understand.[9]

Realizing that age and cognitive development must be considered in understanding the child's comprehension of the meaning of death gives parents an opportunity to help their children grow both intellectually and emotionally, while allowing them to express their feelings in their own way. In studying children's attitudes toward death and dying, Koocher classifies children according to their cognitive states by using Piaget's framework of cognitive functioning.[10] In combining these cognitive levels with an appropriate age classification, the following categories can be used:

1. *Sensory Reaction* (birth to 4 years). The child can sense a loss but cannot understand the concept of birth or death. The child is concerned with present emotions and feelings, has little understanding of time, and needs love and understanding from the parents. No attempt needs to be made to explain the life cycle except to give the child a positive feeling toward nature and life.

2. *Fantasy Reasoning* (5 to 9 years). Children at this stage become aware of both life and death, including the sorrows and joys they can bring. In observing living things and the finality of death, this age group can rarely envision the universality of death. Death becomes personified by egocentric reasoning or magical thinking as they might begin to attribute such natural phenomena to a "bogeyman" or an "angel of death."

3. *Factual Reasoning* (8 to 12 years). During this period, most children witness or observe the death of a pet or perhaps a relative. Not only does the child begin to see some specific causes of death, but also wonders about an afterlife. Most children in this group apply specific causes or factual events to death. Death to them is still a distant phenomenon.

4. *Abstract Reasoning* (13 to 18 years). There is a realization

that death occurs to all living things. Life and death are viewed as part of a natural process of aging, sickness, or general physical deterioration.

No matter at what cognitive age level, it is important for the parent to help the child understand death. When communicating with the child, it is necessary to be honest and open while answering questions clearly. Fear in facing the topic of death openly may cause confusion, fear, or rejection by the child. Perhaps the most important aspect of helping your child understand death is to listen to the child. If a child asks a question concerning death, listen to find out what he or she knows and does not know.

Positive Communication Between Parent and Child

Helping children face death also helps family members deal with their own feelings toward death. Each individual within a family can strengthen and help others face life through the death of a loved one.

There are many positive communication techniques which may be used with children. A selected few follow:

1. Be objective, not technical or complex. One should try to help the child understand death with simple facts. The child's age will affect the amount of information a child should receive.
2. Parents should mourn with the child. Supporting each other will help both, otherwise the child may conclude that you are being secretive.
3. Looking at death together may help families share their hopes, fears, ideas, beliefs, and faith for the future. Death is a test for the family to reexamine their philosophy toward life.
4. Help the child establish a realistic view of the person who has died; help the child establish a memory; however, do not hold onto the past but look to the future.
5. Mourn with the child. This includes not only grieving for the dead person, but also dealing with feelings of loss and

the grieving for a lost relationship.

6. Express feelings; grieving and crying are not a show of weakness, rather they are an expression of feelings.

Many negative aspects of communication exist along with myths and the ways people have attempted to help children cope with death. Some of the negative solutions follow:

1. The phrase "Johnny went to sleep" tends to make a child afraid to go to sleep, afraid that he or she too will die.
2. "God took away Johnny because He loved him." If blame is placed on God, the child may grow up fearing God and lose trust in God.
3. Never use death-related threats, like "clean up your room or I'll kill you." These phrases suggest death as something dreadful.
4. Fairy tales of why a person has died gives a child a false idea. The child should be told the actual reason for the death.
5. Do not shield the child from death; the child may imagine that he or she was responsible for the death.
6. Do not tell a child that the dead person has gone on a long journey. When the person does not return, the child may develop related unrealistic notions.
7. Do not create guilt feelings for the child. Sayings such as "You will be the death of me yet" contribute to guilt. If a parent actually does die, the child may believe that he or she was the cause of death.
8. Do not use expressions like "Drop dead." Any association with death or dying should not be used in talking with a child other than in an *actual* situation of the death of someone or something.

Positive communication between parent and child is important in the development of positive feelings toward life and death. People send different kinds of messages; "I" messages make people feel good and help build healthy relationships and are less threatening. "You" messages tend to make a person feel rejected, put down, or to blame. In a parent-child relationship, the "you" messages can terminate an exchange and produce negative feelings. Examples of some "you" messages:

Child: What is wrong with Grandpa?
Parent: You just wouldn't understand!

Child: Can I help Uncle David to get better?
Parent: You know you cannot help.

Child: I found a dead bird, can we bury it?
Parent: Don't you touch that dirty thing!

Below are the questions reanswered with "I" messages from the parents, which help the child have positive feelings about the situation and about themselves.

Child: What's wrong with Grandpa?
Parent: I'm upset because he is so sick, but Grandpa has done many nice things for us to remember.

Child: Can I help Uncle David to get better?
Parent: I don't know what we can do, except visit him and let him know how much we care; the doctor is helping him.

Child: I found a dead bird, can we bury it?
Parent: I will help you bury the birdie if you find a box.

Summary

A family-centered approach for helping children become aware of death is not so much instruction on death as it is an educational understanding of life. For parents to help their children view death within the broader ecological perspective is to give their children a total picture of the environmental working of nature. Such an understanding gives children a more comprehensive and realistic view of life and death as they find joy and happiness in nature.

1. The family is the major educator of its offspring in matters of interpreting and understanding the life cycle. Parents become the key instruments in shaping and molding their children's awareness of death within the context of their own beliefs. Professionals should not deny families this function.

2. Children at various cognitive age levels will view death quite differently. Even within each developmental stage,

children are unique individuals who grow and develop at different rates.

3. Open and honest communication is imperative. This helps children share feelings of the life cycle in their own way, giving them an opportunity to grow and develop naturally.

4. Parents can and should incorporate an ecological perspective of the life cycle into their children's growth processes. This can be done through informal discussions, family projects, suggested readings, or family activities.

Kubler-Ross emphasizes that children who are given the opportunity to express and discuss their feelings of death openly are more likely to view death calmly and serenely.[11] The ecological perspective will give parents the needed confidence to communicate with their children on topics related to the birth-life-death cycle.

REFERENCES

1. Miller, Peter and Ozza, Jan: Mommy, what happens when I die? *Ment Hyg, 57*:20-22, 1973.
2. Schneidman, Edwin: You and death. *Psychology Today, 5*:44, 1971.
3. McKissack, Jan: On death and pigeon feathers. *J Humanistic Psychol, 14*:79-83, 1974.
4. Fochtman, Dianne: A comparative study of pediatric nurses' attitudes toward death. *Life Threatening Behavior, 4*:107-117, 1974.
5. Goldberg, Stanley: Family tasks and reactions in the crisis of death. *Social Casework, 54*:398-405, 1973.
6. Doyle, Nancy: *The Dying Person and the Family.* Washington, D.C., Pub Aff Pr, 1977.
7. Pattison, Mansell: The fatal myth of death in the family. *Am J Psychiatry, 133*:674-678, 1976.
8. Jackson, Edgar: *Telling a Child About Death.* New York, Hawthorn, 1965.
9. Mills, Gretchen et al.: *Discussing Death: A Guide to Death Education.* Homewood, ETC Pubns., 1976.
10. Koocher, Gerald: Talking with children about death. *Am J Orthopsychiatry, 44*:404-411, 1974.
11. Kubler-Ross, Elizabeth: *Death: The Final Stage of Growth.* Englewood Cliffs, P-H, 1975.

Chapter 13

HOME AND SCHOOL: PARTNERS IN LEARNING

MARION WILSON

Introduction

WHAT would you do to improve achievement of school-age children? Willard Wirtz, chairman of the President's Commission Studying the Scholastic Aptitude Scores, when asked this question, stated that he would restore or build a new relationship between the teacher in the school and the teacher at home. He said further:

> I am convinced that this has to be a partnership arrangement. There are those who would urge that we start being sterner and stricter about attendance, promotions, the difficulty of teacher materials and about holding kids to basics. Those short answers won't help. I'd settle for an alliance between family and school with the expectations that these problems be worked out on a community basis. The schools can't do it all by themselves. We need a closer home and school alliance.[1]

This is the belief under which the Parent-Child Early Education Program in the Ferguson-Florissant School District operates: Parents are a key to the success their children will experience in school.

When the Ferguson-Florissant School District began the study of early education and the possibility of starting such a program in the school district some eight years ago, it was agreed that further schooling for children was not what was needed. As the Superintendent of Schools stated:

> The early education program began because of our frustration with the failures in our educational system and our realization that chief among the basic changes needed were

145

changes in children's response to school. And these depend on children's self-concepts which are developed early in life. So we began this program. Besides, much of what we do in the formal school is remedial in nature.

If an early education program is to be successful, one aspect of the program must deal with the identification of children who have handicaps and are high risks for school success. Second, parents need to be involved with their young child. In this program of early education, both the child and parents are students.

Rationale for Program

In developing a program in early education, several key assumptions were made. These assumptions have served as the core philosophy in the development of the program.

One, the parent is the child's most important teacher. Throughout life, the parents serve as a primary model.

Second, much of what accounts for achievement is not a result of what happens in the school. Coleman, in his 1966 report which focuses on the home environment versus school environment, indicated that variations among students in achievement were determined by family background and that the quality of the home was more important than the school.[2] Christopher Jencks, in *Inequality*, states that elements which determine success in school are a result of what the child brings to school.[3] In the complex world situation in which we live, children learn from a variety of sources, including radio, television, and other people with whom they associate, but they learn primarily from those people in their family unit. A child, during the first five years of life, spends more time in the home than all of the time he will spend in the elementary and secondary schools. During these formative years, as well as later, the parents are the key.

Third, the role to the parent and child is a supportive one. The attitude is not "We know more than you do" but instead it is "Parents, you are doing a great job! We are here not to supplant the home but to supplement the family."

If a child is to be served, concern for him must be translated into services for the entire family. If there are family communication problems, financial difficulties, problems with other children or other family members, the child will be affected. Services to parents of young children are only helpful when health, nutritional, social, psychological, and educational services are combined. Although the basic concern is for the educational progress of the child, he cannot function in this area effectively unless other basic needs are met.

Finally, it is important to identify handicaps or possible learning problems as early as possible. Disabilities have a cumulative effect on subsequent growth and development. By identifying problems early, and providing a specialized program, many of these children can remain within the mainstream of the educational system.

In order to test these beliefs, Ferguson-Florissant developed a program which involved both the school and home working together to provide a program for approximately 700 four-year-olds. The logo, that of a home and school joining hands, describes this approach. Formally known as the Parent-Child Early Education Program and more popularly known as Saturday School, it was funded under Title III from 1971 to 1974. Since then it has been a Developer/Demonstrator project for the National Diffusion Network of the United States Office of Education.

The approach is both simple and complex. In its simplicity, teachers go into the homes for a weekly teaching visit, and children and parents come into the school for a three-hour Saturday session. In its complexity, the staff is continually involved in the process of serving as support, friend, teacher, and counselor, while working with children and parents on an intimate basis over a period of time. The approach is very "grass roots" and demands a staff who care and show concern for other human beings.

The Program

1. At school on Saturdays, four-year-olds attend either a

morning or afternoon class in the kindergarten room of a neighboring elementary school.

2. Parents come into the classroom to teach during the small group instruction periods. Each parent's share is a turn at teaching once every six weeks. Their participation makes possible a classroom ratio of one adult for every four to six children.
3. Teachers go into the home for regularly scheduled teaching visits. Each child receives a weekly home visit and children with special problems receive two visits.
4. At home through the week, parents continue the learning experiences with skill development games and activities. Parents receive weekly activity guides suggesting things to do at home.

The learning activities at home and school focus on the development of skills that will facilitate later learning: language skills, hand-eye coordination, math and science concepts, auditory and visual discrimination, gross motor skills, the creative arts, and social skills.

Growth experiences for parents are an equally important part of the program. They have an opportunity at school and during home visits to observe appropriate techniques for teaching young children and have an opportunity to use these skills.

An initial evaluation of each child's need and abilities is made by his or her teacher and parents before the start of the school year. If indicated, children receive further diagnosis. Teachers develop individual educational programs for children who have exceptional needs.

On Saturdays, three parents take their turn assisting the teacher. Preparation includes meeting with each teaching parent before the children arrive to outline and demonstrate their teaching assignment. Although most of the parent-teachers are mothers, many fathers also participate. All schools have an occasional "fathers only" day. A typical schedule for the students' three-hour school day includes several activities:

Opening Activities — The class meets together for a brief

learning activity and to sing and meet the parent-teachers.
Small Group Instruction Periods — The children rotate in small groups to four learning centers. A permanently stationed parent or teacher conducts the fifteen-minute activity periods for each group.
Creative Play — Children enjoy an independent play period.
Closing Activities — The children reassemble for a song and story.

The parents' active participation at school affords them a unique opportunity to see their child perform in relation to others his or her own age.

The major strength of the program rests in the home teaching visit. Here the teacher has the opportunity to work with a group of two or three children and their parents. Each weekly home visit is an hour in length. Children with special needs receive an individual home visit weekly and are also involved in a group visit.

As the name implies, it is a teaching visit. The primary goal of the teacher is to provide learning activities based on definite objectives for the individual child. During the course of the home visit, the teacher may sing a song, do finger plays, provide a language activity, math game, memory activities, art project, or a motor activity. Usually, approximately five or six activities can be accomplished during the visit. Besides providing the activity, the teacher's role is to provide teaching through motivational skills, positive reinforcement, and sequencing the task. The teacher may introduce the task and then let the mother take over. After the learning time and while the child is choosing a library book, the teacher is sharing the home activity guide with the parent. She briefly reviews the theme of the guide and then points out several things that she would like the parent and child to do together. The teacher also points out how spontaneous learning can occur throughout the daily schedule and encourages parents to use everyday household objects for learning. In fact, many of the learning activities in the home visit revolve around simple objects found in the home.

Home visits provide teachers with an opportunity to individualize the program to meet each student's needs and to know the child in a way classroom contact would not permit. Because she is in the home on a weekly basis throughout the school year, the teacher also becomes a friend to the parent. As this relationship builds, the parent will often confide other concerns dealing with childrearing, sibling rivalry, marital problems, and other family situations. The teacher thus assumes a supportive role as she guides parents into possible alternatives for managing problems.

Teachers have resource consultants in social work and psychology who regularly meet with staff and discuss problems of particular parents. These consultants also observe children in Saturday School and when judged ready by the teacher, they contact parents who have concerns and who seek help. The consultants thus serve a double function: they support the teacher in her role with parents and children, and they provide direct service to parents who ask for help.

The teacher is a member of a team which plans for activities and staff development. It is extremely important that the teacher has the opportunity to share with others because during the time she works in the home she is basically on her own. She needs to have the support of coworkers and consultants so that the *burn-out* syndrome, so typical of those who work in helping professions, does not affect her.

All staff people are allotted two three-hour afternoon segments weekly for staff development and planning. Building planning and staff development into the regular responsibilities lends greater importance to them, and staff members know that the administration has both concern and expectation for their professional growth.

In developing the program for young children, Ferguson-Florissant has devised a method which involves parents and teachers working together with the young child. To support both parents and teachers, consultants are available on a continuing basis. Because of the unique demands of working in the home, teachers partake of constant staff development and team planning. Frequent redefining of her role and support for the teacher are important.

Results

The data was compiled over the three years of program development and was based on the Slosson Intelligence Test, Beery Test of Visual Motor Integration, and the Zimmerman Preschool Language Test. Average gains for all children over the eight months of Saturday School operation were —

16 months in intellectual growth,
15 months in language development, and
12 months in visual-motor skill development.

Even greater gains were made by that third of the children with the lowest entering scores, which included children found to have various problems affecting their learning. These children realized —

17 months in intellectual growth,
20 months in language development, and
16.5 months in perceptual skill development.

The children's feelings about themselves and their relationships with others showed equally significant gains.

Parents showed gains as well. There were statistically significant changes in the parents' abilities to interact with their children, in awareness of the child's needs, and in their use of more appropriate reinforcement and motivation techniques.

Children with special problems or handicaps showed particularly significant progress. Many learning difficulties were remediated by the end of the year. Especially significant gains were made by the children diagnosed as learning disabled, particularly in the areas of language and motor development. By the close of each year, 85 percent were functioning at levels commensurate with their chronological age.

Of the students diagnosed as retarded (frequently due to being educationally deprived), only one in eight still performed within the level of retardation at the close of the year, based on the scores of a number of tests, including the Binet Slosson Intelligence test.

All pupils identified as having emotional problems showed a marked improvement by the end of the year in their behavioral patterns and ability to adjust.

Saturday School's students, thus far tested through fourth grade with McGraw-Hill's Comprehensive Test of Basic Skills, scored significantly higher on all aspects of the achievement test and the total score than children with and without preschool experience.

Of particular note, *those former students with some kind of problem or handicap scored higher than a normal group of children* with and without preschool experience, except in the areas of spelling and language.

In follow-up testing, the children with learning problems, now in fourth grade, for the first time showed no differences in achievement when compared with the rest of their Saturday School classmates, except in spelling.

Of even more interest may be some of the comments taken from parent evaluations in 1977. Asked what they liked best about the home visit and Saturday School, parents commented as follows:

"The teacher and my child loved each other."

"I appreciated the genuine interest and concern shown by the teacher in enriching my child's educational readiness."

"My child gained confidence."

"There was fun in learning."

"My child got individual attention."

"It was a relaxed atmosphere."

"There was a deeper relationship than just teacher and pupil."

"I liked the informality, but my child really learned things."

"Each child was taken at his or her own speed of learning and was continuously involved with something meaningful."

"I liked the learning experience I shared with my child."

"My child came home happy and excited about the things he or she had learned."

"Saturday School was a wonderful learning experience for our entire family."

It is interesting to note that while the primary concern is educational in nature, parents are affected by the concern and interest of the staff. This approach, while stressing educational aspects, has an impact far beyond skills learned. Seven years of developing an approach and process has resulted in a viable approach to early education and success for young children and parents.

Conclusion

The program just described is serving as the foundation for the development of other parent-involvement programs. The school is serving three-year-olds who are considered to be handicapped or high risk for school success, and their parents, through weekly home visits. A home visitor program has also been developed using Title XX funding. This program serves eligible parents of very young children, including teenage mothers or protective custody cases. Home visitors are seen as a friend by the parents. Furthermore, it is hoped that this program will give parents a better understanding of the child and his development, and improve parent-child interaction.

REFERENCES

1. Wirtz, Willard: Academic scores decline: Are the facts the enemy of the truth? *Phi Delta Kappan, 59*:83-86, 1977.
2. Coleman, James et al.: *Equality of Educational Opportunities.* Washington, Department of Health Education, and Welfare, 1966.
3. Jencks, Christopher: *Inequality.* New York, Basic, 1972.

SECTION III
Practice
SERVICES FOR THE DEVELOPMENTALLY DISABLED

Chapter 14

HOME-BASED SUPPORT SERVICES: AN ALTERNATIVE TO RESIDENTIAL PLACEMENT FOR THE DEVELOPMENTALLY DISABLED

GRATIA KOCH

THE forces which compel parents of disabled children to seek residential placement for their children are often not very complex. Sometimes it is just too much work and too much emotional strain to keep a handicapped child at home. Then placement is sought, not because the institution has something special to offer the child but because the resources at home have been exhausted. This is especially true when there are complicating factors such as limited income, more than one handicapped child in the family, or the absence of one parent.

The Family And Child Training (FACT) program was created to help parents keep their disabled children at home by providing certain support services as counseling, recreation therapy, and parent training directly to the family. FACT is a service of Systems Unlimited, Inc., a nonprofit program based in Iowa City, which provides a variety of residential settings for developmentally disabled children and adults. The term "developmental disability" refers to a substantial handicap which occurs before age eighteen, such as mental retardation, cerebral palsy, epilepsy, and autism. The idea for the program first came, appropriately enough, from parents of disabled children who were interested in alternatives to residential placement, and who asked the agency's staff to create a support program. FACT began operation in June 1977.

The program is based on the premise that many parents can

157

and will keep their disabled children at home, if they receive help with the daily care of the child and if some of their emotional needs are met through positive relationships with those who are giving the help. That is, parents need someone to share the load.

The FACT program is also based on the premise that it is almost always more desirable for a child to remain with his family. It costs far less to maintain a child at home than in an institution. More importantly, children who live at home get the intangible but highly valuable benefits of the continuity of relationship with their parents and family.

The FACT program employs a simple service delivery system. The staff includes a coordinator (M.S.W.), a social worker, an educational consultant, and two child care workers. It is a home-based project, so the parents must be involved in decision-making, planning, and monitoring aspects of the child's program. The families served all have widely differing needs and problems, depending on the severity and nature of the child's disability, where they live (the agency serves a three-county area), and many other factors. Most families receive approximately five hours per week of direct contact intervention. This time is used a number of ways:

1. Child care workers visit the home to assist in feeding, bathing, and other daily care of the child.
2. The social worker and educational consultant visit the home to provide parent training in areas such as behavior management.
3. Staff members assist the parents in implementing the recommendations of other agencies including the child's educational program.
4. Staff members counsel with parents about problems they encounter, both related and unrelated to the disability of their child.
5. A recreation therapist, employed by Systems Unlimited, Inc., consults with the program to assist in finding appropriate leisure activities for the child and family.

These services are not primarily educational in nature. Educational services are provided by special education programs within the community. The growth of educational services has been accompanied by a recognition that the child's parents are his or her first and best teachers; that the disabled child especially needs a strong, supportive family; and that this family is likely to have many problems which cannot be solved by educational services alone. Therefore, the FACT program provides support services directly to parents, siblings, and extended family members. Some of these services were formerly available only to children who had been placed in residential or institutional settings.

Referrals are received through the local Department of Social Services. As of this writing, families must be eligible for Title XX services (that is, they must meet low income guidelines) to participate in the FACT program. Because this means that some families have been denied service, additional funding sources are being sought. Once a referral is received, the coordinator makes an initial home visit to explain the program and find out what type of help the parents want and need. Probably the most interesting way to describe the program is to follow a typical referral. Some identifying characteristics have been changed to preserve confidentiality:

Billy is a thirteen-year-old boy who attends a special class for the trainable mentally retarded and lives with his parents and younger brother in a small town a few miles from Iowa City. He was referred to the FACT program by his caseworker from the Iowa Department of Social Services.

During the initial home visit, Billy's mother explained that he was becoming more of a problem as he grew older and bigger, that he bullied his younger brother, and was very difficult for her to control. For this reason, she and her husband were considering residential placement for Billy as soon as possible. She also expressed fears that she and her husband were not providing the best possible environment for him and that he might learn more or do better in some other residential setting. Mrs. T. was eager to try the FACT program while keeping the option of residential placement.

After consulting with Billy's teacher and Social Services

worker, and after observing him at school, the FACT coordinator prepared an individual service plan. A social worker and a child care worker were assigned to the family by the FACT program. Primary goals of the plan included implementation of more effective behavior management techniques at home and utilization of recreation activities to help Billy learn to play cooperatively with his brother and other children. Mrs. T. also requested we help Billy learn to behave appropriately in stores, restaurants, and other public places.

Billy was enrolled in a special Boy Scouts troop, accompanied at first by the child care worker. The FACT staff also took Billy on many outings, often including the younger brother and neighboring children. The social worker began meeting with the parents approximately once a week, to discuss a wide variety of problems. She also visited Billy's classroom frequently to learn what behavior management techniques are employed there and to insure that they would also be used at home.

Mr. and Mrs. T. were given written recommendations for controlling Billy's behavior at home and in public. The family has been included in many of the FACT program activities in order to test these recommendations with the assistance of a staff person.

There has been considerable improvement in Billy's behavior. Mr. and Mrs. T. report that the variety of experiences now available to Billy have helped them feel confident that his needs can be met without placement. They also say that knowing other people are consistently available to be involved with Billy has helped ease the burden of raising him. Although future residential placement may be necessary, it is no longer seen as an immediate need.

The Family And Child Training program is intended to provide support services, to be supportive of the family by acting in the combined capacities of extended family member, teacher, counselor, and friend. Such services must be available at the parents' convenience, rather than according to a rigid schedule. Flexibility is important not only in scheduling but in programming and implementation. Staff members must be willing to help with "daily grind" types of tasks, which wear parents down and make institutional placement seem like a good idea. They must be able to cope with strong emotions, including anger, depression, and frustration of parents who are raising severely disabled children. They must be able to incorporate the child's educational program into his or her daily living activities. Severely delayed children need almost constant help to learn such basic skills as attending to tasks, head control, and eye-hand coordination.

Tina is a two-year-old girl whose diagnosis is "developmental delay, profound retardation." Her five-month-old brother Mike appears to have the same developmental problems. They live at home with their mother and two older brothers in a rural Iowa town.

Mrs. K. and her children were referred to FACT by the local Area Education Agency, provider of special education, and the Department of Social Services. During the initial visit, Mrs. K. expressed a strong desire to keep her children at home. The FACT program was offered to help her, a single parent, with the many problems of raising four children, two of them profoundly retarded, and to help carry out the recommended developmental learning activities of the home teacher from the Area Education Agency, who visits the family every two weeks.

The service plan was written following consultation with the home teacher, Department of Social Services caseworkers, and the staff at the hospital outpatient clinic where the disabled children are seen. An educational consultant and a child care worker were assigned to the family by the FACT program. Their primary responsibilities included the following:

1. To assist Mrs. K. in implementing the recommendations of the home teacher.
2. To provide Mrs. K. with the opportunity to spend more time interacting with her two older children.
3. To assist in transporting the children to and from Iowa City for their frequent medical exams (both Tina and Mike have respiratory and other physical problems).

4. To attend medical and educational staffings with Mrs. K.
5. To assist Mrs. K. with daily child care, including feeding, bathing, etc.

The FACT child care worker and educational consultant visit the family at least twice a week. They do range-of-motion exercises and other developmental learning activities with Tina and Mike. They assist Mrs. K. in keeping a careful record of the children's progress and also free her to spend some time interacting with her two older children.

Tina and Mike have made encouraging developmental gains. Tina can now sit up unassisted and can reach for and grasp objects. However, both children are still severely delayed and require a great deal of work. The FACT program has made a long-term commitment to this family and will continue to assist Mrs. K. with the care of her children. She has reported that this type of assistance has helped her feel "not so alone." She is interested in meeting other parents of retarded children and she has been helpful in getting a small parents' group started.

A home-based program is substantially different from any other type of social work, aid to the handicapped, or educational service. Once the worker has left her desk or classroom and stepped into the family's living room, the rules of the game have changed. The old adage "start where the client is" is transformed from an ungrammatical aphorism into an absolutely necessary first step. Parents of handicapped children have needs which sometimes can hardly be put into words and cannot be neatly capsulized into categories such as "counseling" or "parent training."

Whatever a parent is able to formulate and ask for, within reason, is the first task of the home worker. Sometimes the parents may seem not to know what they need, or to be wrong in their assessment of what should come first. Even so, it is always most helpful to listen to the parents as carefully as possible during the first home visit, and then to start the actual work of the program immediately, focusing on the type of help they request. Other problems, which may seem crucial to the home worker, may be dealt with later.

Eddie is a fourteen-year-old, severely retarded boy. He lives with his mother, older sister, and teen-aged aunt and attends a special class. He was referred to the FACT program by his teacher, who was concerned about his extremely destructive behaviors at school. She had heard that these behaviors were a problem at home as well.

During the first home visit, Mrs. L. indicated that Eddie's destructiveness was not a problem for her, even though he had systematically destroyed every decoration in the house, pulled down all the curtains, and torn all the linoleum off the floor. Mrs. L. requested, instead, that we provide Eddie with a few hours of recreational activity each week. Her heavy work schedule prevented her from doing this.

The educational consultant was assigned to work with the family. She made frequent visits to Eddie's classroom to observe and discuss appropriate behavior management techniques with the teacher. She also began taking Eddie swimming one evening each week. His sister and aunt were invited to come along, and eventually they accepted. It soon became apparent that Eddie's unusual behavior of inappropriate noises and gestures embarrassed the girls and prevented them from taking him to public places. The educational consultant modeled appropriate discipline measures to use with Eddie, such as time-out for misbehavior, and also displayed (or tried to display) a calm acceptance of his retardation. This seemed to help the girls relax and enjoy themselves with Eddie.

Soon the girls were participating in a more structured behavior management program at home. They learned effective uses of reinforcers and were better able to control some of Eddie's behavior.

The consultant talked with Mrs. L. informally before and after each recreational outing. She reported to the mother that Eddie was doing much better at school. Mrs. L. asked if she could observe him in class, and this was readily arranged. Mrs. L. was happily surprised at the degree to which Eddie behaved at school. She expressed willingness to be more strict with him at home, having seen his teacher successfully make reasonable demands of him.

The educational consultant and Mrs. L. have developed a very positive relationship. They talk quite easily about the problems of living with a retarded child. Eddie's behavior, though far from perfect, is greatly improved, and Mrs. L. recently rehung the curtains.

Recreational therapy is especially important in a program designed to enable parents to maintain their children at home. One of the first tasks of such a program is to help the child and family enjoy the time they spend with each other. Occasionally, this can be accomplished by behavior management training, or by helping the parents to be more effective disciplinarians. When the child is simply so disabled that it is no fun to take him places, what is needed is a skilled staff person to go with the family, or to take the child alone sometimes. The child care worker and other staff can help locate activities that will be fun and developmentally useful for the child, and adapt the activities where necessary to allow for the child's disability.

Such activities are a large part of normalization for the disabled. *Normalization* refers not to attempts to "make the child more normal," but to make available to him or her all the things, places, and activities that are a part of any child's world. This concept of normalization has been slow to be implemented in the field because it requires a great deal of work to provide normal experiences for the developmentally disabled. We now recognize that it is a tremendous investment for the child's natural family too, and that they need help.

Home-based program staff can sometimes serve as link between family and other agencies by fostering open communication and by attending staffings and evaluations with the parents.

Chapter 15

THE IMPACT OF HOME TRAINING CONSULTANTS ON THE LIVES OF DEVELOPMENTALLY DISABLED PERSONS AND THEIR FAMILIES: A STUDY OF HOME SERVICE IN RURAL AND URBAN WISCONSIN

Lou Roach

The Task

THE birth of a child is a powerful, often exciting, intimate event in the life cycle of a family. Few happenings prove to be as potent a change-agent in daily living as the arrival of a new member into the family constellation. Anthony Padavano declares:

> It is no easy thing to be a human being. A human life is the most unforeseeable and dramatic venture imaginable. . . . No one knows what a child will become or whether he will even be recognizable in his future. Transformation is at issue in human living. A man can be less than a man or more than a man . . . there is no creature who needs to be healed more often or more deeply than does man. . . . Only life can heal life; only people can save people. . . . Only man can be healed by the word another man speaks to him, or by the thought another man gives him to think, or by the presence of another human being . . . in time of trouble.[1]

Padavano describes the average human condition. Perhaps he describes more specifically the life condition for developmentally disabled persons and their families. Those families face an extended life crisis situation, a never-ceasing demand to bring a handicapped child to fullest capability in a world intolerant of handicaps. Too often these parents deplete their own emotional and intellectual resources prematurely, believing they must cope with the task on their own, convinced that to have borne a less-than-perfect child is their deserved destiny and that to look to others for assistance of any kind would only emphasize their believed inability to be successful parents. When families *do* look to others they may find them insensitive, intimidating, and unrealistic.

Working with these families in what is still a relatively new program in Wisconsin has given me an awareness of the importance of the reliability of professionals and the necessity of one or more empathetic persons who will assist the parents in their work with and planning for a handicapped child. Ronnie Gordon speaks realistically of family needs: "Parents need guidance, they need comfort, and they need to be periodically free from their heavy and lonely burden . . . the needs of the children are great; the needs of the family are often even greater. The needs of the children are frequently met; the needs of the family are too seldom recognized or satisfied."[2]

The work of home training consultants evolves around meeting needs for the developmentally disabled child and his family, inclusive of siblings and grandparents and occasionally other members of the extended family. The home trainer serves as a liaison between the family and the world — physicians, therapists, teachers, psychologists, and the community in general. She or he is a translator of medical jargon, of educational labels, and of psychological tests and measurements.

Home training consultants have no single discipline for their professional training. They *do* have a singular goal for all families: to help in creating an environment and familial awareness conducive to the development of the child's greatest potential. Lending support and encouragement to parents in the ongoing task of caregiving is a secondary goal.

In a 1975 editorial on the handicapped family, Fox explains the feelings of families: "We need one person, someone who could come to us or we could go to him, and he'd have time to talk to us and the knowledge we need."[3]

This is the role most ideally played by the home trainer. Dr.

Stephen Copps, a pediatrician and director of the Western Wisconsin Neurodevelopmental-Cerebral Palsy Center, describes home training consultants:

> My own feeling is that the best person is not particularly specialized in any one field, but someone who is able to take (other's) expertise and knowledge, synthesize it into an effective program and present it in a meaningful way . . . Being a non-specialist, the home trainer is in a good position to do just that for they can act in a manner that is in the best interest of the afflicted person — not what is in the best interest of the certain self-serving institutions or agencies. The home trainer must also have as one of the guidelines for operation the fact that there is *no* patient for whom nothing can be done.[4]

Development of Home Training

Home training is not a new idea. Formalized programs were developed in the United States during the 1930s, 1940s, and 1950s in Massachusetts, New Jersey, Pennsylvania, and Washington, D.C.

In 1957, two new home training programs were begun: one in Washington, D.C., established as part of a clinic for retarded children, was a special project in the Bureau of Maternal and Child Health. The other was a home training program in Ohio, which became a formal component of the Division of Mental Retardation with the passage of Senate Bill 169, which created the County Boards of Mental Retardation. This first home training program served thirty clients in 1957 and had served 3,118 by June 1971. The Nisonger Center and School of Home Economics at Ohio State University developed a program which qualified graduates to be home training consultants. The Division of Mental Retardation of Ohio also has a licensing and certification procedure for home training consultants.

Home training services began in Wisconsin in the late 1950s when the Milwaukee County Association for Retarded Citizens began a program under the direction of Doctor Arline Albright, an educator at Marquette University. Doctor Albright also helped the Racine County Association for Retarded Citizens in establishing a volunteer home training program in 1967.

Home training on a larger scale was initiated in six rural Wisconsin communities under a federally funded project. This project, officially entitled "A Community Services Demonstration Project for the Mentally Retarded in a Rural Area" and popularly known as Project 6, offered home training services to parents for four years. This home training experience was warmly received by parents and proved highly successful. This successful demonstration of home training by Project 6, terminated in 1970, provided a major impetus for the development of statewide home training services in Wisconsin. A Title I grant, awarded in the summer of 1970, allowed several Wisconsin communities to hire home training specialists.

In December of 1970, the Bureau of Mental Retardation became actively involved with home training services and established a position paper on this program. This involvement lasted until the spring of 1974, when the Bureau no longer viewed itself as responsible for the organization of home trainers because of the formation of the county disability boards.

From 1970 to 1974, home training was firmly established in Wisconsin. Regional home training organizations were created throughout the state, starting in 1971 in Southeastern Wisconsin and in 1972 in Central and Northern Wisconsin. These regional organizations provided in-service training to home training specialists, published a statewide newsletter, met in 1972 and 1973 in conjunction with the American Association of Mental Deficiency-Wisconsin Association of Retarded Citizens conferences, and in 1974 formed a subdivision under the General Division of the Wisconsin Chapter of American Association of Mental Deficiency. In 1973, in response to demand for more training, the regional organization began sponsoring institutes quarterly in conjunction with the University of Wisconsin Extension.

During the summer of 1974, home trainers from around the state met to discuss the formation of a statewide association. It was decided to incorporate as a nonprofit corporation and to discontinue regional meetings. At that time, certification by the association and the Division of Mental Hygiene was also approved. In January 1975, the Wisconsin Association of Home Training Consultants in Developmental Disabilities was incorporated.

The Service

The utilization of the individualized home training programs is becoming the norm, rather than the exception, for developmentally disabled youngsters and adults across the state of Wisconsin. At-risk families as well as developmentally delayed children are served by home training consultants. Children with neurodevelopmental problems are also served by programs around the state.

Home training consultants work with a variety of client groups. Some home training consultants are a part of clinic evaluation teams and provide ongoing home programming as a follow-up service. Other home training consultants are carrying out infant stimulation programs with parents. Some consultants staff day activities centers or workshops, provide parent education, and develop programs which improve the daily living situation of the developmentally disabled. In responding to the trends of community placement, there are home training consultants which now provide outreach services to group homes. In some counties where there is a cooperative relationship between community boards and the public schools, the home training consultants work with parents who ask assistance for their school-age children. The majority of service appears to be given to youngsters from birth to three years, and to persons twenty-one years and over.

Initial requests for home training service come from a variety of sources: physicians, county or visiting nurses, extended family members, family, school personnel, social workers, mental health counselors, clergy, early screening and diagnostic centers, and families who have benefited from the program.

Upon referral, trainers check with the recommended family. During a follow-up informal home call, family attitudes and feelings are explored; the disabled person and the family are assessed; and rapport is established between the client family and the home trainer. A foundation for further contact is carefully laid with the provision of information, concise answers to questions, and preliminary suggestions for a possible program for the child or adult. Stress areas and significant problems may be defined during this visit. Unspoken concerns and fears of parents are often explored at this time, as the home trainer listens closely to determine expressed and *unexpressed* needs.

Barbara Loye, a social worker with the community orthopedic rehabilitation program at Central Wisconsin Center for the Developmentally Disabled, observed:

> Home trainers have the most success with families when there is a sensitivity to the family's overall needs, a genuine warmth toward and acceptance of the family, resourcefulness in meeting a variety of problems, a feeling of advocacy for family and child, and an understanding of professional limitations to recognize when consultative services are needed. On the whole, our impression is that the presence of home trainers can and usually does have a positive and beneficial impact upon the families we mutually serve.[5]

If the family indicates a receptivity to service, the program begins immediately. The home trainer seeks out other professionals involved with the family to develop a team approach. The home training consultant coordinates team suggestions and designs and implements the treatment plan.

Consideration is given to three key areas when planning for the child. These include the developmental level of the child; the nature of the parent-child interaction; and the environmental resources and limitations of the family and home. The program helps the parent in improving the child's specific area of weakness and in observing and fostering development. Unless the parents of a high risk child know how to improve the child's conditions, adjustment to his or her problems will remain incomplete. Emotional support is not enough.

Home visits are made weekly; in some cases, twice weekly. During these visits a number of areas are covered by parent, child, and home trainer, ranging from cognitive learning to self-help skills; from explanation of a disability to reassurance about care procedures; and discussions concerning parental attitudes, fears, confusions, and decisions affecting the future of the disabled individual.

This procedure is the rule, not the exception, for home trainers working with developmentally delayed children. During the first three years of life, delay or early signs of retardation must be noted and a plan for intervention begun as soon as possible. "Early intervention *has* been shown to help; it can work to reduce the effects of a handicapping condition, and can do so more surely and rapidly than later intervention. . . . Parents need models of good parenting behavior with a handicapped child and specific instructions for working with the child."[6]

To assist families in developing skills necessary to help their handicapped children is another vital part of the home trainer's task. When parents realize they can develop expertise, become the natural intervention activators, and be the primary change agents for their child, they become confident and more nurturing caregivers. Families develop an awareness of the need for structure and definite goals for them as a unit, at the same time growing more realistically courageous in their attitudes toward the future.

Copps addresses the work of the home training consultant in this area: ". . . they can help families to meet the reality of the situation so that they do not hold out false hope. They can work to help patients and families accept themselves and their limitations . . . the home trainer should never promise what she/he can't deliver. . ."[4]

The families themselves express their reactions to the counseling and intervention techniques demonstrated by home training consultants.

"Finding out that our son is handicapped was a hard reality . . . our son is totally blind, has cerebral palsy and severe brain damage . . . now that we know we can take all the necessary steps to be the most help to our son. The best thing is the help we have received from our home trainer. She has helped us get in touch with the best doctors, therapists, schools and has helped us in finding out about financial assistance."

"Why didn't anyone come to us like this 20 years ago? We've always thought our son could never do anything. The home trainer has changed all our lives."

"I never thought our daughter would be able to feed herself or be with other people. For 27 years, I didn't know anyone would help."

The families of multiply-handicapped children tend to rely on the home training consultant for recommendations concerning special therapy programs. It is the responsibility of a home trainer to provide such detailed information and to assist in the organization of a treatment plan.

Professionals working with a handicapped youngster look to the home training consultant for follow-through. Loye states, "There can be more intensive follow-through on programs developed in inpatient rehab if a home trainer is available."[5]

The liaison role of a home training consultant becomes vital during the transition of a child from his or her program to a school environment. Multidisciplinary coordinator Thecla Tomany speaks of home training consultants as having the ability to counsel parents in the area of decision making for their child's future educational plan. At the time of school entrance, the home training consultant becomes a member of yet another team working in the best interest of a disabled child and the family. If necessary, she or he will assume the role of advocate to obtain appropriate educational placement and specific therapy required for the child's continued development.

Other Considerations

Financial responsibility for home training services in Wisconsin often belongs to unified services or developmental disabilities boards. In some regions, school boards have added home trainers to their staffs. Social service departments occasionally hire home training consultants to assist with their client families. The cost to families, who represent all societal levels, is generally minimal or nonexistent.

Consultants in Wisconsin are now certified annually by the State Department of Health and Social Service, Division of Community Service. Certification requirements vary slightly according to the education and experience of the individual; however, all must have ongoing training in specified areas and also must have a common background in the field of human services.

As home training may be necessary at various points in a person's life, the Wisconsin Association of Home Training Consultants recommends that home training be offered as a county-wide service to the developmentally disabled of all ages and living situations. The program, as it is offered in Wisconsin, is effective in both rural and urban settings.

Home training consultants see the need for professionals to be closely involved with families and their disabled members as a necessary contribution to the achievement and self-actualization of the family group. As long as they can help effect this kind of interaction, home training consultants will continue to be assets in the lives of persons with developmental problems. We believe, with Philip Roos, that "All human beings are considered to be malleable and to have potential for growth and development, no matter how seriously handicapped they might be."[7]

REFERENCES

1. Padavano, Anthony: *Belief in Human Life*. Pastoral Educational Services, 1969.
2. Gordon, Ronnie: Special needs of multi-handicapped children under six and their families. In Sontag, Ed (Ed.): *Educational Programming for the Severely and Profoundly Handicapped*. Reston, Council for Exceptional Children, 1977.
3. Editorial: The handicapped family. *Lancet*, 2:400-401, 1975.
4. Copps, Stephen: *Comments on the Role of Home Training Consultants*. Madison, University Extension, 1976.
5. Loye, Barbara: *Home Training and the COR*. Madison, Central Wisconsin Center for the Developmentally Disabled, 1977.
6. Hayden, Alice, and McGinness, Goel: Bases for early intervention. In Sontag, Ed (Ed.): *Educational Programming for the Severely and Profoundly Handicapped*. Reston, Council for Exceptional Children,

SECTION III
Practice

HEALTH SERVICES

Chapter 16

FAMILY ADVOCACY: IMPLICATIONS FOR TREATMENT AND POLICY

JAMES HYDE JR., ABRAHAM MORSE,
ELI NEWBERGER, AND ROBERT REED

FAMILY advocacy is an approach to the treatment of high risk children and their families which grew out of the work of the Family Development Study at the Children's Hospital Medical Center in Boston.[1,2,3] Although originally tailored to the treatment needs of the study population, which included high risk children with diagnoses such as child abuse and neglect, failure to thrive, accidents, and poisonings, it is now clear that in both concept and practice, family advocacy has a wide range of applications. The public policy implications are particularly worth noting as the diminishing impact of curative medicine on health status and the current emphasis on primary prevention have created an increased concern for addressing causes rather than pursuing the symptoms of illness. The data which led to the development of family advocacy is a therapeutic approach; an exploration of some of its broader policy and treatment implications are presented in this chapter.

Pediatric Social Illness and the Stress Hypothesis

Child abuse and neglect, accidents, poisonings, and failure to thrive are known to have familial, child developmental, and environmental antecedents.[4,5] Together they account for a major share of the mortality of preschool children and often have significant psychological and physical sequelae associated with them. However, there has yet to be developed a rational and universal classification system for these illnesses which would both focus on causal characteristics and direct treatment

177

and intervention more appropriately.

For example, the child and the environment may be forgotten in child abuse and neglect case management, because the diagnostic labels *abuse* and *neglect* focus attention on the hurtful acts and the perpetrators. Clinical approaches to accidents, poisonings, and failure to thrive are often limited by implicit conceptual models of chance occurrence as implied by the names of these social illnesses. They focus clinical attention and treatment on the child's symptoms, while the familial and environmental antecedents and concomitants of the symptom are ignored.

In order to develop a more adequate illness classification scheme for these social illnesses, we designed a controlled, epidemiologic study in which we interviewed 560 mothers and reviewed medical data on their children. Subject children were under four years of age. Cases and controls were matched on age, ethnic status, and socioeconomic status. A maternal interview explored past and present events, realities, and stresses which seemed to us to bear on the capacity of the child's nurturing context to support growth and protect from harm. The central hypothesis was that these social illnesses are related and that their common etiology includes important elements of stress in the family *before, during,* and *after* the birth of the child.

Of particular interest was the impact of stresses on a family's functioning in its current life context. The interview focused on such issues as access to essential services including housing, health and child care, and social isolation of families. We were not surprised to find a high prevalence of these problems in the families of children with the most severe injuries.

We perceived an ethical dilemma: could we possibly ignore the problems which we would identify? Did we have a responsibility, having identified such issues, to offer families help with them? We concluded that there could be no avoidance of this responsibility: therefore, when we began our interviews for the Family Development Study in December 1972, we also began a family advocacy program.

The results of the interview study have been reported elsewhere.[1] In general, the data support the basic hypothesis that differential levels of hypothesized stresses and personal and social strengths contribute to the occurrence of pediatric social illness. They indicate that child abuse is associated with more disparities between stress and strength than the other illnesses studied.

Family Advocacy Defined

Family advocacy is an intervention concept which addresses present-day life-context problems of families. By working to assure access to essential services such as housing, health, child care, education, welfare, and legal aid, family advocacy endeavors to improve the ecologic setting for childrearing and to foster the optimal development and functioning of families. Advocacy services developed by our program did not seek to replace other more traditional forms of social intervention. We were concerned with stimulating more appropriate and productive responses from the service system.

A distinctive characteristic of family advocacy as an intervention process is that it deals primarily, if not exclusively, with the present.[6] Advocacy is distinguished from social casework by this time orientation, by an orientation to direct provision of help rather than counseling, and by the advocate's educational and personal backgrounds. Advocates need not have a college degree, but must be effective people who have learned how to deal with children, adults, professionals, and bureaucrats in a range of institutions.

By working with parents around specific environmental and social problems, advocates help them develop a sense of personal efficacy and control. Parents begin to see themselves not as passive victims but as active agents, better able to control their children. The principal tool which the advocate uses is direct and intensive contact with the family at the time of referral through home visits, telephone contacts, and office accessibility, in order to —

a. develop an open and trusting relationship with the family;
b. agree on the goals and scope of the advocate's involvement with the family;
c. establish a division of tasks such that the achievement of the goals will represent a joint effort between the family and the advocate;
d. increase the knowledge of the people, policies, and systems which are available to assist both the family and the advocates in resolving the problems which affect families;
e. organize data and information collected in the course of helping families, so it may be pooled and generalized to support broadly focused efforts for institutional and social change.

During the first few days after referral, the advocate kept in frequent touch with families, both by telephone and through home visits. As a result of this intensive contact, it often became apparent that the problems for which families first requested assistance represented only the most immediate concerns. Families later were encouraged to use other resources when and where possible, so that a dependency relationship between the family and the advocates could be avoided.

During their work with families, the advocates presented themselves as members of a hospital team working with the family, the other members being the physician providing for the child's medical care, the nurse, and, in many but not all cases, the social worker. The family advocate was seen by the hospital professional staff as an integrator and facilitator who did not rely on a single method or technique of intervention but who tailored his or her approach to the particular problem at hand.

Thus, while a telephone call to a landlord might be effective in having a family's heat restored in one situation, it became necessary in another situation to secure a lawyer and, subsequently, a court order on behalf of the family. Each situation was approached with the knowledge that there is a vast range of methods and techniques available, any combination of which may suit the needs of a specific family but might prove useless when applied to another.

The concept underlying family advocacy is its process orientation. Advocacy is not merely concerned with the tangible measures of success but also with what kinds of problem-solving behavior people learn in the process of addressing a specific goal. The process once learned may be applied to seeking solutions to other problems. In the long run, what an individual learns about his or her ability to effect change in his own life is of far greater significance than the change itself.

A Case History

A three-year-old boy, Scott, was seen in the hospital's emergency room for head contusions which appeared on careful physical examination to have been inflicted. He was accompanied by a woman who said she was a relative, and who explained that Scott had fallen and that his mother was sick and afraid to leave her apartment. He was admitted to the hospital, where signs of previous trauma, as well as a minor bleeding diathses, were discovered. An advocate was assigned to the case and asked to coordinate health care for Scott and his mother.

Attempts to contact the family by telephone were unsuccessful so a home visit was made. At home, a sad, isolated, hugely obese young mother was found living in abject poverty on the seventh floor of a housing project. The neighborhood was extremely dangerous, with crime rate legendary in the city. The building itself was in very unsafe and unsanitary condition. Scott's mother said she was in poor health; her obesity embarrassed her; and she was afraid to go to the doctor because youth in the neighborhood had threatened to break in and steal her few possessions. She said that a relative had hurt Scott and that she was very concerned but did not know to whom to go for help.

Working in conjunction with a state protective service social worker who concentrated on the mother's relationship to Scott, the advocate obtained a commitment from the Housing Authority to relocate the family in an adequate and safe environment. This was accomplished after weeks of activism against the bureaucratic resistance of local housing officials and policies. During this time, many hours were spent with the family in conjunction with the social worker and a community health nurse in a coordinated effort to help the family meet basic needs and responsibilities. As soon as this family was able to move into their new apartment, the mother entered both a new environment and new period of understanding and competency to acknowledge and act on her and her family's needs.

Once the family was resettled, plans were made with the mother to enroll Scott in a child development program and to receive continuing medical care through the clinic where advocates are based. Also, the mother's own medical problems were a source of aggravation. It took several months of intensive contacts with the family to make the right connections within the human service system. Three years later, Scott is physically well and developmentally normal. His mother has lost much weight and she is a happier person. There has been no further abuse. Occasionally, when problems arise, she will call the advocate, discuss the problem, and act appropriately on her own.

Distinctive Characteristics of Users of Advocacy

In order to gain a better understanding of factors involved in a mother's accepting an offer of advocacy within the context of our study, discriminant functions similar to those used in our attempts to identify characteristics of various pediatric social illnesses were calculated to distinguish between the advocacy and nonadvocacy groups.[1] For the entire sample of 560 interviews, a moderate amount of discrimination was achieved (R=31). Of the 121 mothers who made use of advocacy, sixty-two were parents of children with pediatric social illness, including ten cases of child abuse and neglect, and fifty-nine were parents of children in the comparison group. They tended to be characterized by short duration of present marriage; problems with housing; problems with childrearing; and short residence at present address. All of these characteristics have statistical significance. The second and third are indicative of the types of problems with which our advocacy services dealt — housing and child care. The first and fourth — short duration of present marriage and housing — suggest the possible absence of supports needed to cope with environmental problems.

Among the four main variables, childrearing problems and short duration of present marriage tended to characterize the inpatient users of advocacy, while problems with housing and short duration at present address were characteristics of outpatient users of advocacy.

Among inpatients another variable to enter the equation was a history of serious troubles in the mother's childhood, such as broken home, high mobility, or family illness. Among outpatients, underemployment of the father and few people accompanying the mother and child to clinic both tended to characterize the mothers who accepted advocacy services.

Discussion

These findings suggest that environmental forces exert a powerful impact on families, both those whose children bear signs of pediatric social illness and those with other acute medical conditions. Further collaboration for these conclusions is contained in a paper by Jenkins and colleagues[7] in which Standardized Mortality Ratios (SMRs) for the state's thirty-nine Mental Health Catchment areas were ranked according to thirty-four specific independent causes of death. One area in particular, Area 602, ranked highest in excess mortality. Major causes of death for which this area experienced a mortality ratio two or more times that of the rest of the state include but were not limited to respiratory disease, infectious and parasitic diseases, sequelae of mental disorders, pneumonia, cirrhosis of the liver, perinatal mortality, death due to fire, homicide, and other injuries.

Sociodemographic data for Area 602 revealed that across all variables usually used to describe socioeconomic status, this area either ranked first or last: median family income, substandard housing, educational level, etc. "In brief, a composite picture of the social etiology of MHC Area 602 is one of severe economic deprivation, poor housing, a mixture of overcrowding and loneliness, family breakdown, personal disability, and social instability."[7] Of even greater pertinence is that this very area is also characterized by an impressive concentration of primary and secondary health care resources. Clearly the problem reflected in these data does not seem to be one of a lack of health facilities.

Taken together, these findings would seem to suggest that intervention strategies, such as family advocacy which focus on the amelioration of contemporaneous stress and the enhancement of the ability of families and individuals to cope with stress, may prove to be as valuable as other more traditional medical approaches.

Clearly, environmental forces exert a powerful impact on families, both those whose children bear signs of pediatric social illness and those whose children bear signs of pediatric social illness and those with other acute medical conditions. A counseling approach will not suffice to cure the lack of access to essential services, and to attribute the environmental problems to the families themselves is to "blame the victim."

We have seen that family advocacy at the case level can work effectively to reduce stress originating in the real life context and to foster a family's ability to utilize services for their children. The data on the similarities between child abuse and the predicting variables strongly suggest that were advocacy available before the incident, important elements of stress and social isolation might have been reduced. Conceivably, the abuse could have been prevented.

While intervention on behalf of a single family or child may prove efficacious in isolated instances, how does one address the vast cohort of children and families in America whose life context subjects them to such stress? The answer is not in the development of programs directed at increasing the number of hospital beds, or simply expanding the number and size of medical care facilities, but rather through insuring that basic needs of families are met. The magnitude and complexity of the problem demand the development of comprehensive, non-categorical programs aimed at the physical, social, educational, and economic context in which people live. Family advocacy provides an approach to the treatment of individual cases that demands further consideration.

REFERENCES

1. Newberger, Eli; Reed, Robert; Daniel, Jessica; Hyde, James; and Kotelchuch, Milton: Pediatric social illness: toward an etiologic classification. *Pediatrics, 60*:178-185, 1977.
2. Daniel, Jessica and Hyde, James: Working with high risk families: family advocacy and the parent education program. *Children Today, 4*:23-25, 1975.
3. Morse, Abraham; Hyde, James; Newberger, Eli; and Reed, Robert: Environmental correlates of pediatric social illness: preventive implications of an advocacy approach. *Am J Public Health, 67*:612-615, 1977.
4. Gregg, G. and Elmer, Elizabeth: Infant injuries: accidents or abuse. *Pediatrics, 44*:434, 1969.
5. Newberger, Eli; Newberger, Carolyn; and Richmond, Julius: Child health in America: toward a rational public policy. *Milbank Mem Fund Q, 54*:249, 1976.
6. Germain, G.: Time: an ecological variable in social work practice. *Social Casework, 57*:419, 1976.
7. Jenkins, C. David; Tuthill, Robert; Tannerbaum, Saul; and Kirby, Craig: Zones of excess mortality in Massachusetts. *N Engl J Med, 296*:1354-1355, 1977.

PREVENTION OF ABNORMAL PARENTING PRACTICES WITH LAY HEALTH VISITORS

BETTY KAPLAN

Rationale

THE family is a social institution which meets the reproductive, socialization, emotional, and production needs of its members. While individuals continue to have these needs, the family has shifted its responsibility for meeting these needs to others and, in the process, has lost many of its traditional functions to outside institutions.

As Talcott Parsons suggests, the modern family "is more specialized than before, but not in a general sense less important, because the society is dependent more exclusively for the performance of its vital functions."[1] The family increasingly relies on professional educators to teach knowledge and skills necessary for success in society. More responsibility for early child care and socialization has shifted to day care centers, babysitters, schools, and social organizations. No longer does a family independently produce the materials and provide the services necessary for survival of its members. Functions of the family which have survived are the creation of new individuals and nurturing of their development.

The birth of a child involves the integration of an individual into a family unit. The first minutes after an infant is born are crucial, for this is when parents begin attachment to their offspring. "Maternal sensitive period"[2] is the phase coined by Klaus and Kennell to denote this crucial time. During this period the infant is in a quiet, alert state in which his eyes are open, he responds to his parents, and they respond to him by

186

"fondling, kissing, cuddling, and prolonged gazing."[2] This early interaction enables parents to establish a unique, enduring relationship with their infant which is known as *attachment*.

Certain influences on attachment which cannot be changed include the mothering each parent received; relationships with family, friends, and spouse; and past experiences with pregnancy. Those influences which can be altered are the hospital staff's behavior and the hospital policies regarding labor, delivery, and postpartum care. The theory that these factors can lead to mothering disorders has been examined by several researchers.

Doctor Jane Gray and her colleagues recently completed a study in which the mother-child attachment process with its influencing factors was assessed for parenting potential. They utilized a prenatal interview, a questionnaire, and observations during labor, delivery, and the postpartum period to identify a sample of 150 mothers, 100 thought to be high risk for abnormal parenting practices, and 50 thought to be low risk. Mothers were divided randomly into high risk intervene and high risk nonintervene groups. In this study, intervention consisted of pediatric follow-up by a pediatrician, a lay health visitor, and/or a public health nurse in the home. Data from the study indicates that information from observations of labor and delivery interactions was 76.5 percent accurate in predicting parenting potential, and intervention prevented serious injury in a high risk population.[3]

Purpose

Based on the work of Henry Kempe and Jane Gray, the Lay Health Visitor Program was developed to provide extensive outreach services to families with new babies. Traditionally, young families may receive a visit from the public health nurse one to two weeks after discharge and a pediatric clinic appointment in two to six weeks. This overloaded system is often insufficient for young families who may have difficulties in the earliest weeks. Visits from public health nurses are frequently terminated after one or two visits because the family demonstrates no immediate needs or has difficulty expressing needs to unfamiliar people. Families needing extra services must have access to continuous positive and supportive intervention. This intervention can be provided by carefully selected and trained lay health visitors.

Program

Our Lay Health Visitor Program is offered to all mothers of newborns who live in Denver County and deliver at the University of Colorado Medical Center. All mothers are contacted daily on the postpartum ward of the hospital. This intake process allows us to offer services to mothers who do not receive prenatal care and who deliver on weekends.

Important data is collected during the hospitalization and on home visits to assess parenting potential and the family's need for services. This is done by —

1. assessment of labor and delivery room information. Mother-infant interaction forms are completed by labor and delivery room nurses who record parents' verbal and nonverbal interactions with their infant during the first encounter.

2. observation and interview during the postpartum period. During the postpartum period, data is gathered regarding the parents' upbringing, feelings about the pregnancy, availability of support systems, and current living situations. This data is collected from patient interviews, chart reviews, discussions with nursing staff, and direct observations of mother-infant interactions.

3. observation and interview during home visits. During home visits, data is gathered regarding mother-infant interaction, mothers' attitude toward infant, expectations of infant, childrearing practices, availability of support systems, health care plans, and current living situations. Data from home visits is then compared to hospital data.

Assessment of a family's parenting potential and subsequent

need for extra services is based on data gathered from observations made in labor and delivery, on the postpartum ward, and at home. Initially, we examine the parents' reactions at birth: How does the mother look? What does she say? What does the mother do? The father's reactions are also recorded.

Postpartum we again observe the mother-infant interaction, noting the presence or absence of attachment behaviors, verbalizations about the infant, mother's responses to and feelings about caregiving, and her expectations of the infant. At this time, psychosocial information is obtained on both parents, noting educational background, abuse or neglectful background, occupation, current life stresses, and coping behaviors. Availability and reliability of support systems, as well as involvement outside the home, are considered.

Since an individual's behavior often varies from hospital to home, the lay health visitor and her supervisor continue to evaluate these areas. Responses to lay health vistors, such as keeping home visit appointments and utilizing services provided, are included in the assessment of the need for extra services. Also, the use of health care and community services is considered. From this data, the family's strengths and needs are assessed, and further involvement of the lay health visitor and other agencies is determined.

The lay health visitor is a woman who has been a successful mother and who is willing to share her experiences with others. She has qualities of warmth and flexibility which are essential for the development of interpersonal relationships. Her training provides her with knowledge of the basic care of newborns, early child development, home visitation, and available health care and community services.

Because she is not a professional, the lay health visitor is often viewed by parents as less threatening. Her contact with a family begins in the hospital, where she becomes acquainted with the family, arranges a home visit on the first or second day after discharge, and encourages phone calls from parents. This early contact provides continuity from hospital to home.

During the first month of the infant's life, the lay health visitor makes weekly contacts by phone or by home visits. She provides families with information about childrearing and community resources, transportation to health care appointments, and emotional support. In addition, the lay health visitor acts as a role model and companion, often taking the mother out of the home for lunch, coffee, or a walk in the park. This intervention is aimed at developing an alliance with the family and increasing its strengths so that the child may have the opportunity to reach his or her physical, emotional, and intellectual potential.

Initially, a family may refuse to open the door and to keep appointments. Because the lay health visitor has an interest in the family, she continues to visit until the family begins to trust her enough to let her in. Her relationship with the family gives her knowledge and insight into the family's strengths and needs, information which she can share with other community agencies involved with the family. The lay health visitor's relationship with the family becomes the lifeline between the family and the health care system. Each home visitor serves four families through such a relationship.

The hospital-based program coordinator also has a variety of roles. She and the pediatrician develop the initial relationship with the parents during the postpartum period and make frequent contacts with them during the hospitalization. The coordinator is responsible for communicating information about a family to the lay health visitor and the hospital staff. Another task for the coordinator is the review of hospital charts for information about past hospital admissions, clinic visits, and health status. When community agencies such as the Visiting Nurse Service and Social Services are involved with a family, the coordinator contacts these agencies, explains the lay health visitor program, discusses the visitor's role in the family, and in some cases, organizes community meetings to coordinate care for the family. Furthermore, the coordinator organizes all record keeping, obtains information about available community resources, and along with a pediatrician and two research associates, supervises five half-time lay health visitors individually and in weekly two-hour group sessions.

Based on the family's strengths and needs, the lay health

visitor, along with her supervisor, determines the extent of her involvement. During the first month of the infant's life, continuous observations are made of the interaction with the infant, the family situation, and the support systems. When the staff determines that a family no longer needs the services of the lay health visitor, she terminates weekly visits with the family but continues to contact them by phone or in person every three months during the first year of the infant's life. At any point after weekly contacts have been discontinued, if problems are noted by the lay health visitor on return visits, home visits will be reintroduced. Those families experiencing difficulties and requiring continued services will be involved with community agencies and will receive lay health visitor contacts on a long-term basis.

Since the beginning of the program in October 1977, we have visited 140 mothers and families. This number accounts for 75 percent of all new mothers in Denver County. Mothers refuse the program for various reasons, the most common of which is adequate support systems at home. When mothers who refuse the program have perinatal assessments which indicate possible problems at home, they receive referrals to the Visiting Nurse Service and are encouraged to attend clinics where one or two physicians will provide care. In our group of 140 families who received service, there have been no reported incidents of child abuse or neglect and only one suspected child abuse incident. This suspected incident was reported to Social Services and underwent further investigation.

A Case Study

Linda is a seventeen-year-old white female who now lives with her husband and four-month-old son. She has a long history of being abused by her mother and moving from various home situations in an attempt to find a nurturing environment. Her last home situation failed, so she moved to the city and settled down with a boyfriend.

Within a few months, Linda became pregnant. Near the time of conception, she was raped; she therefore feared that this infant would be a product of the rape. Linda felt a great deal of ambivalence about the pregnancy but finally decided to carry the pregnancy to term. She delivered an eight-pound son.

In the hospital, the mother-infant interaction was passive. Linda did not touch or hold the infant. She readily relinquished care of the infant to nurses, the baby's father, or friends. Linda also avoided eye contact with her son. The father's interaction with the baby was positive, cuddling and holding his son whenever possible. Toward the end of Linda's hospitalization, she was able to identify characteristics of the infant which were similar to her boyfriend.

During the initial home visits, the lay health visitor noted continued problems with the mother-child interaction. Linda did not change diapers, was unable to have fun with the baby, and talked about the baby's being mad at her. Jim, the baby's father, assumed these caretaking tasks, talked to and played with the baby, and expressed real pleasure in his son. In Linda's presence, her son did not smile and lay in his bed, face turned toward the wall. Whenever Jim cared for him, the baby would smile and turned toward Jim when he was out of sight.

The lay health visitor made weekly visits and provided Linda with emotional support. She listened to Linda's feelings about the stresses and strains associated with caring for an infant. More importantly, the lay health visitor focused on Linda and her needs, showing her that someone did care and providing emotional support when needed. Through this positive, supportive relationship, she was able to make some changes, and slowly she became attached to her son.

Linda first discussed her growing attachment to her baby when she was hospitalized for a bacterial infection. During hospital visits made by the lay health visitor, she talked frequently of the baby's smile, his daily activities, the tasks he could perform, and how she missed him.

Recently Linda has demonstrated increasing strengths. Independently, she made some positive changes in her appearance, married her boyfriend, enrolled in high school classes, and became involved in a church women's group.

Summary

As discussed earlier, young families often look to the community for satisfaction of needs traditionally met by the family. They look to hospitals and clinics for health care needs. Many families seek food and shelter from social service agencies, and some families must look to the community for emotional support. Realization of these needs is often impeded by the rules and regulations of the system. These families need one person who can act as a liaison between themselves and the helping professions; that person is the lay health visitor. Her intervention will facilitate the use of health care services, thus assuring that families will receive adequate health care, immunizations, and screening and referral for special problems. Widespread utilization of lay health visitors could lead to a trend of preventive health care, a trend which would decrease costs of hospital and clinic services and save human lives.

REFERENCES

1. Parsons, Talcott and Bales, Robert: *Family, Socialization and Interaction Process.* Glencoe, Free Pr, 1955.
2. Klaus, Marshall and Kennell, John: *Maternal-Infant Bonding.* St. Louis, Mosby, 1976, p. 51.
3. Gray, Jane; Cutler, Christy; Dean, Janet; and Kempe, C. Henry: Prediction and prevention of child abuse and neglect. *Child Abuse Neglect: Intl J, 1*:45, 1977.

Chapter 18

FIND: A MODEL FOR HOME-BASED INTERVENTION FOR AT-RISK INFANTS

LaVesta Reeves, Marcia Moore, and Dorothy Manrow

Since 1972, Inland Counties Developmental Disabilities Services, Infancy-Early Childhood Program has been providing case management services for babies and young children who have a developmental disability. The Infancy-Early Childhood (IEC) program began providing services to at-risk infants in 1975. This extension of the program became known as FIND (Follow-up Intervention for Normal Development). Assessment, intervention, and referral services are provided through home visitation by a counselor who coordinates a comprehensive, individualized program of assessments and interventions using community health care resources.

A one counselor service has grown to six counselors, with a Prevention Services Coordinator currently being recruited for outreach and educational services. The geographic territory served by the agency and this program includes four counties, both metropolitan and rural areas, with a population of 1.4 million.

Development

FIND was developed out of the concerns of four agencies which provide maternal or child health services. The primary follow-up services needed by infants and families were available, but the system was not working for maximum benefits. The four agencies were Loma Linda University Medical Center Neonatal Intensive Care Unit (NICU); county health nursing services in Riverside and San Bernardino; Crippled Children Services (CCS) in these two counties; and Inland Counties Developmental Disabilities Services (ICDDS), a private, nonprofit agency under contract with the state of California.

The NICU was concerned with the need to assist parents when discharging infants home, after having spent considerable time and expertise toward survival of the infant. These infants had difficulties during labor and had low birth weight, birth defects, or other complications. Staff found the infants were often a tremendous burden on the family; there were emotional barriers to overcome in the transfer of the infant to the home, and there were expenses and care needs which the family was unable to provide without support. With an NICU crib capacity of forty infants from a large geographical area, home visits after discharge were impossible for hospital staff to assume.

County health nurses were attempting to accept about 1000 referrals annually from the NICU and three intermediate care nurseries with no additional staff allocated for at-risk infants. The nurses were unprepared to assist these families and fragile infants, being without resources for special needs. At-risk follow-up was not mandated by the state, and health department requests for additional funds and staff were not being approved.

CCS was often the agency providing diagnostic and treatment services for these infants. Problems encountered were failure to keep appointments, lack of transportation, and the realization that many of the infants were not being referred for evaluation soon enough to allow for optimal treatment.

ICDDS was discouraged by referrals of children who might be benefited by early intervention but had received none and by parents who were not requesting evaluation and counseling services. The parents had ignored the developmental delays in the child or did not know where to find help or had spent several years shopping for services. Often the agency evaluated a child who was not yet developmentally disabled, but how could the agency deny preventive efforts for such a child?

These agencies kept interacting in attempts to deal with problems faced by these infants and families caught up in this maze of an ineffective service system. After a number of thwarted efforts to obtain state funds to coordinate and effect more adequate programs, the agencies, in a last ditch effort, offered to set up a coordinated program. The NICU staff would schedule weekly discharge planning sessions and invite the other three agencies to review cases identifed as high-risk; the health department would provide a home assessment prior to infant's discharge and general health care services to all families of infants leaving the nursery; CCS would continue to provide medical care, funding, and therapy; and ICDDS obtained trustees' approval to broaden its services of case management to include at-risk infants.

Funding and staff commitments of these agencies were developed locally but within the framework of their state or private program. Except for CCS, all were without specifically allocated funds for at-risk infants. However, each agency assumed a share of the costs under their current budgets at that time, based on their belief that preventive efforts save money. The structure of these early meetings has been continued by quarterly council meetings for sharing concerns, program modifications, planning, and inservice training.

A Canadian consultant recently stated: "The time may come when we need to accept the fact that the missing ingredient is not always a case of more money . . . we may have the necessary human and financial resources to do the service job, but only if we learn how to mobilize (or remobilize) the resources of the existing special and generic agencies. . . ."[1]

In the Inland Counties area, this time had come. Community agencies would mobilize the resources: FIND was one of the resources of one of these agencies.

Description of FIND Program

Babies with a risk of becoming developmentally disabled have no label, and rightly so. Many of them, it is hoped, need not become disabled. Although most of the infants are delayed in developmental milestones, or are born with a birth defect, parents expect their infant to be normal. The FIND program staff believe that initially, and for as long as is realistic, these parents should not be exposed to situations which introduce the idea that their infant is expected to develop in a way other than normal. The philosophy of case management with the at-risk infant and family is centered around encouraging positive parent-infant attachment; acquainting the family with their child's development; and with techniques, such as infant stimulation, therapy, or other accepted treatment modalities, to enhance the child's development.

The goals of the FIND program are twofold. The primary goal is prevention of developmental disabilities. The program has not yet undertaken a study to prove the hypothesis of this goal, but research is being considered by the coordinating agencies. The Kauai study suggest that the critical period for prevention and intervention is before damage is done, as early as possible after birth.[2] The secondary goal is early screening, assessment, and intervention of at-risk infants. This might also be described as early case-finding of disabled infants. *Early* is the key word. Delays of a few weeks or months in the life of an infant may be critical for assuring adequate parenting or initiating treatment. Medical tendencies to delay diagnosis, plus parents' resistance to labeling, create a situation which denies services, thus this alternative approach has potential.[3]

The following objectives support FIND's activities: (1) to encourage parent-child attachment; (2) to teach parents the principles of infant development; (3) to guide parents in establishment of realistic goals for the infants; (4) to provide assistance in giving and obtaining child care; and (5) to coordinate an infant care plan with parents and the appropriate services.

These objectives relate specifically to the parents who are the primary caregivers of the infant. There is no intervention with an infant except with the parents' or guardians' consent and involvement. With the support system, parents are enabled to parent more effectively. Most researchers with infants find this approach, rather than specific activities with infants, the most promising avenue in providing developmental gains.[3] Klaus and Kennell have reported on the impact of early separation of mother and infant when intensive care is needed, and advise early promotion of parent-infant interaction.[4] There is little or no transference of normal childrearing practices to the deviant child without guidance from outside the family.[5] It has also been learned that parent education makes the greatest impact when imbedded in a comprehensive system of social change in housing, food, income, medical services, and power.[6]

A 1977 review of more than forty longitudinal intervention research programs for high risk children has reported these findings: (1) parental involvement increases the effectiveness of early intervention; (2) effects of a stimulating or depriving environment appear to be most powerful in early childhood when the most rapid growth and development take place. Since the child's primary locus during these years is the home, home-based intervention programs appear to be one of the most appropriate and effective methods of providing services.[7] Also, the value of intervention for infants born to mothers whose IQ are below 80 was demonstrated by Heber.[8]

Most of the infants served by FIND are discharged from intensive care nurseries following birth. Only a few infants are referred directly by community physicians and parents. Some referrals are initiated by ICDDS counselors whose adult client, being developmentally disabled, is experiencing difficulty as a new parent.

Referrals to FIND are accepted according to professional judgment of need and possibility of subsequent developmental disabilities, based on newborn assessments, parental capabilities, and known morbidity rates.

A number of research studies have provided guidelines for determining who is at risk: 31 percent of newborns have symptoms of neurological or growth abnormalities which are at risk for school failure six years later.[9] The incidence of neurological sequelae of mental retardation, motor deficits, and seizures in survivors of neonatal seizures is still approximately 35 percent, although mortality from this has decreased from 40 percent to 15 percent since 1969.[10]

In 1963, Lubchenco described an inverse relationship between birth weight and subsequent handicap.[11] More recent findings show low birth weight infants with intact survival as high as 78 percent.[12] Smith and associates have predicted potential risks through analysis of a series of assessments, including

Apgar scores, Brazelton, and other assessment results.[13] Utilizing behaviors, Escalona identified an infant syndrome of hyperactivity, low frustration tolerance, and gastric distress which signals potential dysfunction.[14] The Brookline study recommends looking to prescriptive need, rather than risk, for failure as criteria for follow-up.[15]

FIND referrals fall into the categories of neuromedical, socioeconomic, and parenting-potential factors. A diagnosis or label is not necessary, only the risk and the fact that a potential for normal development has not yet been ruled out. Those infants with a diagnosis of developmental disability who need services bypass FIND and are routed directly into the Infancy-Early Childhood Program of ICDDS for case management.

Loma Linda University Medical Center refers infants to FIND based on specific criteria. Kaiser Hospital and the two county medical centers base their referrals to FIND on mutual planning based on infant needs. Counselors accept referrals from discharge planning for the agency Intake Coordinator, who opens a case record into an at-risk status.

Staffing

The objectives of FIND are implemented by counselors, who are each responsible for thirty-five to forty cases. The counselors are public health nurses, pediatric nurse associates (PNA), or master social workers (MSW) with medical orientation. These disciplines are effective since the primary skills needed are counseling, developmental evaluation, and coordination with medical personnel, focusing on pediatrics. Every counselor in FIND has previously been a counselor in the Infancy-Early Childhood Program and is well-qualified and motivated in the role.

Cases are assigned according to discharging hospital, which facilitates continuity of communication with the discharge team. Supervision is provided by a Program Manager with a Master of Public Health degree and an Assistant Program Manager with a MSW. They also share responsibility for the Infancy-Early Childhood Program, and this dual management allows for smooth transition of a case from FIND into the developmental disability service, if this should be necessary. PNAs also relate to a medical preceptor, who is a staff pediatrician and who is available for consultation on medical or physical concerns requiring immediate attention. The preceptor co-signs physical assessment reports and assists as needed in contacting the child's physician. In order to meet the needs of the Spanish- and Chinese-speaking persons in the area, two counselors are bilingual. Translation and transportation are substantial needs of the families in these case loads.

Staff attend quarterly meetings which FIND coordinates with the other agencies. Counselors are encouraged to attend at least two work-related conferences during the year.

Infant Assessment

No one assessment tool can be used to screen an infant for developmental status. However, evaluation in a number of different behavioral areas can be quite useful in determining the functional category of the infant such as "normal, suspect, or abnormal."[16] Also by eliciting "signs" in the baby which are precursors of a developmental defect, it is possible to intervene in the home situation with the infant in an effort to prevent or ameliorate the potential disability.[17] Counselors are guided in administration of and referral for assessments by the readiness of the family and the infant. An infant asleep or ill is seldom appropriate for evaluation. A home in a crisis, or involved with other concerns, cannot benefit from a teaching experience. In fact, a poorly timed assessment may only increase stress in a family. Parents are always informed of the evaluation being performed, and the reason for its use.

Assessment tools used by the FIND staff include the ICDDS Infant Assessment, Physical Assessment, Denver Developmental Screening Test (DDST), Harrison Mother/Infant/Family Behavior Tools,[18] and Bayley Scales of Infant Development.

The Infant Assessment incorporates a social assessment, health and medical history, and a nursing assessment of the infant's problems and needs, with a plan for intervention. The

DDST has been most satisfactory to the staff in its ability to assist in teaching principles of child development. Some parents are even taught to use the test themselves, in order to anticipate developmental steps. A physical examination can teach parents the norms, even when all findings are negative.

The Bayley Scales of Infant Development are used by all FIND counselors to determine mental, psychomotor, and behavioral development. Bayley correlations with later mental developments are limited,[16] but the tool is effective in assessing broad categories of function.

Since the parent is the basic caregiver, a parenting assessment is critical in looking at the outcome of the child. The Harrison tools used by FIND counselors in assessing parent-child relationships categorize adaptive and maladaptive behaviors in mothers, infants, and families. A satisfactory and comprehensive developmental screening system is only useful if it plugs into practical intervention programs.[19]

Interventions

Throughout the overview of the FIND program, the use of interventions has been mentioned in regard to services offered to infants in the program. *Intervention* is used to mean any action taken in behalf of an infant or family which pursues normalization and the developmental model. Each intervention then is intended to be a positive influence, one that encourages parenting behavior and subsequently enriches the infant-parent relationship. Most importantly, there is recognition of the need for interventions which do not unnecessarily expose the probable normal infants' families to situations which would introduce the idea that their child is expected to be other than normal.

Interventions in the FIND program are planned individually for each infant and family, beginning in the discharge planning session at each hospital and continuing in the home and community. The counselor visits the family as often as needed, but at least four times a year. The at-risk infant population has such diverse characteristics and handicaps that a set of standardized interventions is not realistic.[20] Each intervention is initiated by the counselor to focus on the normality of the infant and the parent-child interaction. There is no magic in interventions. They are based on a foundation of child development, counseling skills, and common sense. FIND gives parents a copy of the *Baby Exercise Book*[21] to use as a guide when playing with their baby, an area frequently overlooked when assisting parents.[22]

There are three central themes for planning interventions:

1. Supporting the family in adjusting to and working with an infant who may have been critically ill or who is entering a less than optimal environment.
2. Promoting each infant's development to its optimum. Most often there is more that is normal about an infant than is abnormal.[23]
3. Coordinating services to the infant and his or her family so needed services are secured in a thoughtful and sensitive manner.

FIND counselors generate continuity of care by communicating closely with the infant's doctor, accompanying parents to medical appointments, and interpreting medical information to parents. By sharing all documentation with the infant's primary physician, the counselor reinforces support to the family. In some remote areas, infants may not have adequate medical services available, and might never be brought back to the pediatric clinic at the hospital except for the counselor's intervention.

Case Recording and Disposition

Each infant accepted for follow-up in FIND becomes an open, active case of ICDDS. Each case record is marked "at-risk" and remains open until twelve months of age, adjusted for prematurity. At that time a team conference is held with the parents and all team members involved.

The Infant Assessment is updated quarterly and other assessment recording is entered into the record as administered. At the time of the team conference an Individual Development Plan (IDP) is completed with the family and involved agencies; the summary is recorded; and copies are sent to the child's primary physician, agencies involved, and the parents.

Copies of assessments and records of treatment and care by other agencies are requested with parents' written consent. These are added to the case record to complete the follow-up documentation.

Closure of a case is based on the normal development of the infant and/or lack of criteria for eligibility for ICDDS. A transfer to the IEC Program is the recommended plan for those infants with a diagnosis of developmental disability or severe developmental delays.

By the time a child is twelve months old, the assessment process has begun to demonstrate significant problems or it has identified the child who has escaped developmental handicaps. The program is not intended to screen for all neurological handicaps, learning disorders, and communication disabilities. Gross developmental disorders and a number of preventable medical conditions will normally be identified by this age, developmental delays documented, and needed treatment initiated. Parenting patterns are generally established, and a method of relating to agencies and services has been learned by the parents.

At-risk factors are recorded on a brief data collection form, confined to questions which counselors or hospital staff can be expected to gather without reference to instructions, and designed for computer analysis. Client confidentiality is insured by an identification code. This collection is effective for local planning and research.

Evaluation

A statistical review of cases summarizes the FIND program. Evaluations utilized include a cost effectiveness review and a service system evaluation.

From January 1975 through December 1977, FIND has followed a total of 363 at-risk infants. Table 18-I presents a statistical summary. For the 59 percent who were closed at one year of age as *not developmentally disabled,* it is impossible to label this group as *normal* since there may be other handicaps. Of the infants who died during the year, eleven of the fourteen were suspected or definitely developmentally disabled. If this number is added to the 23 percent figure for developmentally disabled infants, this brings the total of at-risk infants assessed as developmentally disabled to 28 percent. It is important to note that these identified infants are from a selected high risk target group, not the general population.

TABLE 18-I

CASE DATA ON 363 AT-RISK INFANTS

Cases Served

Status	Number	Percent
Cases Receiving FIND Services	148	40
Cases Completed FIND Services	215	60
Total Cases Served	363	100

Cases Completed FIND Services

Disposition	Number	Percent
Cases Closed (Not D.D.)*	126	59
Cases Closed (Died)	14	7
Cases Transferred to IEC†	50	23
Cases Inactivated (Moved)	25	11
Total	215	100

* Normal development, or condition other than D.D.

† Developmentally disabled or manifesting severe delays and in process of evaluation.

For the 59 percent of infants who do not have a substantial handicap, the questions include the following: Did intervention prevent a disability? If follow-up was longer than twelve months, would more infants be identified as disabled? At quarterly council meetings of involved agencies the present concerns are centered on initiation of a research study. A study might answer other questions as well: Which interventions have a positive influence on the infant, and which are detrimental? Has intervention had an effect on preventing child abuse and family disintegration? There has been little research on stresses on the family with a high risk infant during the months following discharge.[24]

ICDDS is analyzing data on infants who received services in the past three years to determine which identifiable characteristics were present in infants followed by FIND who were later diagnosed as developmentally disabled. This very loose method will determine the highest risk factors for the Inland Counties Region. The Brookline study indicated risk was different depending on "when and how" a child was evaluated.[15] Due to "marked regional differences in risk factors" [25,26] this information may not be useful for replication.

A cost accounting of the program shows a client cost of 1783 dollars per year. This covers costs of salaries of staff, fringe benefits, special supplies and equipment, respite care, and private infant education. This does not cover costs of administrative overhead and transportation, which has been a major cost due to the size of the area. This figure also does not account for the salary of a new health education coordinator staff position.

Since funding for client services by the agency is available only after exhausting all other avenues of support, the most frequent source of funding is through private insurance, group health care programs, CCS, and Medi-Cal funding. It is obvious that the accounted cost is only the basic cost of staff, plus the unique needs of the infants not covered by other sources.

Program Benefits

Early problems experienced by agencies and families have almost been forgotten. Except for the obvious benefits of screening and assessment, there have been other benefits, not all anticipated. One of these is the motivation of FIND and IEC staff toward their work. Accountability of staff has increased due primarily to motivation and team effort. Parents have a ready resource when they need a listening ear, a helping hand, or a pat on the back. The coping energy of the parents of infants later found to be developmentally disabled appears to be more adequate than in those families without such helps. Numbers of referrals have consistently increased as FIND staff contributed to discharge sessions, and as physicians found the service helpful to client, families, and themselves. Parents have expressed satisfaction at team conferences, in letters to administration, and when interviewed by local news media. Another benefit has been in establishment of agency-to-agency relationships which carries over to the developmental disability program (IEC).

At the request of the FIND program, an evaluation was completed by the University of California, Los Angeles, Neuropsychiatric Institute Research Unit. The tool utilized was the Program for Analysis of Service Systems (PASS). The analyists recommended that administration and funding sources be detached from deviancy programs; that services to outlying areas be increased; that more effective in-service training be developed for counselors; and that a consumer participation aspect be added to the program.

Immediate plans for FIND include consideration of specific criteria for referral based on the regional data study of highest risk factors; outreach services to smaller hospitals, schools, and the general public; a parental evaluation questionnaire; additional specific screening, such as child abuse and lead poisoning; a clearly defined follow-up for FIND graduates through childhood; and active communication with the state Maternal and Child Health and Developmental Disabilities Sections regarding potential name changes from "disabilities" and "crippled" to nondeviant names. Other areas to be addressed will be nutritional consultation, more active involvement of county mental health services, potential inclusion of local volunteer child abuse prevention groups, and compilation of an in-service training manual.

With local agencies, FIND will continue to pursue the potential for research within our area, and to review findings of other researchers in the field.

REFERENCES

1. Roeher, G. Allen: Canadian perspective. In Tjossem, T. D. (Ed.): *Intervention Strategies for High Risk Infants and Young Children.* Baltimore, Univ Park, 1976.
2. Werner, E.; Bierman, J.; and French, F.: *The Children of Kauai.* Honolulu, U Pr of Hawaii, 1971.
3. Tjossem, T. D.: Early intervention: Issues and approaches. In Tjossem, T. D. (Ed.): *Intervention Strategies for High Risk Infants and Young Children.* Baltimore, Univ Park, 1976.
4. Klaus, M. and Kennell, J.: *Maternal-Infant Bonding: The Impact of Early Separation or Loss on Family Development.* St. Louis, Mosby, 1976.
5. Godrey, Cathleen: Sensory motor stimulation for slow to develop children: A specialized program for public health nurses. *Am J Nursing, 75:*57-59, 1975.
6. Gordon, Ira: Early child stimulation through parent education. In Stone, L.; Smith, H.; and Murphy, L. (Eds.): *The Competent Infant.* New York, Basic, 1973.
7. Stedman, D. J.: Important considerations in the review and evaluation of educational intervention programs. *Research to Practice in Mental Retardation, Care and Intervention, I:*100, 1977.
8. Heber, R.: Results of the Milwaukee Project. *Science, 171:*1227-1228, 1971.
9. Denhoff, E.; Hainsworth, P. K.; and Hainsworth, M. L.: The child at risk for learning disorders. *Clin Pediatr, 2:*164-170, 1972.
10. Volpe, J. J.: Neonatal seizures. In Volpe, J. J. (Ed.): *Clinics in Perinatology, Symposium on Neonatal Neurology, 4:*56, 1977.
11. Lubchenko, L.; Delivoria-Papadpoulas, M.; and Searls, D.: Long-term follow-up studies of prematurely born infants. *J Pediatr, 80:*192-197, 1977.
12. Dweck, Harry: The tiny baby: Past, present and future. In Dweck, Harry (Ed.): *Clinics in Perinatology, Symposium on the Tiny Baby, 4:*425-430, 1977.
13. Smith, A.; Flick, G.; Ferris, G.; and Sellma, A.: Prediction of developmental outcome at seven years from prenatal, perinatal, and postnatal events. *Child Dev, 43:*495-507, 1972.
14. Escalona, S.: *The Roots of Individuality: Normal Patterns of Development in Infancy.* Chicago, Aldine, 1968.
15. Levine, M.; Polfrey, J.; Lamb, G.; Weisberg, H.; and Bryk, A.: Infants in a public school system: The indicators of early health and educational need. *Pediatrics, 60:*579-587, 1977.
16. Matheny, Adam: Assessment of infant mental development. In Volpe, J. J. (Ed.): *Clinics in Perinatology, Symposium on Neonatal Neurology, 4:*192-197, 1977.
17. Lipsitt, Lewis: Sensory and learning processes of the newborn. In Volpe, J. J. (Ed.): *Clinics in Perinatology, Symposium on Neonatal*

208 *Home-Based Services for Children and Families*

Neurology, 4:180, 1977.
18. Harrison, L.: Nursing interventions with the failure to thrive family. *Am J Maternal-Child Nursing, 1*:111-116, 1976.
19. Meier, J. H.: Screening, assessment, and intervention for young children at developmental risk. In Tjossem, T. (Ed.): *Intervention Strategies for High Risk Infants and Young Children.* Baltimore, Univ Park, 1976.
20. Kass, E.; Sigman, O. W.; Bromwich, R.; Parmalee, A.; Kapp, C.; and Haber, A.: *Educational Intervention Strategies for High Risk Infants and Young Children.* Baltimore, Univ Park, 1976.
21. Levy, Janine: *Baby Exercise Book.* Westminister, Random House, 1974.
22. Finnie, N.: *Handling the Young Cerebral Palsied Child at Home,* 2nd ed. New York, Dutton, 1975.
23. Tudor, Mary: Nursing interventions with developmentally disabled children. *Am J Maternal-Child Nursing, 3*:25-31, 1978.
24. Sonstegard, L.: Parental adjustment to their high-risk infant. *Perinatal Press, 1*:6-7, 1977.
25. Butler, N. R. and Bonham, D. G.: *Perinatal Mortality: The First Report of the 1958 British Perinatal Mortality Survey.* London, Livingston, 1963.
26. Niswander, K. R. and Gordon, M.: *The Women and Their Pregnancies, The Collaborative Perinatal Study of the National Institute of Neurological Diseases and Stroke.* Philadelphia, Saunders, 1972.

SECTION III
Practice

SOCIAL SERVICES

Chapter 19

THE LOWER EAST SIDE FAMILY UNION: ASSURING COMMUNITY SERVICES FOR MINORITY FAMILIES

MARYLEE DUNU

Background

FOR many people, poverty is not just a lack of income. It also involves a deprived and defeatist state of mind, a persistent lack of capability for improving one's situation, and an inferior or dependent position in society. Major social institutions reinforce these maladies, even when those institutions are specifically intended to alleviate poverty, in any number of ways:

The provision of public assistance to the poor in ways that increase or emphasize their dependency, rather than stimulating feelings of adequacy or efforts at self-improvement.

Exploiting the ignorance of the poor by imposing on them higher costs than other people pay for similar goods and services, particularly interest rates for merchandise purchased on credit.

Imposing prices for housing in the low-income area which is far more expensive in relation to the quality of service received, especially in nonwhite areas, than middle or upper income areas.

Providing fewer opportunities to families to improve their housing because most lenders will not provide mortgages for either purchase or improvement in very low-income areas, even if the borrower has good credit.

Providing schools of lower quality with the least qualified or experienced teachers and often the oldest building and equipment.

211

Providing low quality of city services such as garbage collection and police protection, as measured in quality of output.

Inadequate police practices which maximize the probability that young people, particularly nonwhites, will develop official police records for acts that would not create such records in higher-income areas.

Insensitivity of social and public agencies to the scope and depth of the client's problems.

Unavailability of comprehensive services to the problematic family.

The Lower East Side Family Union incorporates the concepts of case management, integration of services, monitoring, and self-help networks to assure community services for vulnerable families, primarily Hispanic, Chinese, and Black, in a deterioriated area of New York City. The Family Union model is essential in an urban society where there are a myriad of institutions, agencies, and services. Its flexibility makes it easily adaptable to other communities. This chapter is designed to explain the salient features of the Lower East Side Family Union model.

This model is the result of a process which began with a concern about the continuing deterioration of the family in an urban society. Beginning in 1971, there were real concerns about the growing cost of child welfare services in New York and even greater concerns about the increasing disruption of the family unit through prolonged placements and inadequate preventive services. Efforts by various individuals, as well as the Citizen's Committee for Children, led to recommendations for a shift in focus from a placement orientation to direct work with vulnerable families at a neighborhood level. These recommendations were coordinated with similar proposals from the Human Resources Administration for decentralized services with community participation. The Human Resources Administration is the superagency which coordinates all of the public social welfare agencies in New York, with a special concern in decreasing child neglect and family breakdown which is so prevalent in the ghettos of New York City.

These recommendations were closely related to the interest of administrators of settlement houses and human service agencies on the Lower East Side, who were also concerned about the fragmentation of services. Eight of the most influential agencies were able to identify generation after generation of families exhibiting destructive family patterns. In order to break this vicious cycle, the agencies agreed to establish the Family Union, under a grant from the Foundation for Child Development. Initially, the focuses of the Family Union were to —

1. strengthen the families who are folding under the weight of extreme internal and external stress;
2. minimize the intervention of the juvenile justice and welfare systems because of their contributions to family breakup; and
3. prevent, where possible, the placement of children outside the neighborhood.

The early work of the Family Union was designed primarily to assess the problems faced by both the families and institutions. During this period certain observations were made which shaped the LESFU intervention model.

First, there seems to be an inappropriate emphasis on child placement in the New York child welfare system, evidenced by the incredible amounts of money paid to foster care agencies. A report from the Office of the Comptroller for the City of New York, Bureau of Municipal Investigations and Statistics, states there are over 29,000 children in foster care in New York City at an overall cost of more than 280 million dollars in 1977, for an average cost per child of almost 10,000 dollars.

This emphasis is also reflected by the tremendous fear and distrust parents have of child welfare workers. Most of them have expressed in any number of ways their belief that child welfare workers have a vested interest in removing the children from the family constellation.

Second, there is little or no integration of existing services. Most agencies have operated autonomously without feedback on the appropriateness or effectiveness of their services. Fragmentation and rigidity of services are based on very real factors, such as the goals and objectives of the agency, specific services of the agency, resources of the agency (staff, funds, etc.), effectiveness of agency's services, and staff commitment and involvement.

Early in the program a woman known to sixteen agencies was located. This is the illustrative case of a forty-four-year-old divorcee who was wandering through the streets of the Lower East Side with her six-year-old daughter who was not attending school regularly. Both mother and daughter were dirty and unkempt. When the Family Union entered the case the family was known to the following agencies: Mobile Crisis Unit, adult day care facility, public school, private school, synagogues (2), municipal hospitals (2), public clinic, settlement house, Income Maintenance Center, Public Housing Authority Office, child protection services agency, State assemblyman, and a legal aid agency.

The tragedy in this situation is all these agencies felt they were providing services for this family, when in reality none were. The LESFU entered the case because a neglect petition had been drawn against the mother and the court was threatening placement of this child unless someone took responsibility for the case. It was agreed that the Family Union would provide a suitable treatment plan for the situation which would include —

- housing stabilization.
- financial stabilization.
- home management and child care training.
- education and tutoring for the child.
- medical attention for both the mother and child.
- psychiatric examination of the mother.
- recreational activities.
- legal services.

The plan was to formulate a coalition of service providers who would perform certain tasks and/or services, coordinated and monitored by the LESFU worker. The other agencies who were not directly involved in the treatment plan were encouraged to step out of the case situation and asked to call LESFU before service was given to the client again. The major problem with the previous handling of this case situation was that these agencies planned *for* not *with* the client. Because this woman was not involved, she moved from agency to agency seeking services with no redress of her problems. In a sense, these agencies were participating in the disorganization of the client.

Another observation made by LESFU staff centered around the fact that the people in slums rely almost exclusively upon public provision of health, education, and welfare services because there is very little else available to them, except for churches and some voluntary community action projects. Public agencies have been mandated to provide such a wide range of services that they are almost "bursting at the seams."

Agencies are beginning to strangle in their own network of services. For example, Matthew Wald, writing in the September 19, 1977, issue of the *New York Times,* documented that it takes an average of 25.3 days to receive *emergency* help from the New York City Department of Social Services. People who are unemployed, without food, or about to lose their homes or utilities face "unconscionable delays." Of course, such a delay is not agency policy, but because of the endless red tape and paper pushing, what should take, at the maximum, 2 days stretches out to 25.3 days. According to this same article, persons applying for nonemergency help actually received service in 23.9 days.

Because of this, many vulnerable families see the bureaucracies like Department of Social Services and the New York City Housing Authority as agencies of control rather than agencies of social responsibility. Each of these agencies dictates specific rules and regulations one must follow before service is granted. However, compliance with these rules does not necessarily assure the provision of service. Because of this, many clients are unable to use the services of these agencies. Therefore, it becomes the responsibility of an agency like LESFU to advocate for the client, especially in those agencies which are absolutely essential to the conduct of urban living such as finances, housing, and physical and mental health.

Wald also observed that informal neighborhood supports are no longer as functional and strong as they were in the past. Nuclear families are separating more quickly from their extended families. Problems of substance addiction, unemployment, crime, delinquency, neglect, physical and mental illness, retardation, and family discord seem to be the major pathologies that strain the resources of the family unit. Families seldom have the necessary skills or resources to cope with the breakdown of the individual members. Help for the family must become a shared responsibility, with neighbors and friends providing specific concrete services on an as needed basis.

Because LESFU recognizes that informal supports must be cultivated and strengthened where possible, part of the work involves the building of these supports. For example, the Union has set up babysitting cooperatives, used skills of talented community residents in negotiating the various systems and bureaucracies, and arranged for overnight and weekend emergency child care.

In one case, a maternal grandmother in her late sixties, who had been granted custody of her granddaughter because of the mother's drug addiction, was afflicted with a stroke. Staff had been working with the grandmother because of difficulties with the thirteen-year-old granddaughter who was refusing to go to school and was beginning to be rebellious. At the time of the grandmother's stroke, the Family Union worker was able to place this child with a neighbor who had several children of her own, including two teenage girls. This neighbor had shown some interest in the girl during other periods of stress. The plan for this family included the following:

- Stabilizing the child's custodial care.
- Stabilizing the child's income.
- Arranging child care fees.
- Recommending and supporting certification of home as a foster care home.
- Counseling the child.
- Managing income for the woman during hospitalization.
- Maintaining public housing apartment.

• Assisting in funeral arrangements.

The Family Union is currently working on permanent plans for this child. The mother of the child and other relatives continue to be unresponsive. The child has made such a good adjustment to the situation that subsidized adoption may be a real possibility.

These observations and experiences served as the basis for the current Family Union model, which is the product of an expanding, comprehensive commitment to working with the urban poor who are primarily from minority groups and at high risk of losing their children to the child welfare or juvenile justice systems. The model is designed to maximize social work practice with chaotic, disorganized families in the increasingly urban and impersonal multiethnic communities in New York City.

The LESFU Model

LESFU is currently being demonstrated on the Lower East Side of Manhattan, an area where many European immigrants first settled during the early 1900s. The area continues to be one of the most densely populated and multiethnic communities in New York City.

The Family Union is a semiprivate and public community-based early intervention project. It is composed of a board of directors, an administrator, and four teams responsible for providing brief direct crisis intervention services while identifying, locating, and contracting for long-term services. Three of the four teams include a team leader, five caseworkers, five homemakers, and a receptionist/typist. One of the direct service teams is stationed in New York City Bureau of Special Services for Children, one of the five social work agencies under the umbrella of the City's Human Resources Administration. Special Services for Children (SSC) is the mandated child welfare protective services agency for the City and State of New York.

The fourth team of workers is composed of a team leader and a combination of paid and voluntary community residents. One of the goals of this team is to develop community-wide

participation and involvement in meeting needs identified by
the residents.

Except for the team leaders who have master's degrees in
social work, most workers are community residents who bring
with them a wide range of knowledge and experiences which
reflect the dreams and aspirations of the community, as well as
the trials and tribulations. Each team reflects the ethnicity of
the total community it serves. Team I serves primarily Hispanic clients, has a majority of Hispanic workers, and is
headed by an Hispanic social worker. Team II serves primarily
Asian clients and is headed by a Chinese-American social
worker. Team III, which serves primarily Black and White
American clients, is headed by a Black social worker. This team
has a full complement of workers who are outstationed from
two sections of the Human Resources Administration. Team IV
has a clientele which is predominantly Hispanic and consists of
a bilingual social worker and all Hispanic workers.

While the Union believes that ethnicity is an important
factor when dealing with socially deprived clients, it is not the
most important factor. The most important ingredients are
worker skill and effectiveness, which are enhanced by the com-
pulsory training sessions.

Agency philosophy, another important factor, views people
as living within a set of social and environmental systems. The
systems approach makes possible an organized view of the individual in his or her multiple interactions with all the forces
that shape life, from the type of employment to ways of childrearing.

A Case Study

A typical case which illustrates this philosophy was a five-
year-old boy admitted to a municipal hospital for sickle cell
anemia crisis, precipitated by the stressful environment in
which he lived. The boy had to remain in the hospital several
weeks for a full diagnostic work-up. After discharge, he would
require monthly routine medical treatment and follow-up.
During his hospitalization, his mother spent most of her time

there visiting and seeing to his needs, impressing the doctors, nurses, and other social work staff as a concerned and interested mother. On several occasions, however, it was obvious she had been drinking, and the social worker in the hospital had to evaluate this mother's ability to care for the child.

The evaluation revealed that the child's living conditions were atrocious; he and his mother lived alone in a semi-abandoned building, a third floor walk-up without heat, hot water, or electricity. Because her welfare had been illegally cut off and all of her efforts to have it restored fruitless, the mother had been supporting herself by begging for food from friends and casual acquaintances. Fearful of the child's physical condition and wanting him with her, she had not enrolled the child in school. While all of this was overwhelming for the mother, the quality of her child care had not suffered. The hospital found this child to be emotionally and physically fit, except for the effects of the sickle cell anemia crisis which was out of the mother's control.

It was apparent this child should be with his mother, but could not because of the environmental forces involved. The case was referred to Special Services for Children, who were prepared to place the child. Fortunately, the hospital social worker knew of the work of the Family Union and referred the family.

Involvement with this family concretely illustrates the approach of person-in-systems. Staff found this mother had been diagnosed as a chronic alcoholic and because of this, eight of her nine children had been placed in foster homes. This mother had been known to three foster care institutions. None had offered any casework services, but because this mother had wanted so desperately to keep this boy, she had greatly modified her drinking habits. The first step was to engage the mother in a workable treatment plan which began with a signed work agreement. The work agreement or contract emphasized five basic services to keep this family together:

- She must be immediately reinstated to the welfare rolls which would require legal representation.
- She had to be relocated in more suitable housing, which

required involvement with the New York City Housing Authority, the Department of Buildings, and the Department of Relocation.

- She had to enroll in and attend an alcoholic treatment program.
- She had to begin to plan for permanence of the five children remaining in child care.
- She had to plan for immediate custodial care of her son who could not remain in the hospital.

The second step required discussion about the probable success of the five goals, particularly the welfare and housing issues. It is obvious these two agencies are so enmeshed in bureaucratic red tape that it sometimes takes weeks or months to get from one step to another with something like a simple application. It was agreed the boy could not be returned home until these two problems had been resolved. Temporary placement was therefore inevitable and was accomplished through a written contract between the client, Special Services for Children, the municipal hospital, a child care agency, and the Family Union.

In this contract, the client agreed to keep all appointments with all parties involved, and to cooperate in all aspects of the agreement. Special Services for Children agreed to accept a time-limited agreement regarding the child's placement. The municipal hospital agreed to keep all parties informed of clinic appointments, and to schedule appointments in different clinics back to back so the child did not have to come to the hospital two or three days per week. The child care agency agreed to place the child in a foster home situation on a temporary basis with the stipulation that the child would be returned as soon as the mother was rehoused; they also agreed they would not initiate new obstacles to the return of the child unless all parties were in agreement. The Family Union agreed to support the efforts of the client as well as coordinate the activities of the other service providers.

The placement went according to plan and the child was returned to the mother within three days of the mother's occupancy in a new apartment.

Unique Features of the Model

One of the unique features of the Family Union model is the use of the team leader in not only program planning and administration but also board participation and strategizing. The executive board is made up of representatives of the various settlement house and agency administrators in the community, as well as community residents. The team leaders, a training specialist, a social historian, and a researcher serve as consultant to this board. The Union director and the team leaders meet regularly to assess, plan, and evaluate the effectiveness of policy and practice of the agency. This provides almost instant feedback from and to the direct service teams and points up increased needs to modify or invent new patterns of delivery of services (strategies) and approaches to service and collaboration.

As stated before, direct services of the agency are provided through the individual teams. Each team member has specific tasks which he or she must perform with a clear purpose of working toward the agency's major goal, that of keeping families together by helping them use existing agencies and institutions more effectively. One innovative aspect of the model is the use of homemakers as part of the team with social workers. The homemaker's responsibilities include child care and home management, and the teaching of parenting, child care and home management skills to the unaware or overwhelmed clients. The homemaker is a very important part of the team, as she spends more time with clients and augments casework treatment with families. Much of her work revolves around enlarging, backing up, reinforcing, or otherwise implementing the treatment process between the caseworker and client, which facilitates diagnosis, case planning, and development of treatment plans.

The receptionist/typist serves as an administrative assistant to the team leader. In addition to helping manage the physical operations of the team, he or she is also responsible for initial screenings of calls, walk-ins, and inquiries.

Another unique feature of the LESFU model is its flexibility in handling diverse case situations. Because of funding patterns and policies, most agencies require clients to fit very specific requirements, making it impossible for any one social agency to have enough services to assist the severely needy family unit. The Family Union has expanded its delivery of services through its use of convening, contracting, and monitoring with other service providers. To provide maximum integration and efficient utilization of existing resources, and the clout to monitor and enforce family service contracts, LESFU has been developing a neighborhood services network based on agency contracts. These agency contracts, which are negotiated at the board level, provide a unique way of integrating existing services without promoting a serious backlash from the established agencies. To date the Family Union has contracted with such diversified agencies as Henry Street (the largest settlement house in the United States), Gouverneur Hospital (a community-based municipal hospital), Special Services for Children, and the Federal Probation Services (which deals with women returning from the federal penal system); in addition, contracts are negotiated with twelve other agencies.

Beyond the obvious function of these contracts to provide and monitor services, they also include an agreement for joint planning and training as well as exchange of information. Because of the experimental nature of the LESFU model in its training and development, there is a strong commitment to staff, melding community residents, public welfare homemakers, and caseworkers with professional, public, and private social workers. Training is regular, intensive, and comprehensive. Recognizing the demands on the worker in the powerful but also vulnerable position between the family and service providers, training is geared toward an interactive approach. The training themes, topics, and concerns are directly related to this sensitive position. The Family Union social worker must be able to engage, plan with, and advocate for the client without encouraging the client's dependence; to counsel resistant families and conduct family and provider agency meetings; and to monitor the service providers without stepping over them.

The training consultant, a Columbia University professor, was responsible for the early work in designing the model. Training sessions are a blend of basic theoretical concepts, case material from the agencies, and dealing with realities of the changing socioeconomic stresses of urban living. There have also been several trainers who provided sessions on very specific themes and topics. Such continuous input has helped staff broaden their thinking and approaches. In an effort to deal more effectively with the needs of each group, the staff have been divided into three major training units: the caseworkers, the homemakers, and the team leaders. Occasionally, these groups may meet together depending upon the focus, content, or theme of training.

Some of the content themes have been designed to increase skills in the following areas: assessing high risk status, monitoring, collaboration issues with families and agencies, convening meetings, using the strength of the team structure, outreach and motivating, normal growth and development, decision making, writing contracts and work agreements, the use of goal attainment scales, and recognizing potential class action suits.

In addition to these training sessions, the team leaders have the responsibility for development of the workers through individual and group supervision on a weekly basis. In these sessions, cases are reviewed carefully, to insure that essential elements of the family service contracts are well planned, understood, and executed at a pace acceptable to the client.

Effectiveness

Given all of these unique features, the logical question could be posed: What are the Family Union's results? In 1977, Family Union worked with 420 families, nearly 90 percent from minority backgrounds. Of this number, 193 were determined to be high risk for family breakdown. Only 11 of these families required placement services for their children, involving a total of 22 children.

Because of continued involvement, 17 of the children were returned home from placement in an average of two months. According to the Goldin report, previously noted, the average length of stay of a child in foster care is six years, with many spending much more time in foster care. Also, many children move from home to home, often with harmful effects to their social and emotional well-being. This, at a cost of from 5,000 to 13,000 dollars *per child,* seems wasteful if placement can be avoided. The preventive work of the Family Union, through its integrative and service network, is costing less than 1,500 dollars *per family* for a year.

The LESFU model is an effective response to the need of assuring community services to high risk families in a densely populated neighborhood in New York City. The model is readily adaptable to other settings. However, to successfully replicate the model, social work practitioners and program planners must recognize the increasing complexity of family problems, must understand the need to effectively provide and coordinate efforts of a variety of agencies, and must be thoroughly committed to the fullest development of the individual and the family.

Chapter 20

THE MENDOTA MODEL:
HOME-COMMUNITY TREATMENT

MARY ANN FAHL AND DONNA MORRISSEY

THE Home and Community Treatment Program (HCT), which has been in operation since 1969, had its origins in the residential setting of Mendota Mental Health Institute. Preadolescent boys were separated from their families, neighborhood schools, and peer groups, and brought to this residential treatment center to live so treatment could be provided on an intensive basis. For some of the boys, the treatment center was the last hope; the school and the community agencies had been attempting one sort of treatment after another with discouraging results. Some of these children had been detected before kindergarten as needing special services. Sincere attempts were made, but at ten or eleven years of age they were still in need of a more intensive or different kind of treatment. The children carried the gamut of diagnostic labels, from childhood psychosis to adjustment reaction of childhood. The range of behavior problems was wide: from classroom disruption, defiance, property destruction, assaultiveness, and bizarre mannerisms, to intense fears and delays in physical/motor development. Upon admission to the setting, the child underwent elaborate behavioral and psychological assessment, and individually tailored treatment plans were implemented with a high degree of interstaff consistency.

The well-trained staff members were often able, in a relatively short time, to effect many desirable behavior changes in the children. There were problems with the residential approach, however, problems that actually argued against the treatment gains being maintained once the child left the highly consistent milieu. Because the disturbing child had been selected as the one to enter the institution, the responsibility for change was really borne by him, rather than the problem-causing environment: the family, the school, the neighborhood. With the child out of the home, parents' motivation to change sometimes abruptly diminished. With children coming from distant parts of the state, it was difficult for parents to be at the Center at critical times and for sufficiently long periods to learn from treatment staff what was effective treatment for their child. Thus, the child continued to grow and change within the residential milieu, while the parents' and community's readiness to maintain those changes and to teach additional coping skills lagged behind. Because of this lag in the parents' and communities' abilities to take over as mediators of change for the child once he left the residential setting, the changes in the children's behavior could not be maintained in the natural environment, nor could they be strengthened. It was not unusual for a child to be discharged after about eighteen months of treatment, to reappear three months later with the original problem.

The final goal for these children was more adequate functioning within their own families and neighborhood schools. Training children to live within the institution was incongruent with this goal. Large amounts of staff and child time were spent in the integration of the child into the residential setting and reintegration into his natural environment. Within the institution, the children had only other deviant children as peer models; they were unwittingly being taught more varied antisocial, unacceptable behaviors. While the problems of some children were severe enough to warrant highly specialized treatment in a residential setting, others came to the Center because their home communities were often not prepared to meet their treatment needs.

Donald Stover, a psychologist who directed the residential program, weighed the problems of institutionalization against the benefits.[1] It seemed that the same intensity of services could be provided to the child in his own home and school and thereby eliminate the problems accompanying institutionalization. Stover conceived a program in which the clinicians would become a roving band of change agents, going into homes and schools for as many hours as necessary each day to effect the desired treatment goals. The locus for change would be in the individual's natural environment. The mental health professional would not be the only *treater* but would work with those individuals within the child's environment who could better effect desired changes.

Two Arizona researchers, Roland Tharp and Ralph Wetzel, had also become discontented with the degree to which the helping professionals had not fulfilled their promises.[2] They felt that a treatment model which could maximize the full helping potential of the child's social environment was needed, and that such a model ought to dovetail with the accumulating research on the utility of behavior modification. They constructed such a model and chose to conduct the demonstration with a group of behaviorally disordered, underachieving, delinquent and predelinquent youths. Their book, *Behavior Modification in the Natural Environment,* became a guide for the staff at Mendota as they proceeded to leave the comfortable familiarity of the residential setting and move into the unknown environment of the client.

Another researcher who influenced the development of the Home and Community Treatment Program was Gerald Patterson of the Oregon Research Institute. Patterson and associates were testing the viability of providing treatment for families of disturbed children within their homes and schools.[3] He developed an empirical approach to implement a social learning theory model to problem families. In addition to his interest in providing efficient and effective intervention, he developed tools with which the therapist could assess his progress toward stated goals. This behavioral coding system that permitted more precise measurement of interactional patterns within the family and school environments has been a major influence on the work.[4]

Many other clinicians and researchers have worked on refining the applications of social learning principles to human behavior, contributing to our understanding and skills.[5-9]

With the knowledge and encouragement that two other programs were being conducted elsewhere, the residential team *re-*

tooled ideas, goals, and procedures to begin exploring an alternative approach to treatment of emotionally disturbed children known from then on as the Home and Community Treatment Program (HCT). Initially, for a random sampling of children who had been referred to the residential program, nurses and aides were assigned to the home or school for blocks of time to directly manage the child's behavior in these natural settings. Staff members from other disciplines contributed their skills in approximately the same way as they did in the residential program; for example, teachers did academic tutoring, social workers counseled parents, and occupational therapists structured play time. It became apparent that this model was duplicating roles already found in the community, such as teachers and teacher aides. Additionally, all staff members working with the child wanted to share in working with the parents, and the parent counseling staff members felt they wanted to be better acquainted with the child's problems and behavior patterns. Based on these needs, a team approach was evolved. Several years of evolution resulted in a case manager/-team member model, to be outlined later, in which any staff may learn any aspect of the treatment process, regardless of academic background.

The initial focus on eight- to eleven-year-old children shifted to younger children, ages three to ten, with emphasis on the preschool child. The older child had usually been identified several years earlier as being somehow deviant. It was, and still is, difficult to determine exactly when a child is in need of professional help. Generally, more research data is needed to ascertain early patterns of coping which lead to deviance in later life.

About the same time the move was made to work with families with younger children, several other developments led to greater contact with the community. The development of visual aids and the HCT child management techniques sheets advertised the HCT ideas and program, both in Wisconsin and in other states. A second development was a course on parenting skills which originated in response to a Department of Social Services need to offer parenting education to court-referred families. These two activities, offshoots of the initial family treatment process, led to training other community agency staff to teach their client families new interaction styles and ways to change their own behavior to enhance their children's positive growth.

Continued shared work with local providers of educational, social, and mental health services provides HCT staff with realistic feedback about the needs and constraints of diverse Wisconsin communities. The central location of HCT, in the Mendota Mental Health Institute, gives the staff flexibility to combine clinical evolution of a treatment model with its dissemination through contractual shared work with community-based agency staff members. The following description of the clinical model is one which is practiced today; refinement and growth of the model of practice continues, based on the synthesizing of new information from research findings.

The presenting problems of the children referred to HCT are varied, but the aspect of the problem focused on is the adult/child relationship; therefore, the first contact includes as many of the family who live together as possible. The family usually sees the HCT film, "Home and Community Treatment: Activating Family Change," followed by a review of the situation as viewed by the family members. They are asked to consider their involvement in the program for a week before making the decision because involvement calls for many hours of time, willingness to try new ways to relate to their child, and willingness to let staff members come into their home. If the decision is to proceed with the treatment process, the family signs an official application for admission and the first contract for the month-long evaluation phase is outlined.

Formal evaluations are scheduled, including standardized sensory integration tests, cognitive skills evaluation, and language skills assessment. An appointment for the consulting child psychiatrist to interview the referred child, or several children if it seems valuable, is arranged. Physical and dental health is ascertained through contact with the child's pediatrician and dentist. Home observations are arranged for three or four different time periods to obtain specific behavioral counts of parental directives, child compliance, and parental follow-through, combined with less formal notations in order to present the family with specific vignettes.

A critical point in the process is the case planning meeting held after the evaluation is completed. At that meeting, two or three hours are spent synthesizing all available materials, speculating on the nature of the problems, what contingencies are keeping the family system operating, and what treatment plan would be offered them during the next phase, which is the first treatment contract. At this point, the formal record is prepared including nature of the presenting problem, social history, developmental and educational history, evaluation measures used, psychiatric diagnosis, short- and long-term goals, and staff members handling the case and their roles.

While the average number of months a case is open is 9.7 months, the intensive treatment usually lasts four to six months: *Intensive* in this case means sharing about six to eight contact hours with the family per week, with several additional hours in the school if there is a demonstrated problem there. Each two or three weeks a new contract or statement of mutual expectations is outlined, giving both staff members and family a time to assess progress, to confront each other about disagreements, and to outline the goals for the next period of time.

The first treatment period includes a didactic portion, conducted at the Institute, in which staff members present the theoretical construct of antecedent-behavior-consequence on which all of the further work is based.[10-13] Reading through the relevant HCT visual aids, roleplaying a situation seen during home observations, or doing structured exercises involving direction-giving and appropriate consequences are all used to introduce the concepts. Staff members work directly with the child in activity sessions to build a relationship and to find out how the child learns, including how directions are understood, how effective is social reinforcement, and how the child responds to limit-setting. These activity sessions serve as modeling sessions for the parents to observe the child management skills which they will be expected to learn; parents usually gather the same kind of data on staff members as was taken on them in their home in an effort to have them focus on the adult behaviors being demonstrated rather than on their own child(ren). The family may be asked to write down information about the occurrence of specific problem behaviors at home which will be programmed later. While the reliability of parent-reported data is known to be questionable, asking parents to record behavioral events can serve other purposes, such as (1) learning to describe behavior specifically and discreetly, (2) giving them a competing task to attending to the child's deviant behavior, and (3) providing the parents with a more realistic view of the amount of time the behavior actually occurs. Since parents always record a competing positive behavior as well as a deviant one, they practice scanning the child's behavioral repertoire for socially desirable behavior as well as deviant ones.

During the second treatment phase (which may or may not be the second contract), skills learned at the Center are practiced in some time periods at home, arranged to fit the family schedule, with some sessions including only one parent and child, and sometimes both parents. Scheduling and logistics of these sessions can be part of the family's problem, especially in families where future planning happens rarely, and where every new request is seen as a crisis. The ability to praise compliance and positive behavior is set as a predetermined goal, such as 60 percent of the total times possible with the view of shaping towards other goals. Staff members work out with the family members how a cue can be offered to remind them that now is a time to give verbal praise. Coupled with the ability to give verbal praise is the ability to ignore minor but coercive behaviors. Taking the parent into another room, engaging in conversation, or getting the parent started on a physical task are some techniques used to help the parent learn to ignore such behavior.

Consequences for severe acting out behaviors such as hitting, destroying property, or running away may be included from the beginning. Parents need immediate support for behaviors of major significance, if they are to see success and continue the learning process. In such cases, cost response programs are usually used in which the child can *earn* for demonstrating performance of competing behaviors; for example, if darting away from the adult is the problem, asking permission and listening to the adult may be defined as the desired behavior and reinforced by tokens or marks, exchangeable for material reinforcers at some point. Withdrawing points or tokens for the problem behavior provides a penalty which can be immediate and matter-of-fact. Teaching the parents to employ a formal *time-out* procedure may need to go on simultaneously; such time-outs need to be coupled with positive parental feedback, and introduction of the time-out procedure is usually withheld until there is demonstrated evidence that parents are indeed giving more praise.

Teaching too many new skills at once can be confusing to parents; a step-by-step introduction, practice, and mastery of sequential skills seems as important in learning social skills of child management as in any other learning process. Demonstration or modeling of how we expect parents to perform, and risking failure in front of them, is an important element of the teaching process. Schoolwork, activities of ordinary living, play tasks, and household chores are some of the events which can be used for parental practice of child management skills. Talking aloud with the parent(s) about the problem-solving steps we are doing together is a step toward the final goal of problem-solving new situations by the parents themselves using the child management skills to help solve the problem. Often one of the family goals is to increase each spouse's support of the other; consistency in implementation of child-rearing practices is helped by open communication between parents.

The last phase of treatment stresses the parents' increased ability to handle daily problems on their own, with only our verbal input. The two to three month phase-out period before the discharge date is set gives parents a chance to consolidate the new learning. Even though the family may be discharged, the emotional investment and trust built up by this time is great and if further problems arise a team member is usually called to help sort out the "forest from the trees."

The persons who participated in building the Home and Community Treatment model represented many different disciplines and viewpoints. The heterogeneity of that group, with nurses and aides, teacher and occupational therapist, social worker and psychologist, seems in retrospect to have been a major strength. Heterogeneity continues to be the guiding principle used in determining position classifications of the group as a whole as well as in the makeup of treatment teams or project teams. The concept of working in *teams,* of shared decision-making and assignment of tasks, was also a concept brought into the HCT model from the earlier years as a residential staff.[1] While some issues seem slow to be resolved by expecting the group process to act on them, the mutual understanding and willingness to implement the outcome are well worth the effort. Other positive aspects of team functioning include (1) the validation of ideas and procedures which can go on among several persons and which keeps a better focus both in treatment and in the educational processes and (2) persons with different views and strengths which provides a vehicle for the growth of each individual on the team. Different combinations of staff members are used so that the growth of the entire team occurs with some evenness. While some efficiency may be lost in the team approach, staff members' continued capability to function at a high energy level and to be productive over many years is part of the trade-off. One-time presentations about child management skills may be done by an individual staff member, but even then we try to get a local provider of service to share the presentation with us. It is costly to have to orient new staff members repeatedly; in a complex social group such as HCT the time needed is about a year before the varying and complex tasks can be learned to implement treatment, plus another year to learn how to do the educational and consultative aspects of the job.

Six disciplines are currently represented on the seven-person HCT team: social work, psychology, special education, early childhood education, occupational therapy, and nursing. The specialized knowledge and skills which each person brings from their discipline ensures the families that all aspects of their functioning will be taken into account, including their physical health, learning capabilities, advocacy for seeking services, and adequate play and leisure pursuits. Students from the disciplines represented on the team, as well as from guidance and counseling and behavioral disabilities, experience the treatment process with experienced staff members and learn through an apprentice model how to influence adult-child interactions in the natural environment.

As mentioned earlier, the distribution of responsibility and work tasks occurs on the basis of competencies demonstrated in the treatment process and on the basis of the personal comfort and challenge desired by the individual. Tasks which require travel as well as administrative unpleasantries are shared by all; no one is expected to do all the unpleasant tasks nor is allowed all the glamorous jobs. Each person is expected to be a case manager on at least one case, plus a team member on another one or two cases, and team members work with the family about an equal amount of time. During a weekly case planning meeting, the team decides who will do which tasks in the therapy process. Documentation is also shared by all, but the case manager is responsible for ensuring that all documentation is accomplished. Each consultation or education project request is reviewed by the entire team, with the assignment determined by previous experience, distance and time needed, type of task requested, and other assignments already made.

An area of concern for groups providing mental health services, social services, or any of the human services is that of staff *burn-out*. Low morale, passive resistance, high job turnover, and increased illness or exhaustion can be symptoms of this burn-out syndrome. Prevention is more effective and includes administrative acknowledgement and the support of providing adequate vacation time; encouraging strong distinction between job and personal life; keep work loads to forty hours per week; and by providing job diversity. Other considerations which are helpful include interpersonal support of team members, participation by all in decisions of work assignments, and occasional group meetings to look at the group process. The ability to feel somewhat in control of one's own destiny within the group counteracts the frequent feelings of helpless frustration experienced after meetings with a family when no progress seems to have been made. Treatment is a slow, painful process with little job satisfaction for a long while; efforts to provide job satisfaction above what clients provide must be a high priority endeavor if the group is to continue over time providing high quality services.

Dissemination of our ideas and skills began with training students from the beginning of the program. The apprenticeship style of teaching field students includes a period of orientation seminars about aspects of the process they would experience when they began working with a family. This model was used by HCT when community agencies began to ask for consultation on difficult cases. Actually, the consultation work in local guidance clinics started when an arbitrary geographical distance limit was set for the families who could receive direct treatment services from HCT. A distant professional group may have heard of the intensive treatment services offered and wanted to refer a family directly, but the limited geographic range helped provide the rationale for offering consultative assistance. The current practice is to contract for an educational/consultative experience with a local group, for a period of six months to two years. Either HCT or the group revise the contract or break it if situations should arise which would throw the original agreement awry. A short didactic introduction to the treatment process, followed by work with one or more of their families beginning almost immediately, approximates the field student training model used within the HCT program.

Because of the distribution of the HCT child management visual aids referred to earlier, and the request from the local Department of Social Services to help them teach child management skills to court-referred families, a parenting skills course was developed. Currently, local professionals can request training in conducting this course by scheduling three courses: the first one with trainees as participants, the second taught jointly with the local trainees taking as active a role as they feel comfortable with, and the third taught by the trainees

with consultations only, with or without the HCT staff's physical presence. Individual presentations of the course are made at
professional meetings, at parent groups, and at student classes.
A movie, filmed in 1975 and 1976, serves to introduce HCT's
ideas about child management and family treatment and has
been rented by groups across the country.

Education in parenting skills and intensive family intervention seem to be ideas whose time has come. While many people
are expressing interest in this model, much work still remains
in cost analysis, long-term effectiveness, and education for parenting in the general population.

REFERENCES

1. Browning, R. M. and Stover, D. O.: *Behavior Modification in Child Treatment.* Chicago, Aldine, 1971.
2. Tharp, Roland and Wetzel, Ralph: *Behavior Modification in the Natural Environment.* New York, Acad Pr, 1969.
3. Patterson, Gerald: Behavioral intervention procedures in the classroom and in the home. In Bergin, A. and Garfield, S. L. (Eds.): *Handbook of Psychotherapy and Behavior Change.* New York, Wiley, 1969.
4. Jones, R.; Reid, J. B.; and Patterson, Gerald: Naturalistic observation in clinical assessment. In McReynolds, P. (Ed.): *Advances in Psychological Assessment.* San Francisco, Jossey-Bass, 1975.
5. Bandura, A. and Walters, R.: *Social Learning and Personality Development.* New York, HR&W, 1963.
6. Hawkins, R. P. et al.: Behavior therapy in the home: amelioration of problem parent-child relations with the parent in a therapeutic role. *J of Exp Child Psychol, 4*:99-107, 1966.
7. Bernal, M. E.: Behavioral feedback in the modification of brat behaviors. *J Nerv Ment Dis, 148*:375-385, 1971.
8. Mahoney, M.: *Cognition and Behavior Modification.* Philadelphia, Ballinger Pub, 1974.
9. Meichenbaum, D.: *Cognition-Behavior Modification, An Integrative Approach.* New York, Plenum Pr, 1977.
10. Berkowitz, S.: *ABC's of Behavior Modification, Leader's Guide.* Baltimore, Behavioral Information and Technology, 1972.
11. Becker, W.: *Parents Are Teachers.* Champaign, Res Press, 1971.
12. Patterson, Gerald and Gullion, M.: *Living With Children: New Methods for Parents and Children,* rev. ed. Champaign, Res Press, 1971.
13. Patterson, Gerald: *Families,* rev. ed. Champaign, Res Press, 1975.

Chapter 21

THE EFFECTIVE USE OF
VOLUNTEERS IN HOME-BASED CARE

HARRIET GOLDSTEIN

THIS chapter concerns itself with a child welfare agency, the Association for Jewish Children of Philadelphia, established through the inspiration of a single volunteer, Rebecca Grats, as she gazed one wintry day upon a group of orphan boys selling matches on a street corner.

Founded 127 years ago, the agency is steeped in the tradition of voluntary service. Through changes in programs and personnel, the thread of services rendered by agency volunteers has been steadfast.

Historically, the exclusive function of the Association had been placement of children who, it was believed, needed separation from their own parents, placements in foster family care, group homes, and adoption. Women with problem pregnancies were also provided service.

Approximately twelve years ago, the Association began a systematic approach to develop services that could prevent placement of children, including services to children living at home; family day care for children under three; after-school day care for the upper-aged latent and early adolescent child; and a life-skills program for the markedly disordered family. Additionally, a primary drug prevention program in the Philadelphia schools reaches about 7,000 children and 3,000 parents annually through group counseling sessions. Most recently, the agency was awarded a contract to remove twenty-five children from a state hospital for placement in community-based foster homes.

The AJC Population

Only about a quarter of the families that come to the Association for Jewish Children are intact; the remainder are separated, perhaps living with someone other than a spouse, or have experienced death, divorce, or desertion. Some are reconstituted families. Many of the parents have severe character disorders, are borderline psychotics, or exhibit sociopathic qualities. Problems include psychiatric hospitalization, prison records, drug abuse, and mental retardation. Some of the parents have lived primitive, disorganized lives and have become isolated from their kin and community. The families are largely blue collar, with an income level range from public assistance to "genteel poor." There are a few higher salaried families.

The consequences of such family life are apparent in problems of early childhood development in relationship and behavior disorders, and among adolescents, in running away, sexual acting out, suicide attempts, antisocial behavior, and drug use. School failure is common and educational deficits severe, despite intellectual capacity. Many of the families have been engaged in a long-time referral/re-referral cycle with many agencies. "Although their need for services is most urgent, these families tend to reject or resist help. They have traits which tend to serve as barriers to effective treatment, and they are also likely to exhibit an antipathy toward institutions, thus placing an additional obstacle in the way of effective services."[1]

A Treatment Approach

To cope with these particular families and children in a home-based program, the Association developed an approach in which the agency was viewed as the client's *extended family*. This approach is supported by the use of a range of social, educational, and clinical services designed to create corrective experiences in living.[2,3]

Succinctly, this concept suggests the following:

1. The agency is in the position of helping parents rear children, and services must reflect that task.
2. Support is required for the day-to-day development of children to help them cope more effectively and to acquire social competence.

3. Work with parents starts with assessment of parental capacity: the quality and degree of nurturance; the family life style; homemaking skills; the fun enjoyed in the home; the religious atmosphere; the cultural aspirations.
4. Some parents require help learning how to express the positive feelings they have for their children, and how to deal with their sense of inadequacy. Children need to understand the parental deficiencies, becoming psychologically freed to develop improved relationships.
5. The parenting concept requires direct, obvious, concrete, and demonstrable evidence that people care not only about the children but the adults as well.
6. Realistic expectations, modest goal setting, and commitment are required of the helpers involved, as needs and deficits of the client population can be endless.
7. Many people are required to fulfill the many roles and tasks of *extended family*. Volunteers are helpful in meeting these service needs when appropriately teamed with professional staff.

Volunteers as a Resource

In 1966, assessment of client needs at the Association led the agency to look to volunteers as an additional resource for service. There was recognition that members of our Board of Directors and our active volunteer group had performed many direct and indirect services to our clients and to the community. However, volume of clients was increasing, treatment approaches were growing, and differential manpower was required.

Agency candor is required in looking at the needs for an enlarged volunteer group because the psychological, interpersonal, and situational forces that motivate professional leadership to make extensive use of volunteers can also mitigate their use. For effective employment of volunteers, hard questions need to be raised.

Will the professional staff accept working with volunteers? The efforts to use volunteers in new areas and to promote them to new levels of responsibility can be met with caution, resistance, and rejection. Unclear division of responsibilities between staff and volunteers can result in a lack of lines of accountability and authority.

Will the professional staff be able to give up some of the contact with clients? The professional loses some of the rewards and personal satisfaction that comes from client feedback. Some emotional satisfaction is lost to the worker who may view the volunteer as having the satisfactions and the heart of the relationship.

Does the professional staff have competence as trainers and consultants? The staff may become aware of lacks in these areas and recognize that they do not possess these skills. Professional staff's feelings of inadequacy may be fostered if they sense that "indigenous volunteers have skills and know-how that professionals lack, and that many volunteers today have professionally trained skills from their own areas of competence which represent major resources beyond the expectations of the professional."[4]

What about professional standards and quality service to clients? There is concern about potential danger to clients from insensitive, unskilled helpers not trained in the dynamics of human behaviors and appropriate treatment modalities.

What about issues of confidentiality? This has been a basis of tension between volunteers and professionals which has excluded volunteers from the inner workings and records of many agencies.

Can the myths about volunteers be answered? "They don't get paid — so they come and go as they please." "They meet their own needs — not those of our clients." "They hire us, they think they are better than we are, and they can fire us."

Can the practical issues of office space, insurance, supervision, and budget needs be met by the agency?

Naylor has suggested that the "keystone of voluntary activities is the concept of sharing work: of volunteer-staff teams carrying joint responsibility for tasks, projects, or continuing work." She continues that "professional staff is responsible for giving expert and innovative leadership, for carrying on the part of the work specifically delegated to staff, and equally important for giving advice and arranging the supportive services required by the volunteer counterpart."[5] The feelings of professional staff about volunteers are very influential in determining the quality and the quantity of their participation.

The agency's volunteer program operates on several assumptions:

The need for services for clients is expanding and will continue to intensify. Client need will outstrip the training of professional and paraprofessional workers.

The service needs of many clients is a home-based program can be met by the sheer "humaneness" of a personal response; thus, a person-to-person program is itself therapeutic.

The economic base will not be available for supporting the training and maintenance of complete staffs of paid workers in home-based care, nor would they be willing to be used in these functions even if paid.

There is an increasing number and potential of volunteers. More and more persons with useful skills and with great sensitivity and commitment are available. Often their knowledge and skills complement those of the professional.

Organizing, coordinating, and facilitating the use of volunteer resources is a challenge for professional leadership. This can be as exciting and stimulating as collegial or client relationships.

Volunteers need to be assigned specific tasks and need to be connected to specific staff members. Roles and expectations of volunteers require clear definition and a support system built in for appropriate execution of them in order to insure service and volunteer satisfaction.

An agency climate needs to be established that demonstrates to the volunteer his or her value and contribution. Volunteer identification with the program and progress of the agency is vital for client service and volunteer and professional job satisfaction.

Ongoing training mechanisms and communication requirements must be built into the system for volunteers and for the professional staff as well.

A director of a volunteer program is essential if the program is to have plan, continuity, and worth. Such a person is the key in recruiting, selecting, integrating, and training volunteers and in developing ongoing program direction.

In using volunteers, an agency requires an attitude as serious as looking for paid employees. There is a need for a range of opportunities, and interests and skills of volunteers require matching with role assignment.

Task Assignments

It takes careful and practical planning to develop good work experiences for volunteers. Job titles and job descriptions need to be drawn and qualifications for each volunteer category considered and defined, such as those for the home-based program at AJC:

Case Aides — to work directly with a caseworker on an assigned portion of a case or on a sustained basis with a child or parent. For example, consistently visiting lonely or depressed women, teaching household management and shopping, sitting with a young child, demonstrating authority concepts to parents, parental role modeling, and assisting parents in securing family medical and dental care.

Recreational Aides — to plan and supervise group and special individual activities for children, i.e. outings to museums, sports events, and the theatre, shopping for clothing, running a play group for young children, conducting an art therapy group. Such recreational aides have been used heavily in the agency's after-school day care component of the home-based program.

Big Brother/Big Sister — to provide the child a specialized individual program offering a sustained relationship. These volunteers have been especially useful for children in single-parent homes.

Drivers — to escort specific children on a planned, individualized basis for service appointments. Volunteers are expected to observe the child's behavior, interact with him or her, and report observations to the worker.

Educational Assistant — to teach individually assigned

children or parents in a specific subject. This volunteer is expected to work with the caseworker as well as the agency's educational psychologist who designs the remedial program. Other educational assistants work with the agency's clinical and educational psychologist in administering intelligence and educational testing.

In addition to these direct client assignments, volunteers provide indirect services to the home-based program in the following ways:

Administrative Assistants — to serve in the agency's reception and clerical departments; to type correspondence and complete special mailings; to assist the paid secretarial staff for the agency's branch office that serves the home-based clientele.

Child Advocacy Committee — to become familiar with current legislation affecting child welfare programs; to engage in letter writing and in-person contacts with the political structure; and to join other community groups advocating on behalf of children.

With the completion of such an inventory of the jobs, it is then necessary to determine a manageable unit of work; the benefits to the clients; the degree of job satisfaction for the volunteer; and the interface of the tasks of the volunteers and the professional team members.

Recruitment

The crux of any service program is people. In recruiting volunteers, the Association determines that people with special skills and talents are needed. Standards have to be established and maintained and careful screening and evaluation is required with a right to rejection. Matching of a volunteer to client problem or agency use is essential.

Men and women are sought who can relate well to children, who can communicate with adults, who have a flair for creativity or detail work, and have patience and nurturant qualities. Volunteers are recruited who can work well with children on either an individual or group basis. It is made clear that volunteers are expected to be consistent in their approach and are required to maintain confidentiality. Because of the nature of the long-term service provided, commitments of several years' duration are expected from the volunteers.

In some service categories, the volunteers need special talents. Experience in typing, filing, and stenography is essential to be an administrative assistant. A driver's license and a car is useful in several categories. It is expected that tutors have a B.A. degree, preferably in education, with teacher training experience considered valuable.

More important than specialized skills of the volunteers is their personal capacity to work with children and parents who have many needs. The responsibility of bringing up children is not spectacular; it is difficult to parent children and grown-ups who must also be parented at times. Results are slow, and frequently there is little glamor to the task.

The volunteer's motivation becomes critical. Altruism is a part of the motivation of most volunteers. However, some volunteers do so to improve their own technical knowledge and to test a possible career. Some student volunteers do so looking for data or research possibilities.

Doctor Aaron Levenstein has suggested, in an analysis of why people work, that man is a social being, interdependent with other men, and developing relationships with people at four levels of his existence. (1) The first level of relationships is self: I must live with and be comfortable with my self-image, the work I do, and the volunteering I do must be right for somebody like me, appropriate to a person of my education and experience, consistent with my ideals and objectives, my likes and my prejudices, my loyalties and taboos. (2) The second level is relationships on a one-to-one basis with another person: This is probably the strongest single force moving a person toward involvement in a particular organization and into a place within it. (3) The third level concerns relationship to the organization itself: I feel more effective within an organization whose ideals and purposes are consistent with my own values. (4) The fourth level is the feeling of contribution to mankind: I come to realize my obligation to all people.[6] Providing these levels for volunteers minimizes recruitment and retention problems, as does realistic understanding and acceptance of the volunteers' motivation.

To secure a wide range and sufficient number of volunteers, an ongoing plan of recruitment must be maintained. The easiest and most popular way to recruit new volunteers is through those who are already in the organization and are having a good experience there. An agency should also be involved in the community's volunteer bureau.

Sometimes there is group motivation: a small group of members of another organization volunteer together to carry out a task. For example, a group from one of the fellowship lodges in the community is responsible for planning outings for children at the Association. Members of the Alumnae Association for the Agency are working in pairs on certain aspects of the volunteer program.

Other methods of recruitment are the mass media, speakers' bureau, flyers posted in local neighborhood shopping centers, and letters sent to unions. In collaboration with other agencies involved in recruitment, special college groups are addressed, service organizations are made aware of the agency's programs and volunteer needs, and religious groups are involved in the agency's search for volunteers.

Implementing and Sustaining the Program

The director of volunteers is the hub of the program. Skilled in recruitment, evaluating, and matching, the director creates an ongoing development program which meshes the volunteer's identification to a specific service category with the overall function and purpose of the agency.

Requests for volunteer services are made by a staff member to the director whose first task is to recruit and match the volunteer to the designated service. Further, it is the director who provides the volunteer with his or her initial orientation and who answers questions and concerns. She or he becomes the bridge to the staff member who defines the specific service assignment and with whom the volunteer works. Together, the volunteer and staff person examine and reexamine the client's wants and together plan for their fulfillment. The volunteer is apprised continuously of the scope and dimension of the client's treatment requirements so that he or she may fit his function into the service. Honesty and trust between volunteers and staff strongly enter the picture. The volunteer is provided with feedback for his or her performance and guided in participating in the client's service goals.

The director of volunteers is aided in planning a training program by a steering committee, composed of representative volunteers from each service category. A yearly calendar of events is scheduled. Group meetings, held about once every ten weeks, provide an additional technical knowledge base and are similar to professional staff in-service training. Seminars are provided on such topics as —

- "Treatment Modalities — Fact or Fad, the Psychoanalytic Approach, Behavior Modification, and Family Treatment"
- "The Adolescent — Understanding his Growth and Needs"
- "Relationship — How to Achieve It"
- "The How-To's of Interviewing"
- "Tutoring the Unmotivated Child"
- "Child Abuse"
- "Bright Child — Poor Achiever"
- "Client Needs — Your Needs — How Do They Fit?"
- "Your Agency IQ — What Is It?"

These are practical meetings geared to help the volunteer better understand his or her role and the dilemma of the clients. Volunteers are informed about the children in care, their history and background, and their current pattern of functioning.

Another learning experience for volunteers is periodic trips to related social agencies and institutions for collaborative understanding of the broader social service system. An agency newletter is a mechanism for communication with volunteers. Further, the agency seeks to honor volunteers through an annual evening of recognition and hosts three general meetings to solidify agency relatedness.

Summary

To complement professional staff, the Association has developed a volunteer program which includes inventory of its jobs; inventory of volunteers; a recruitment plan; selection, matching, and placement of the volunteer; induction and supervison of volunteers; arrangement of a comprehensive and unified training program; and provision of volunteers with opportunity for self-growth and movement in the program.[5]

In so doing, agency clients have benefited from an increased service delivery system and from viable demonstrations that people do indeed care. Further, the volunteer-professional relationship has flourished based on clarity of functional roles and a full acceptance of the unique necessity for each in an integrated approach to helping troubled families. Through such partnership, opportunities are provided for deeper experiences and for responses to human need.

REFERENCES

1. New York State Charities and Associations: *Multi-Problem Families: A New Name or a New Problem?* New York, Social Research Service, State Charities Aid Association, 1960.
2. Taylor, Joseph: The child welfare agency as the extended family. *Child Welfare, 51*:74-83, 1972.
3. Goldstein, Harriet: Providing services to children in their own home: an approach that can reduce foster placement. *Children Today, 2*:2-7, 1973.
4. Rainnov, E. and Lippit, Ronald: *The Volunteer Community.* Washington, NTL Learning Resources, 1971.
5. Naylor, Harriet: *Volunteers Today — Findings, Training, and Working With Them.* New York, Associated Pr, 1967.
6. Levenstein, Aaron: *Why People Work, Changing Incentives in a Troubled World.* New York, CC Pr, 1962.

Chapter 22

HOMEBUILDERS' APPROACH TO THE TRAINING OF IN-HOME THERAPISTS

DAVID HAAPALA AND JILL KINNEY

Introduction

HOMEBUILDERS is an intensive family crisis program.[1] The goal is to provide an alternative to foster care or psychiatric hospitalization for families experiencing severe crisis.

Target families are those where both family members and referring agency personnel assess the situation as requiring out-of-home placement unless change begins immediately. Referrals come from the juvenile court, schools, child protective services, and many other community agencies. Once a client has been referred, Homebuilder therapists are on call twenty-four hours a day. Families are seen for a four- to six-week period. Therapists accept no more than two intakes a month and have no more than three families at a time on their caseloads. Clients are seen almost entirely in their homes or at their schools.

Homebuilders began in October 1974. Original funding was from the National Institute of Mental Health and general monies were from the parent agency, Catholic Community Services, with additional funds now from the Office of Child Development, Title XX, and the Weyerhaeuser Foundation. Original staffing was three therapists and has increased to six full-time and three part-time therapists. Concerns about staff burnout and rapid turnover have not been supported.

During the first three years, Homebuilders saw 207 families involving 311 potential placements in foster or psychiatric care. Follow-up is for one year. To date, 96 percent of these families stay together until their crisis is passed and 86 percent are still together one year after intake without additional Homebuilder involvement past the crisis. Almost all those remaining together say they are very glad they did.

Characteristics of Families

Perhaps the best way to describe the families seen is to cite the problem list of the most recent referral. Although not all cases are as dramatic as this, the case does depict the issues we confront.

1. The mother was suicidal.
2. Five of their seven children were retarded.
3. The father had had a heart attack last spring and had had two strokes since then.
4. Three months before, the mother's rectum had burst. She had been patched together but was unable to have sex and said it felt like firecrackers going off inside her. She also had serious liver problems. She was using many, many drugs — sometimes more than had been prescribed.
5. They still had custody of a thirty-year-old son. He had run away two weeks before and was suspected to be in jail in Ohio. They were upset about not knowing how to handle his money without getting in trouble with the state or risking his getting cut off public assistance.
6. They were trying to get custody of their grandchildren whose twenty-seven-year-old mother was committed to a psychiatric hospital, partly for indecent exposure and prostitution. Her husband, who was in prison for rape, was trying to get custody of the children. The grandparents did not want this to happen.
7. Their twenty-five-year-old son kept trying to kill his girlfriend and was in and out of jail.
8. Their twenty-one-year-old son was going to have to go to jail in two weeks if he could not pay off fines he had accumulated for shoplifting.
9. Their eighteen-year-old son had been run over by a school bus when he was four and was unable to talk. They were worried about how he would ever take care of himself.
10. The fifteen-year-old daughter drank, smoked, lied, did no chores, sassed everyone, and stayed out late.

11. The thirteen-year-old daughter was restricted to her room for one year because she lied, stole, sassed, and did no chores.

These people had been in family counseling for twenty years at a mental health clinic in Tacoma.

This case was terminated in early November 1977. A follow-up telephone call done by the research assistant in February revealed that the mother was very pleased with the way things were going. She was continuing to have some physical problems, but they were improved. Fighting had greatly decreased. Both teenage girls were reported to be in the family home and involved in counseling. The eighteen-year-old son had a job and an apartment of his own. The older daughter was out of the hospital and living independently. The mother felt the overall situation was under control and much more pleasant for everyone.

There are several factors in this program which contributed to success with this case:

1. It helps that clients are in crisis. Family members are more willing to experiment with new ideas and new behaviors than they are when their pain seems more bearable.
2. It is good that almost all of the treatment is done in the home. It makes a difference how a person assesses a situation if he or she can really see what is happening. Also, there are many opportunities for therapists to model and shape new behaviors in the environment where they will need to occur. It is possible to watch new treatment plans being implemented and to help with revision to ensure successful experiences in trying new ways of responding.
3. It helps to be so easily available to the families. Staff have spent dozens of hours with many families. This can be the equivalent of months of therapy in traditional outpatient clinics.
4. Staff have many resources available to them. All staff are well acquainted with community resources. Much time is spent coordinating efforts of currently involved agencies. One girl had fifteen different case managers. In other cases, clients are *not* involved with agencies that could be helpful to them.

Staff Training

Homebuilders staff are trained in Parent Effectiveness Training, behavior modification, assertiveness training, values clarification, Rational Emotive Therapy, and fair fighting. It is useful to have several options when working with families.

In Homebuilders, as in any home-based service for children and families, line staff are the most important resource. Their job is much more demanding than if they were able to sit behind a desk and have clients come in for fifty minutes a week. Staff who go into clients' homes must be able to function well in unstructured, unpredictable, and sometimes dangerous situations. They must be able to juggle their own needs and the demands of their personal lives within a schedule that can adequately provide for the sometimes overwhelming needs of their clients.

Staff in this program, and in others, go through some extremely painful and trying times adjusting to this type of work. Work on the training package was begun because it was believed information was available which could make the transition from more traditional service delivery to in-home services more manageable and more productive for all.

There are several components in the training. First, expectations for staff performance with clients are defined: make sure no one gets hurt; stop the disintegration process occurring within the family in order to begin to work toward more positive interaction; obtain enough information so an accurate assessment of the total situation can be made by the therapist and the family members; introduce options for improving the situation; and implement at least one option that resolves the present crisis and, hopefully, prevents another crisis from occurring.

To meet these goals it is useful to consider three important aspects of the Homebuilder program: staff attitudes and beliefs about what is done; process concerns or the way things are done; and content issues concerning what is done (a variety of interventions, approaches, or methods).

A more complete description of these areas is presented here, along with examples of techniques helpful in teaching various concepts. Covered are assumptions and beliefs considered to be helpful, as well as process skills and content of teaching material.

Assumptions and Awarenesses

We currently do not have enough data to declare any family to be hopeless. We must continually challenge others' pessimistic predictions in order to give any family who is interested a chance to work things out. Some of the situations which are the most difficult for new therapists are cases where psychiatrist, psychologist, or M.S.W. (someone who should know) diagnoses a client as psychotic or, perhaps worse, "unmotivated" or suggests the case is hopeless.

Many, if not most, of Homebuilders' cases meet these criteria. Most are not hopeless. Prediction in the social sciences is not advanced enough to tell us which families do not deserve a chance. One of the principal advantages we have at Homebuilders is that there are several staff members who have seen many severely disturbed families make significant changes. It is important that new therapists be encouraged to remain as open as possible to the surprise and wonder of finding out how many families are not hopeless, despite all the reasons we have for deciding that they should be.

Giving clients hope is part of the therapist's job. We in the mental health field may need to accept more responsibility to modify negative attitudes or encourage people to challenge their feelings of hopelessness. We need to become as skillful as possible in finding ways to become an encouraging resource in the situation, rather than doing all the things therapists can do to make clients feel even worse about themselves and more overwhelmed and confused by their situations. Value-laden assessments and therapists pushing their own ideas of what should happen can be particularly instrumental in leading clients to give up on their problems. Paradoxically, we can give hope by not pushing hard on the notion that the family must stay together. We tend to do best when we offer people in crisis assistance in clarifying what they really want. This is another way of saying that we try to be accepting of their feelings and confused thoughts. These are some of the factors which seem to provoke hope for many families.

If the clients are not progressing, frequently it is because we are not working on the problem of highest priority for them. Usually, it is an assessment issue for the family, not a motivational issue.

Often therapists feel time pressure to implement their own agenda. One thing we ask therapists to keep in mind is a comment by Carl Rogers. Supposedly, a student once asked Rogers what he could do in five minutes with a client; Rogers responded, "Five minutes' worth." It is usually helpful if we will allow the clients to define *where they want to go* and *how fast they can get there*. It is not our job to define this. It is our task to help the family clarify these issues.

We have the potential to elicit more feelings of helplessness and inadequacy. Taking too much responsibility for restructuring and redefining how their lives ought to be can make the family less certain and more confused, and even less able to work constructively.

It is important, in developing therapist compassion and flexibility for the therapist, to realize there are many valid ways of viewing reality. A greater variety of options for assessment means that therapists are more likely to find strategies which "fit" for each family, since each family will be different. The therapist's own frustration and anxiety will be reduced because he or she will not be dependent upon the family buying into the solution. The therapist will then be less demanding of self and the families.

Therapists may be most effective in dealing with families when they acknowledge and utilize their own strengths *and* weaknesses. Therapists are not perfect. This is no problem. In fact, sometimes it is beneficial for the therapist to admit and accept his or her vulnerability. The client is often more likely to begin taking personal responsibility, as well as ultimately trusting the therapist more, because of his or her honesty about such imperfections. Another benefit is the therapist's opportunity to model self-acceptance in the realm of his or her own limitations.

We emphasize compassion as opposed to the deification of procedures. Over-technologizing is becoming more common in our profession and sometimes results in the "handling" of clients. Handling a client refers to the practice of going rigidly by a prescribed therapy rule at the expense of the client. The relationship is most important and we are not likely to learn how to "do" therapeutic relationships according to any set procedures.

Family members usually *really* do want to make it as a family. When they hurt each other, it is often because of (1) lack of information — they know of no other way to proceed or (2) wrong information — they think what they are doing will pay off in the long run, or they misperceive intentionality. They frequently take too many things personally. Much of the behavior they interpret as mean, rotten, or sick is really neutral in nature. It is nothing to be taken personally. For instance, the teen did not miss second gear in his parents' car to upset them. He just made a mistake. As family members gain more information about each other, we are often surprised at how nice they can be and how much they really do care for each other.

It is most helpful when we view family members as colleagues. They have the best and the most data about their situation. They can tell which strategies and interventions are going to fit best with their values. This attitude is contagious. By modeling courtesy and desire to cooperate, the therapist can set the mood for families to try similar patterns among themselves.

People really do the best they can do. This attitude reflects a contagious optimism. Being optimistic is believing that families are trying, in their own homespun, beautiful, error-filled ways, to make things work. This is the mindset promoted in Homebuilders' training.

Second, saying that people really do the best they can gives all of us permission to accept ourselves where we are and, at the same time, work towards becoming better.

Values Clarification exercises are quite helpful in steering people into some of these assumptions.[2,3] For example, one exercise asks participants to list three helpful people in their lives. Under each name they are requested to list what the person specifically did which was helpful. The most common responses are listening without butting in, good eye contact, nonverbal acceptance, touching, and not pushing to do something before it is time.

Another exercise is used to help therapists become more compassionate. They are asked to list five things their clients do which are irritating to them. They can list three possible good reasons the clients might have for doing these things. Therapists are then asked to check those annoying behaviors they have emitted themselves, along with their reasons for doing so. It is usually sobering to realize how much struggling we are all doing in trying to live our lives the best we can.

The training staff likes these methods because they help the therapists discover for themselves the desired attitudes and techniques. It almost always seems more effective if they learn from themselves or each other.

The staff attempts to describe behavior of the participants, instead of labeling those behaviors, when they do things not understood. The interactions between trainers are strong models for desired behavior. The different mindsets are discussed before and after role-playing situations; first as therapists lacking many skills, and then role playing again as therapists with increased competence. The people in training are usually good at picking up the importance of therapist attitude in allowing for cooperative and positive interaction.

Process

Process skills are critical to doing a good job with families. The Homebuilder program has been influenced heavily by the process skills advanced first by Carl Rogers[4] and, more recently, by Thomas Gordon.[5]

These process strategies are actually methods used in the here and now. They are the way we calm people, the way we get information, and the way we relate to the clients. "Active listening" and "I message" techniques allow the counselor to make genuine contact with the client in the present, without judgment or blame. The counselor, through these methods, comes to understand the client more accurately and generally facilitates the client's self-understanding.

The power and effectiveness of these process skills emanates from the fact that they are so much a part of the therapist's own self. Richard Farson has made an interesting observation in this regard. According to Farson, the process skills developed by Rogers cannot really be thought of as techniques, in the commonly accepted use of the word, because these methods become part of the therapist's personal style and pattern in communication. Other techniques used in therapy are much more separate from an individual's style. They are obvious and cumbersome, such as charting, family meetings, and family sculpturing. In this way, we may think of process skills as techniques to do away with techniques and to get us down to a more basic and human level of interaction.[6]

The *how* of process skills training relies heavily on the modeling of trainers, as well as practice among the participants in role-play situations. An exercise is used to improve listening. The therapists are asked to pair up and take turns playing a particularly difficult client, while the other tries to facilitate the interaction. They are then told to give feedback on very specific behaviors which were or were not helpful in calming them or clarifying their thoughts. Trainers provide individual coaching for therapists who are having a rough time. Sometimes the change in client behavior can be very dramatic when the therapist stops blocking and is able to facilitate. It is much more effective for student therapists to witness this shift than it is for them to be told about it.

To teach therapists to present their point of view without being punitive or threatening, participants are asked to write down a one or two sentence statement which they might use with someone who is causing trouble in their life. They then share this statement with a partner who gives them information on how it feels to be on the receiving end of the message. Participants are asked to use that information and try to improve their messages by considering these points:

1. They want a statement which retains the other person's self-esteem.
2. They want a statement which does not damage the relationship they have with the other person.
3. They want to let the other person know very clearly what he or she is doing which is problematic.

Participants then take turns trying out their sentences again. In the discussions which follow, it is always fascinating to use how closely their insights fit the guidelines for "I messages" suggested by Gordon.

Content

The content phase of training follows the process section. The training is structured in this way because it fits the movement of Homebuilder involvement with clients. Hopefully, therapists enter the home with a functional framework and awareness, move into helping the clients understand themselves better, collect pertinent data by listening, and then come to the point of first discussing and then testing possible interventions. This phase is called content phase of training because therapists look at the concrete options, which are many and varied, that could be utilized in helping families make the kinds of changes they desire for their situation.

Therapists are encouraged to use many different theoretical approaches to resolve the issues providing difficulty for their families. For example, behavior and modification, assertiveness training, Rational Emotive Therapy, relaxation exercises, cognitive restructuring, hypnosis, paradox, mood control techniques, systematic desensitization, or fair fight techniques might be discussed. The rationale for appealing to the variety of methods is to attempt to respond to the individuality of each family and to increase the therapist's sense of flexibility in his or her work.

"Brainstorming" is utilized in this phase. The participants in the workshop are called upon to generate possible interventions. This reinforces the notion that they already have many options available to them. Participants almost always suggest a wide variety of ideas and trainers include others. For cases where therapists are feeling too overwhelmed to rely on their own creativity and knowledge bank, a resource book is utilized which has many common client problems categorized with many options that have been helpful in the past.

If the participants are unfamiliar with a technique, the trainers then demonstrate the intervention. Additionally, participants are encouraged to attend workshops on topics which seem interesting to them.

In summary, the following are important when training home-based personnel:

1. Provide an atmosphere which makes use of action-oriented exercises to learn about in-home work. Abstractions are not as helpful in producing experiences into which participants may tap at a later time.
2. Attempt to make values and beliefs explicit. These assumptions are part of any training program. It is easier if everyone knows what they are.
3. Make use of the enormous wealth of knowledge which each participant brings with him or her to the training session. Everyone feels much wiser because of this and it engenders greater compassion.
4. Design training in a flexible manner which will allow trainers to respond to the here and now needs and feelings of the participants.

REFERENCES

1. Kinney, Jill; Madsen, Barbara; Fleming, Tom; and Haapala, David: Homebuilders: keeping families together. *J Consult Clin Psychol,* 45:667-673, 1977.
2. Simon, S.; Howe, L.; and Kirschenbaum, H.: *Values Clarification.* New York, Hart, 1972.
3. Simon, S.: *Meeting Yourself Halfway.* Niles, Argus Comm, 1974.

4. Rogers, Carl: *Client-Centered Therapy*. New York, HM, 1965.
5. Farson, Richard: The technology of humanism. *J Humanistic Psychol,* in press.

Chapter 23

SERVICES TO CHILDREN
IN THEIR OWN HOMES:
A FAMILY-BASED APPROACH

THEODORE LEVINE AND ELIZABETH McDAID

WHILE the provision of services to vulnerable children and families in their own homes is not new to the field of child welfare or to Youth Service, Inc., the approach described here is singular, if not unique. The creation of a family-based service built upon sound child welfare principles will be described in terms of (1) the organizational context and assumptions out of which the service program developed; (2) the client group served, staff roles, and services rendered; (3) outcomes and costs; and (4) the ramifications of the work in regard to practice, policy, and values.

Organizational Context and Assumptions

Youth Service, Inc., a voluntary child care agency, has been providing community-based *placement* services for deprived and delinquent adolescents since 1952. The agency has offered residential care, group foster care, and individual foster care services, supplemented by an alternative educational program and counseling services to the families of the adolescents served.

Since Youth Service, Inc., opened its first residence, the agency has stood firmly for a philosophy of care and a standard of behavior. Our child placement services have stressed clearly defined staff roles, structure in the living situation, full provision of the youngsters' basic needs, the importance of choice for adolescents, and the provision of casework services, primarily through the use of M.S.W. social workers.

Certain assumptions are made about the agency and the

client group:

1. Clients have the capacity to develop a sense of self-value, in spite of early deprivation.
2. The client must experience a structured, clear, external reality in which the agency maintains sound standards of care.
3. The realities of daily living provide consistent opportunities from which people can learn and can increase their sense of self-value.
4. Opportunities for casework services will be used positively by most clients.
5. Development of an increased sense of self-worth takes time.
6. The agency will be willing to experience stress from the client and from staff in order to allow the enriching process to take hold.

These assumptions have formed the basis for this agency's *placement service* for many years and are probably similar to those held by many voluntary child care agencies. However, many of the standards of care which are held as being absolutely essential to sound provision of placement services have been diluted when services are provided to children who live at home.

In January 1974, through the generosity of the William Penn Foundation, Youth Service, Inc., received a grant to develop a family-based service which was to provide services to families and children in their own homes. In essence, Youth Service, Inc., proposed a service which would transfer resources and skills of child care and social work staff to the homes of needy families. Plans were to operate on the above assumptions, as supplemented by the following points:

1. Some children entering placement could be better served if the appropriate quality and quantity of concrete and psychological services provided to the child in placement could be provided the youngster at home. The family unit would be viewed as the major focus of needed support and strengthening.
2. The provision of concrete and casework services to family

members must be agreed to by the parents.

3. Disorganized family life, while a function of psychological stress, is also a function of lack of goods, services, and experience in implementing the routines and elements which go into family organization.

4. Parenting and family management skills can be taught and learned. The teaching and learning, however, will be most effective when taking place within the current reality of family life.

5. The costs of the service will not be inexpensive. However, the cost of serving an entire family will approximate the cost of placing one child outside the home.

Program Description

The Family-Based Service is designed to help neglectful families learn to provide for the healthy growth and development of their children. The members of the family are offered an opportunity to set individual and family goals, to learn new methods of managing their homes, and to provide proper physical and emotional care for their children and themselves.

Most families are referred by the city public welfare agency when one or more children are facing placement or are already in placement. The families are usually in crisis; immediate intervention on an intensive basis is needed.

Characteristics of Families Served

The families served share common identifying characteristics; most importantly, all families have a long history of physical or mental abuse or gross physical neglect of *both* parents and children. Many of the parents exhibit characteristics used to identify abusing parents.

All families served have a long and unsuccessful history of connections with other human service organizations. In attempting to secure responsive service, the families have often "shopped around" the city, with medical records at several hospitals, housing applications at several offices, and open cases at many agencies. Children from the same family may be in foster placement with several agencies and visiting and return home plans may be uncoordinated.

Another characteristic of the families is the lack of knowledge of parenting skills. The families live in a familial and community vacuum, with few acceptable social skills and few, if any, social ties. Family relationships are tenuous: often extended family members are also in trouble and are dependent on the client family.

In summary, the families may be described as (1) isolated from positive interpersonal connection; (2) living with a great deal of environmental stress; and (3) unable, without help, to break the proverty/deprivation/abuse cycle.

Intake

Families are accepted for service on the basis of both family and agency commitment that positive change can occur. When the referral appears appropriate, the referring worker is asked to duplicate and send any pertinent material from the case record and to meet with the family to inform them that the referral was made. A decision is made by phone as to whether the agency can work with the family.

The Family-Based Service supervisor contacts the family head and makes an appointment, either in the home or, if the family is without housing, in the office to explain the program and to obtain the parents' initial reaction. If the parent wishes to pursue the intake process, a second appointment is made at which all children are asked to be present. During that visit, each member is asked to describe goals that he or she would like the family to accomplish with the service. Families are accepted for service based on three criteria: those who say they want help; those who can set some goals which are appropriate for the agency to respond to; and those where the parent or family head is nonemployed during daytime hours, so that the team members can work along with them in their daily schedule. The subjective opinions formed during the intake process are used by the supervisor to make a beginning diagnosis and suggestions to the team on how and where to start with the family.

The supervisor forms a diagnosis and beginning treatment plan and then makes a third visit to introduce the family care worker and social worker to the family. The family's goals are reviewed with additions discussed and agreed to, and the roles of the team are explained in detail. A contract is signed by the family head and agency social worker, agreeing to hours when the family and team members will be working together and setting the date for the first evaluation of service by the family and staff.

Staff Roles

The staff is organized into units of one social worker and four family care workers, with family care workers serving two families, spending two full days a week with each. The social worker supervises the four family care workers and is responsible for providing social casework services to the eight families in the unit.

The family care worker reports directly to the family home on the scheduled days, where she concentrates her time and efforts on working with the parent(s). Activities with the parents include teaching and helping with household and child caring tasks, assisting the family with use of outside contacts and community resources, and providing necessary material goods for the family. In addition to being both teacher and helper, the family care worker is also a motivator. She must give hope to the family that reasonable goals can be accomplished; serve as a role model; and provide relief for the parent to pursue personal interests by caring for the children at appropriate times. The importance of these qualities is reflected in the way the worker is viewed by the families: she is the key staff person to most of those served.

As a supervisor, the social worker provides case management services, plans and implements the casework plan, interprets agency policies to the family care workers, teaches, and interprets family interaction for the workers.

The weekly sessions are directed at developing personal goals for each family member, discussing and interpreting individual behavior, knowledge and acceptance of self by family members, and relieving marital/family/child stress. Social workers also run the mothers' group meetings.

The social worker serves as the follow-up worker after family care work has terminated. The worker provides occasional counseling and keeps the family involved with office activities, to which all families, active and closed, are invited.

Outcomes

The question of outcomes in a service program such as we have described is complex. In one sense, we could report no failures. We could say, in those situations where placed children were unable to return home, or where after a period of service the children nonetheless had to be placed, that indeed Youth Service, Inc., had provided a valid and helpful service. One could seriously maintain that an opportunity was provided to a family which proved unable to utilize it, and that the county child welfare agency could be more certain that placement was not arbitrary but was indeed indicated.

Measures of success depend on the frame of reference of the evaluator and the point at which he enters the family's process. Typical of the caseload is the situation in which conditions have gone from impossible to tolerable.

Even in some families where the placement of those children designated as vulnerable at intake did not occur, there were some other children already in placement or placed subsequent to the agency entering the family's life. Some of these children are severely retarded, brain damaged, or psychotic. In one situation where placement was required as a result of the death of a parent, the teenaged son is making excellent use of a Youth Service, Inc., group home. We suspect life has much brighter prospects for him since his mother's death and his placement. Situations like this do not lend themselves easily to categories of success or failure.

Again, the issue of outcomes is quite complex; someday the

staff hopes to be able to conduct major research. Until that time, however, the following information is available:

Since October 1974, the agency has worked with fifty-four families. As of August 1977, sixteen were still active, including two reopenings, and forty cases have been closed.

Eight families were accepted whose children were in placement at the time of referral. The parent(s) requested that the children be returned home; while the placement agency staff accepted the motivation of the parent(s), they also felt that a great deal of intensive work was needed to establish a suitable home, or in several cases, to find a home or apartment that children could visit before returning. In three of these eight families, the children were not returned, on specific recommendation to the agency that the parents were not mature enough or stable enough to provide basic care to the children. In the other five families, the children were returned after an average of three months of work with the parent(s), and the home stabilized into a healthy environment for the children. Work with these families continued for two and one-half days per week, for an average of a year after the children were returned.

In the thirty-two families with children at home at time of referral, the referral was precipitated by impending placement of the children, either by request of the family or as determined by the public child welfare agency staff to be in the best interests of the child. Each family was offered the Family-Based Service as one which could be used to stabilize the home and prevent placement of the children. For ten of the families, family deterioration was too extensive to reverse, and after four months the agency recommended that placement planning proceed.

Six other families did not reach the goals of stabilization. Improvement was substantial, to the extent that placement could not be justified; however, there was question about the overall welfare of the children.

The goals of stabilization of the home and enrichment of the family supports were realized in sixteen of the families. These families are the "success stories," in which parents, children, and staff have been in touch from time to time, and in which the staff and family are mutually respectful of the work that was accomplished. Continued contacts are used to help the family through an occasional crisis and to confirm the ongoing stability of the home.

Costs

In the developmental stages of the service program, it was determined that service to the entire family would be provided at a cost not to exceed that of service to one child in the residential program. During the fiscal year 1976-1977, the cost of residential service for an adolescent at Youth Service, Inc., was approximately 15,000 dollars per year per child, for long-term, twenty-four hour care. The yearly five-day-a-week cost for a family in Family-Based Service was 9,360 dollars. Almost 11,000 dollars was expended in one year for basic essentials for families. Although representing a small portion of the budget, these expenditures reflect the philosophy of the service in a concrete way: it is not necessary to place in order to provide basic services.

During the 1976-1977 fiscal year, service was extended to families averaging 3.5 children, for considerably less than the cost of serving one adolescent in residential care. Apart from comparative dollar issues, the question of the use of dollars to supplement a family's capacity to function, rather than to substitute for a family's capacity to function, must be considered.

Practice

After three years of establishing and providing the Family-Based Service, experience has illuminated a host of practice, policy, and value issues.

There is a need to sharpen the collective capacity for making sound judgments as to which families can make use of certain components of the service. Are there in the caseloads the elements of a beginning family typology? If so, what are the elements which enable some growth in some families to take place?

The staff is intrigued by the role and place of the men in the lives of these mothers. In over 50 percent of the families served, there is an active adult male who plays a role with the family. He may be the husband and father; however, he is often a "paramour," a "stepfather," an "uncle," or just a friend. He is usually not listed on any forms, nor is he mentioned at the point of intake. The staff learns of him and relates to him as they work and develop relationships with the family. Since these men seem to play a critical role, it may be necessary to learn more about them, their needs, aspirations, and levels of functioning.

The relationship of the concrete help to the psychological supports provided by both family care and casework staff needs considerable exploration. Experience points to the presence of severe emotional damage, immaturity, and relationship problems in the client group which cannot be swept away by the presence of new mops, helping hands, and an added washing machine. On the other hand, the most skillfully offered psychological service, without concrete help and provision of goods and teaching, will likewise fail.

While the need for both components has been established, there remains a series of questions surrounding the staffing of this program. Should we attempt to hire trained M.S.W.s to serve in the family care worker role? Are there B.S.W. or other human services personnel who could provide both the psychological and concrete services? There are also questions of supervisory structure, staffing patterns, and use of neighborhood volunteers.

Serving multiproblem families on their own turf is exceedingly draining and demanding. The family care staff, and to a lesser extent the social work staff, must work in the most trying and stressful situations. Unsafe neighborhoods, unsanitary homes, lack of decent toilet facilities, plus a range of bizarre and antisocial behavior from extended family and neighbors, are not unusual. It seems essential that there be personnel practices, including adequate vacation, sick leave, telephone coverage, and petty cash resources, which recognize these stresses. Trust and office backup are essential services which the agency must provide.

The staff have provided examples of personal courage and dedication to the families and the agency. However, a very few staff leave early, have the family cover for them, and continually seek the path of least resistance. Situations where the agency attempts to meet comprehensive needs of clients may stimulate dependency needs of some staff to a degree which impairs their functioning. Recruitment of new people, retention of good staff, and release of those who have difficulty functioning are ongoing tasks.

Social Policy

Family-Based Service has pointed to several problems of a social policy nature. The caseload includes many individuals and families who have been known to the complete range of public and private agencies in our community and who seem to be prime examples of the well-known, often-decried "lack of service integration."

When funded solely by private foundation money, funds may be utilized for concrete services, including home repairs, furniture, emergency food, and rent and utility bills. This seems totally consistent with the fundamental notion that a child needs a sound living environment with caring adults who have the necessary means of providing care.

After the private foundation grant expired, a Title XX contract from the Commonwealth of Pennsylvania Department of Public Welfare was obtained. These funds, while critical to the family-based program's survival, brought with them service constraints. Title XX provides social services only; other funds must be utilized for material aids.

Since the agency was viewed as providing service to children in their own homes, it was not permitted to perform services other than those designated for children in the state Title XX plan. For example, such services as housing location and chore services, which are not included under services for children, could not be included in our Title XX contract.

An essential issue is the need for the development of social policy, and from it a program which speaks to the impact of the family and its needs on the client, as well as the impact of the client on the family. It is difficult to conceive of any target group of individuals where the availability of supports of a concrete and psychological nature to the family cannot be an important factor.

Values

Although the practice and policy issues are important, the answer to these questions will not eliminate a host of ethical or value considerations. Do we, once we have the necessary capacity and data, decide to use our resources only for those families who can change and grow? Can we accept the fact that for some families the issue is maintenance and prevention of further deterioration, with no real possibility for change? Should all families, by virtue of the fact that they are vital to the nation's stability, be extended service?

The world of the clients and those serving them is not a neat system of rights and wrongs. While not amoral, and while rooted in an agency value base for all services, staff members have advocated, angered, pressured, and "bent the truth" in behalf of the families. In dealing with this dilemma, individual needs of the client are considered in combination with the agency values.

Conclusion

Some children need to be removed from their own homes. Such major surgery, however, should only be implemented based upon a judgment that the family and the child's condition is such that concrete and psychological service to the family will not alter the need for placement. Supports must be made available to assist families in fulfilling their historic role and function.

While this Family-Based Service operates in the urban Northeast, the basic format and conceptual framework is applicable to other geographic areas. The content of the services and precise client need and behavior may differ; however, the focus remains on the family and the provision of concrete and psychological services. Communities recognize the need for a range of child placement options; similarly, a spectrum of methods and services for enabling families to fulfill their role should be developed.

Chapter 24

FAMILIES PROGRAM DESIGN: GIVING FAMILIES RELEVANCE IN TREATMENT

Michael Ryan

THE chapter title, "Giving Families Relevance in Treatment," may be misleading. Perhaps a more accurate title would be "Recognizing Families' Relevance in Treatment," or "Building on" or "Responding to the Relevance Within the Family." Professionals who deal with families tend to find resources within the family, rather than introducing them. Virtually all therapeutic changes emerge from the *family's* activities, rather than those of the therapist.

The first aspect of relevance in individual or family therapy is the self-reflective observation that something is wrong. This self-diagnosis can take many forms depending on the sophistication and the trouble of the individual or the family. The observation in itself is not yet treatment-oriented. To be treatment-oriented, the diagnosis must be made in a context of wishing that the situation were not so, and that things might be different. A father recognizes that he has a great deal of anger toward one of his teenage sons; he must move on to some formulation that he does not like things that way and he must wish the relationship were different. It is this recognition and the wish that the relationship be different that places an individual or a family on the threshold of treatment.

The next step leading to the treatment is the decision to *go public*. The decision to go public, to approach a friend, a pastor, or a structured therapeutic resource begins a dynamic process which should ultimately return the individual or the family to a self-directed living process.

These initial steps taken by the family (*something is amiss; it might be different; let's seek help*) begin the process of therapy. The first two steps may be internal and lead to numerous efforts of the individuals themselves. The third step of seeking help often elicits community response. The family conditioned to failure may well approach these problems negatively. They may introduce their own hopelessness to the agencies. If not conditioned to failure, they may more easily begin therapy from a position of initiative.

If a family conditioned to failure requests services, it is rare for the community to respond seriously, and without something significant happening, the family will not likely achieve productive change. The family has given up, and the community attitudes may be reactive, predisposed by the family's position.

If the negative attitude of a family is accompanied by a great deal of pain, the family may become desperate and seek radical solutions. The sense of hopelessness prevails, but because the pain is so great, something must be done. Under the force of desperation, radical solutions are considered. These may include running away, suicide, divorce, spouse or child abuse, a nervous breakdown, or requesting separations or removal of a "problem child" from the home. The two essential choices in such an atmosphere of desperation are (1) abdication, running away, or breaking up the family or (2) enlisting the tools of power within oneself or within the community in the hope that compliance or resolution can be eventually achieved. In either case, desperation can not only lead to despair but it may also lead to the ravaging of the family unit. The community often accepts treatment intervention only when the family is ready to give up or relinquish its own efforts, and the community may at this point exclude the family from involvement.

Nathan Ackerman urged us not to ignore or exclude the family as a social and emotional unit. In 1937 he stated:

> None of us live our lives utterly alone. Those who try are doomed to a miserable existence. It can fairly be said that some aspects of life experience are more individual than social, and others more social than individual. Nevertheless, principally we live with others, and in early years almost exclusively with members of our own family.[1]

There is less tendency to ravage the family in situations where the family goes public with a positive rather than a negative approach. The family may be capable of initiative, in the sense that there exists some receptiveness or openness that does not place the helper in a position of uselessness nor enlist his or her powers to effect radical changes that may in no way be therapeutic.

Regardless of the initial stance of the family — whether hopeless, desperate, or one of initiative — its first relevant involvement in treatment has begun. The helpers may forget the relevance of the family in treatment and may overreact to the solutions, or lack of them, that the family presents. They may play into the sense of defeat experienced by the family. The best response, however, is to maintain the initiative within, which may not have been verbalized by the family. The therapist should be alert to possible conscious or unconscious diagnostic efforts of the family. In fact, we are all familiar with the ability of family members to unconsciously set forth the initiative stance, acting out the family dynamics. A fourteen-year-old girl involved in drug abuse and sexual promiscuity somehow selects the same age and type of men with whom her mother is associated. This selection not only points toward family dynamics, but it quickly provokes the mother to demand some changes. We must carefully await or seek out the initiative of the family before commencing a treatment regimen, or we run the risk of building upon the family's irrelevance. In *The Family Crucible,* Augustus Napier says:

> . . . we are convinced that successful therapy isn't something that is "applied to" the person or the family. Therapy, for us, is related to a growth process that takes place naturally in lives and in families. We assume that the will and the need to expand and integrate experience are universal; and the family that enters psychotherapy is simply one in which that natural process has become blocked. Therapy is a catalytic "agent" which we hope will help the family unlock their own resources. Therefore, we place great emphasis on the family's own initiative, assuming that if they cannot discover their own power to change themselves, therapy will have no enduring effect.[2]

Many service programs seem to reinforce the irrelevance of

the family members. Certainly it is difficult to see how the family as a unit can be any more than peripherally involved in foster or institutional care or in the individual therapies. Many such service programs assume that their major challenge is to compensate for or even reverse some of the effects attributed to inadequacies of the family's behavior. The further a child could be removed or insulated the better. Such agencies were rejecting the relevance of families, their self-diagnosis, and perhaps also their primitive treatment efforts. Their programs are advanced as an alternative to the family. We are now speaking of an alternative to the alternative, an alternative to institutional, group home, and foster care. We have come full circle.

The program design of FAMILIES of Iowa immediately responds to the family's relevance. An effort is made to respect virtually all of the bureaucratic decisions that a family makes in running its day-to-day operation; the place the family lives, jobs that are held by family members, the church attended, the various community relationships which have meaning to the family, choice of schools, and selection of medical or legal assistance to list a few. The family also is respected in its essential role of socialization of its offspring, the growth process alluded to by Napier.[2]

Embracing the principle that the family is the appropriate practical and therapeutic resource for a child dictates several elements of the design of FAMILIES' intensive in-home service. The acceptance of the family's relevance in treatment requires that the agency design reconsider such questions as turf, or where the service will take place; agency organization; the expertise and flexibility of the staff; and the family's role in accepting the service, the therapist, goals, and the various treatment approaches.

There are a number of practical and therapeutic reasons for providing the service within the home of the family. These reasons outweigh the advantages of in-office designs or placement. As a logical consequence of family-focused therapy, FAMILIES' program design accepts the family's turf for several practical reasons. The essential reason, and the one most instrumental in bringing the experimental agency into existence, relates to the deficiencies of placing a single member of the family. Institutions are few; some are great distances from the families needing service. The distances prevent good coordination with other family members and with community-based efforts. The child is identified as *the problem,* and placement usually means loss of positive as well as problematic relationships in the child's community. The grouping of such children with other delinquent or emotionally disturbed children often serves to strengthen their identity as "mental" or "hood," and pathologies are frequently expanded rather than ameliorated. The practical advantage of serving the family in the home preempts many of these obstacles.

There are several therapeutic advantages in offering service on the family's turf. The total family and significant community people can be more readily involved. Coming to the home automatically includes all family members; some or all of these may be involved in the problems. Members may have vested interests in perpetuating the conditions, or they may have important ideas about the eventual resolutions. Not to include them negates their importance and places an additional burden on those members who are involved in the treatment process. They must not only uphold their part of the bargain; they must take it upon themselves to invite others to change. Accepting the family's turf is no guarantee that you will succeed in engaging everyone in treatment, but it does improve the chances.

Another advantage is that the family's home may be more secure. The families may already be, as Napier says, frightened or angered at social agencies or intimidated or afraid to travel; or it may be difficult to get all of the members to make the effort to go to a centralized office. While Napier recognizes the advantages to providing service on the family's turf, he seems to prefer the certain shifting of gears that may be necessary, and perhaps the initiative that is implicit when a family ventures out to the therapist's office. FAMILIES' program design does not lose this initiative, as members may still avoid involvement by leaving and reentering. These actions can be quickly related to both by the therapist and the family members.

The family's turf also provides a realistic training ground. Family interactions will be visible and observable, not just spoken about. Presence of workers within the home may allow for a variety of service efforts: modeling, teaching new ideas, and ultimately practicing them on the spot. Many opportunities occur for teaching, including power struggles, where principles of *Parent Effectiveness Training*[3] might be enlisted; arguments where fair fighting[4] might be helpful; and teaching and practicing the parenting techniques outlined in the *Home and Community Treatment* manual.[5]

FAMILIES' decision to provide services in the home and community mandate other elements of the program design. The accessibility of the family to the therapist, and the therapist to the family, requires that they be geographically close and that sufficient time be spent by both the family and the agency to accomplish the goals. Professionally trained staff are assigned service responsibilities in those counties in which they reside, and each county serviced is represented by board members who hold the administrative responsibility over the total agency. This community-based feature of the design shortens the distance between resources and families in need, and the agency becomes a very real part of the service structure in each of the communities. The *in-home service* becomes a *home and community service* assisting the family both with its internal functioning and its relationships within the community.

This centralized approach gives families access to professional teams within institutional or hospital settings. FAMILIES assigns at least two therapists to each referred family and makes a commitment to include other disciplines and other professionals in the overall treatment approach selected by the family. This design feature coincides with principles outlined in *Multiple Impact Therapy With Families.*[6]

While allowing for traditional staffings and consultation with one another and with selected specialists, the program design does not include the traditional supervision. Supervisory roles and responsibilities are compensated for by the team approach where various staff members can be called in and utilized on a prescription basis. Both the director and the treatment coordinator are involved in such team efforts, which eliminates some of the hazards of the traditional supervisory models. Program designs that respect the relevance of the family in treatment make the special expertise directly available, which avoids behind-the-scenes speculations in which the family may not be able to participate. When diagnostic thinking and planning take place openly in the presence of the family, they too are part of the process. The family encounters an agency or a program design that accepts the family itself as the therapist.

Initially, even though the approach is different and the family now has a team of individuals who have committed themselves to involving the family, the family or its members may attempt to act out their convictions of defeat. The very behaviors or treatment efforts that caused agencies to respond with protective removal will be displayed in full view. A few families may maintain superficiality, but because of the daily availability of the family therapists, the real world quickly emerges.

In some families, the chronicity, disorganization, and sense of goallessness will make no sense and may well elude even the experienced therapist. In multiproblem family situations, virtually all workers begin to wonder why they did not listen to the family's early requests, as they find themselves inundated, perhaps overwhelmed, by the family's sense of defeat. Simultaneously, however, the family may begin to bring out some elements of initiative and strength to accomplish change. A bag of tricks may be helpful to reinforce such early positive efforts of the family.

Within the first few weeks, some time may be given to serious observation and formulation of hypotheses. Although the therapist benefits from constructing a generalized approach, assignments or initial treatment ideas are essential in responding to the relevance of issue-oriented families.

In one particularly disorganized family that had been known to social agencies for generations, it was obvious that both mother and children continually engaged in destructive interaction. Because so many of the children could be reduced to tears and because the mother was resorting to tranquilizers, it became obvious that all were trying to accomplish something. A game was staged whereby the children were to receive one dollar for being present at the family meeting and talking about the family. The destructive interaction was so fast and furious that the children were informed they would be fined a quarter out of their anticipated dollar for each destructive attack they made on a family member. One sibling was called a "retard;" a fine was levied. Another was called a "mental;" a fine was levied. One child derided another because of his fine; a third fine was levied. The children controlled their destructive behavior for the remainder of the meeting. The mother was quickly impressed that the children could behave differently and admitted to frequently referring to her teenage daughter as a "slut" and a "whore." The family began to understand what they had been doing to one another, and a decision to extinguish the name calling and hitting was made. Upon accomplishing such change, even though minimal, the family began to consider additional issues with some initiative.

In families where children are under the age of eight or nine, parenting techniques are immensely helpful. The learning theory approaches of the Home and Community Treatment Project in Madison or the Adlerian Step Program are often utilized by staff. Several families have initiated in-home service because a child was uncontrollable, prone to temper tantrums, or perhaps even the object of abuse. When a parent employs a new bag of tricks and gets desired results, he or she recognizes that they have had something to do with effecting compliant behavior, where previously there had been no compliance. The parent will be encouraged by not needing to resort to threats, shouting, or physical attacks. This change may allow the parent a beginning of self-esteem to replace the previous disrespect for his or her role as parent. Parents are thus establishing a treatment program for their child and developing consistent and improved habits for themselves.

Equipping parents with new parenting techniques has a simultaneous effect of avoiding any direct rumination on their painful sense of inadequacy. They begin to experience a new relevance as parents. This relevance may not occur without resistance, but being in the home allows therapists to invite test runs by parents or to model the desired behavior. Occasionally, a parent may freeze up over the simple request to give a child a specific praise. When this occurs, it is very possible that although the praise is not forthcoming, the parent is prepared to attack more comprehensive concerns. It also occurs that when the praise indeed is forthcoming, it unleashes a flood of emotion from a child who had been feeling very much alone. The child finds the family milieu more in tune.

In some instances where children have experienced frightful or bizarre behavior, the attitude of the parent is "You should have to put up with what I do." Bizarre behavior can be frightening to parents, but the terror dissipates when therapists are willing to be in the home and when parents have achieved the ability to respond relevantly to this behavior. Although task oriented or issue oriented initially, these reeducation approaches almost always are accompanied by dynamic changes as well.

Those families who are initially issue oriented often may become dynamically oriented and those families who are dynamically oriented at the outset can learn to cope well with issues. The well-organized family, good at "therapy games," may invite you to enter the labyrinth of confusion without taking proper steps toward issues of concern perhaps to the child or the community. It may be necessary to invite the family into running several programs. Some can be very practical in nature, while the other is theoretical. Many families are quite capable of implementing such programs and eventually working out problems.

Whether a family initiates service on a prescription basis, working on identified issues or on an immersion basis seeking total overhaul, relevance in treatment is both pervasive and immense. In point of fact, as a family progresses in its ability to cope and respond to one another, their role in the treatment enriches their vested interest in making things work. The treatment staff, too, rather than feeling they have had very little to do, recognize they are engaged in hundreds of ways in the multiple efforts of the family. They are educators; they are experts; they are sometimes referees. They are friends attempting to support the best efforts of the family and its members.

In the last century, Georg Wilhelm Friedrich Hegel advanced his philosophy of thesis, antithesis, and synthesis. The growth process seems to follow this pattern quite accurately. The family living process may be considered the *thesis*; its reflective ability or its therapeutic efforts the *antithesis*; and the resolution of the two result in new patterns of living, *synthesizing* the first two. This synthesis would become the new thesis, subject to continuing antithetical thoughts and resulting in new growth levels as life progresses.

If therapeutic agencies are in a position to be this intimately involved in the life processes of individuals and families, the nature of their alignment with the family should be a known quantity. While working with a mother of four children who had just been returned to her from foster care placement, the six-year-old wet his pants and was lying on the living room floor kicking and screaming. The author asked the mother "How will you be handling this?" Her response was "After you've gone." The author then asked her what she would do when he left, and she said, "I'll whip him, only social workers don't like to see that. They will take your kids away." This indictment assumes that all professional assistance may be offered with the risk of irrelevance. The insight of this mother is not necessarily off-center. The bulk of expenditures for service are made available on the condition of family break-up, rather than on the condition of family relevance. In the recent publication of The Carnegie Council on Children, *All Our Children*, Ken Keniston states:

> Despite the long-term reduction in familial roles and functions, we believe that parents are still the world's greatest experts about the needs of their own children. Virtually any private or public program that supports parents, effectively supports children. This principle of supporting family vitality seems to us preferable to any policy that would have the state provide children directly with what it thinks they need.[7]

REFERENCES

1. Guerin, Philip: Family therapy, the first twenty-five years. In Guerin, Philip (Ed.): *Family Therapy: Theory and Practice.* New York, Gardner, 1976.
2. Napier, Augustus and Whitaker, Carl: *The Family Crucible.* New York, Har-Row, 1978.
3. Gordon, Thomas: *Parent Effectiveness Training.* New York, Wyden, 1970.
4. Bach, George: *The Intimate Enemy.* West Caldwell, Morrow, 1969.
5. *Home and Community Treatment.* Madison, Mendota Mental Health Institute, n.d.
6. MacGregor, Robert: *Multiple Impact Therapy With Families.* New York, McGraw, 1964.
7. Keniston, Kenneth and The Carnegie Council on Children: *All Our Children: The American Family Under Pressure.* New York, Har Brace J, 1977.

Chapter 25

IN-HOME FAMILY SUPPORT SERVICES: AN ECOLOGICAL SYSTEMS APPROACH

Douglas Stephens

For the past fifteen years divergent trends have developed addressing children's problems and their treatment. Only recently has the treatment focus been changing from the individual client to the family unit as a client. Family systems theory, asserting the primary focus to be the social contexts that contain the variables which shape group and individual behavior,[1,2,3] has become a respected approach toward understanding human social problems.

Much of this change in treatment perspective can be attributed to an increasing emphasis on maintaining the solidarity of natural social units within the community.[4] Institutionalization is not regarded as the sole solution for individuals and families in crisis. In fact, the current emphasis on deinstitutionalization in some states[5] has prompted social services policy makers to investigate alternatives to placement.[6] Consequently, human services professionals have tried to provide a wider spectrum of treatment alternatives to cope with problems of high risk clients and their families.

One of these alternatives is family therapy.[7] Family therapy has become a frequent treatment choice of professionals working with troubled families. It can be defined as the treatment of those natural units such as parents and children, spouses, or members of the extended family, which are perceived as a group, with the purpose of improving their functioning as a family unit.[8] While family therapy usually occurs within an office context, practitioners have begun questioning the limitations of this aspect.[9] Home-based services to families, including family therapy, have become options which address some of the environmental limitations of in-office counseling. The intensity of home-based services create far-reaching possibilities for individual and family change not found with some other family treatment alternatives.[10]

It is the intent of this paper to report on a home-based program which attempts to assist high risk, multiproblem families that have received many human services yet have remained dysfunctional. The program has been a demonstration project by Iowa Children's and Family Services, in Polk County.

The Contextual Variables

The Community

Des Moines, Iowa, is an urban community, with a population of approximately 200,000. The city is situated in Polk County, which in 1970 had a population of 286,101. A further important factor is that Polk County is considered by many to have an unusually high divorce rate. While reports may vary somewhat, Polk County has, in recent years, an average of one out of every two marriages ending in divorce, compared to one out of every four nationwide, according to 1973 city records.

The Agency

Iowa Children's and Family Services has specialized in services to children since its beginning in the late 1800s. However, during the past eight years there has been a growing trend to counseling and support with families. This expansion of services included the establishment of an Emergency Homemaker Program, with most of its referrals coming from the Child Protective Unit of Polk County Department of Social Services.

The agency (hereinafter referred to as I.C.&F.S.) felt that greater coordination of its various counseling, placement, and supportive services might be possible through an intensive in-home family service. Funding was secured through Comprehensive Employment Training Act grants and an allocation from the United Way of Des Moines. This funding allowed I.C.&F.S. to assess the need for an in-home family service program in Polk County, through a demonstration project, beginning in mid-June, 1977.

The Workers

There have been numerous studies regarding the effectiveness of paraprofessional workers with troubled families.[10-14] Mental health centers and family service agencies often are staffed with a high proportion of skilled paraprofessional workers who provide direct therapeutic work with families as their clients. In-home services, as envisioned by I.C.&F.S., entails a very intense, time-consuming involvement with each family. Therefore, in light of the need for maximum service provision, as well as limited agency funding, I.C.&F.S. employs workers with bachelor's degree training in social work or psychology. The workers vary in their experience levels, but the degree of formal training is relatively similar.

Such selection of workers who have not had graduate training in social work or psychology is in accordance with the philosophy of this program; intense in-home counseling and support of multiproblem families requires a willingness by the family workers to be informal in their clinical treatment, to allow for a more rapid engagement with client families.[15] Day-to-day problems within the community, as well as at home, are addressed with each family on an intensive basis by the worker. This requires enthusiasm, persistence, and commonsense intervention which may be sometimes lacking in the efforts of graduate workers.[14]

Agency support for staff family workers is imperative. The geographical proximity of the workers' homes allows for frequent contact among the in-home staff at the agency. Additionally, one hour of individual supervision and two hours of group supervision are provided each family worker on a weekly basis. Semimonthly case conferences provide intake staffings and continuing education. Solid support between family workers is quite prevalent, with peer support often being the essence of group supervision sessions. This allows for greater depth and flexibility for training considerations through experiential learning modalities.[16,17]

The Client Population

High risk families with members who are strong candidates for placement in institutions, group homes, or foster care are the population for which this in-home family service is designed. Their problems are so comprehensive that intensive work with each family, as a system, is presently the only apparent alternative to placement of individual family members. Even when a family member may be removed for placement, the systemic operations of the family invariably create a new scapegoat, to renew family homeostasis.[18]

The presenting problems in high risk families may include juvenile delinquency, school truancy, alcoholism, incest, marital strife, physical abuse and neglect, or the institutional placement of children. Emotional ties between family members are excessively strained and sometimes severed, contributing to isolation and mistrust in stressful circumstances. Poverty, unemployment, and low socioeconomic status constitute environmental problems that prevent improved family functioning. As these families attempt to remedy their problems, they often utilize the services of numerous agencies, yet rarely are able to successfully coordinate these services. Eventually the families become so entrenched in the maze of human service systems that they reinforce the community's image of them as high risk and multiproblem. Often they remain in this scapegoat position, woefully dependent upon systems external to their system.[14,19]

High risk families have certain structural and interactional characteristics. Although they have a wide range of functioning, from disengaged to enmeshed, high risk families are characterized by difficulties in their communication between various family members. Inflexibility when confronted with change, and development needs, results in dysfunctional responses and incomplete communication processing.[20] Within such disengaged families, the boundary between the family system and the external community is porous. Family loyalty between members is tenuous at best, even with problems concerned with outside systems, such as juvenile court or the public school. This generates confusion in family functioning. Family members are either emotionally or physically distant from one another, precluding the support needed to surmount particular problems. These disengaged families are underorganized and are prone to collapse when chronic stress becomes intolerable, either to family members or to environmental systems.[21]

Extreme closeness between family members is characteristic of enmeshed families. Undifferentiation and lack of autonomy is prevalent, inhibiting the tolerance of self-growth by adults and children alike. Unlike the disengaged family, the enmeshed family consists of interactional patterns which create a rigid external boundary, protecting it from ideas of change, yet perpetuating amorphous generational boundaries within the family system.[22]

The manner in which high risk families request assistance is characteristic of their problem solving within their unique family system. Scapegoating and expulsion of the identified client are often attempts to resolve family stress during a crisis. Once this process is begun, homeostatic adjustment makes it extremely difficult for the identified client to either regain a position in the family or develop age-appropriate autonomy. Community efforts can often contribute to this dysfunctionalism for such families.

Unless a coordinated treatment plan is implemented among all human service agencies working with a high risk family, perpetuation is granted to the conflicting pattern of "assistance" from numerous helping systems. Once this conflicting pattern is reinforced, the family's dysfunctionalism becomes chronic. Frequently this chronicity is a by-product of the poor communicative efforts between family and helper systems. The family, however, carries the burden of labeling within the community, partially due to uncoordinated treatment elements.

Treatment Program

Theoretical Orientation

An expansive treatment approach is necessary when working with high risk families. Viewing the family system as a client may not be sufficient for treatment effectiveness, as environmental variables and forces must be also considered. Numerous authors have outlined what can be called an *ecological family systems approach* to treatment.[11,14,23,24,25] In this approach, intervention is directed toward changing the problem-solving efforts of troubled families which perhaps have heretofore been ineffective. These efforts have a patterned structure that needs to be altered at the point where it is maintained, whether within the family system or at the interface of the family and the helping systems.

This ecological systems approach addresses the whole range of everyday difficulties of living for family members at home and in the community.[11,14,25,26] The family worker operates as a teacher, advocate, and counselor, guiding families in functioning effectively with exterior systems. This modality requires analysis, by the family worker, of helping agency systems' interplay with the family, as well as the family system's own unique structure. Creating flexibility in rigid, sometimes maladaptive, service efforts is a continual task.[9,19,21,24,27]

Support from extended family, friends, and community helpers is needed by high risk families. Therefore, the family worker attempts to construct a social network of people which may aid the family in its struggle with social isolation and hopelessness.[14,28,29,30,31,32] Crisis-oriented counseling and restructuring of community relationships with a family may often produce positive change by averting chronic patterns of dysfunctional interaction.

A method encompassing systems theory and appropriate techniques is used by in-home family workers.[20,33,34,35] The structural family therapy approach is well suited for the ecological systems intervention which is engineered by an in-home family worker. The structural family model suggests goals for therapeutic intervention within the family system, as well as in the community. The family worker becomes actively involved with the family in its experiences, while restructuring the dysfunctional transactional patterns in order to change the family system. Altering the positions of different family members within the system produces a change in their subjective experiences and their problem-solving abilities as a family.[36]

Service Design

An intense involvement and alliance with a troubled family requires much time and emotional stamina on the part of a family worker. Therefore, service delivery centers around a caseload of four to five families per family worker. This allows for a weekly average of six hours direct service per family. However, the initial alliance-building requires much more time within the first two weeks, which is referred to as the observation phase.

The observation phase is crucial to the treatment program. It immediately follows an intake visit by the referring worker (if there is one), the in-home family service supervisor, and the assigned in-home family worker. The family worker arranges day and evening times with the family for the purpose of a two week, twenty-hour observation of family dynamics. It is usually opportune to arrange appointment times that coincide with the active periods of the family's everyday routines. This allows a more realistic assessment of their problem-solving abilities and the implication of treatment possibilities. Naturally, the initial stages of these two weeks are seemingly artificial, with some families presenting a somewhat rose-colored image of their home life. However, patterns of interaction remain the same, even though content issues may be restrained in intensity. Also, with the family worker assuming an indirect stance within the home, the family often assesses the worker as less threatening perhaps than previous professional helpers. This is an asset, as it lays the groundwork for a potential alliance with the family.[37,38]

The family worker then proceeds to write a detailed family assessment covering important treatment concerns including marital subsystem functioning, parental subsystem functioning, children subsystem functioning, socioeconomic functioning, family relationships (alliances and splits), communication patterns, and conflict resolution styles. A summary and recommendation section is detailed, outlining long-range, general goals for family treatment. These goals may include the addition of a homemaker, marriage or family therapist, tutor, day care services, etc., all of whose efforts would be coordinated by the family worker.[39,40] Additionally, for those families where a member has already been placed outside the home, a goal may involve the eventual return of that member to the home. This necessitates coordinated objectives which often are directed by the family worker, yet stressing shared interactions between the family and the child placement workers.

After presenting the assessment in case conference for comments and suggestions by remaining in-home staff, the family worker shares with the family a treatment plan which is specified and reassessed thereafter on monthly intervals by the worker. The family worker's direct involvement, beyond that of coordinating any appropriate auxiliary services, includes supportive counseling, teaching alternative parenting skills, and serving as a family advocate within the community.

Working intensively with family dyadic and triadic communication patterns is a continual counseling responsibility for the family worker. Problem behavior is regarded by the worker as symptomatic of the family system's dysfunctional patterns of interacting.[41] Therefore, treatment efforts are directed toward restructuring boundaries and patterns within the family, as well as between the family and environmental systems.

Evaluation

As with any new program, the evaluative measures are in a trial stage. Nevertheless, there are certain standards that already appear to be advantageous for this in-home family service program.

Monthly goal sheets are devised for each family. These entail earmarking two or three specific behavior changes which are referrents to the more general goals and objectives established within the family assessment. Monthly goals are subdivided into short-range and long-range goals, the latter considered within a time frame of one month. These short- and long-range goals are scored, following the target date, on a five-point scale:

1 = Little or no progress toward goal
2 = Partial progress toward goal
3 = Substantial progress toward goal
4 = Goal attained
5 = Goal exceeded

Efforts at measuring overall treatment performance with a terminated client family are still in process. The program uses a goal attainment sheet to rate general behavioral gains for adults within a family, though not necessarily just the parents. This sheet, unlike the monthly goal sheets, is filled out following the family assessment and is not scored until the family terminates with in-home service.[42] In addition to the goal attainment sheet, a six-month follow-up phone call or home visit is planned for each terminated family to obtain a status check on the original presenting problems. Additional evaluative steps are expected to be developed in accordance with the securing of funding contracts.

Clients

A family may begin in-home service either through a self-referral or referral by a community agency. If a family is being referred by another agency, it is important that the referring agency prepare the family regarding what in-home service entails. In-home service is regarded as a voluntary service, with the family and family worker possessing the mutual right to terminate service either when the presenting problems are resolved or when the service seems to be at an impasse. The voluntary aspect of this service is often difficult for families and/or referring agencies to adjust to readily. Nevertheless, it has proven, even in court-related cases, to be an asset for the family worker and the client family.

Referrals are appropriate in most cases. The primary criterion that is restrictive is that the family not be presently involved with other in-home family treatment services. What constitutes a family is relatively flexible for this program. As long as there is at least one adult and one child under eighteen years of age living together, that arrangement is considered a family system.

Throughout the period under discussion, from late June 1977 to December 1977, a total of twenty-six families were served. Three families terminated service during the observation and assessment phase, prior to direct treatment. One family left the state concurrent to the completion of a family assessment. Two other families terminated services after three months, with substantial progress made toward the goals established during assessment. The remaining twenty families continued in direct service.

The families served contained a total of forty-three adults and eighty-nine children. Six of the children were in placements prior to in-home family service. Of these twenty-six high risk families, 46 percent of the families were functioning at such a level that if no positive changes occurred in the family, at least one and possibly several of the children in the family had been identified for potential placement. During the six-month period, six were removed for either institutional or foster care.

It has been estimated that the cost of placement to Iowa taxpayers for all twenty-six children earmarked initially as potential placements (9 foster care, 8 group care, 9 residential or institutional care) for one year would be about 332 thousand dollars. On the other hand, in-home intervention on a preventive basis for those twelve families for a year (assuming the family service continued that long) would be about 4,000 dollars per family or a total of 48,000 dollars. While costs would vary somewhat according to the particular needs of a family, these figures demonstrate what the cost might be to maintain an intact family unit and to help develop the ability of that family to function adequately on an independent basis.

Conclusion

For years, human service agencies and professionals have labored to serve clients and their families. Only recently, however, has the trend turned toward aiding the entire family unit, within its ecosystem, in a rehabilitative and preventive manner. The development of in-home family treatment services appear to be a successful modality for counseling troubled youth and families that have incurred the myths of their communities. Provided referring agencies do not ignore the coordinated effort necessary to help dysfunctional families, it may be possible to someday diminish the high number of high risk, multiproblem families that exist in urban centers. The future for this change appears promising.

REFERENCES

1. Janchill, M. P.: Systems concepts in casework theory and practice. *Social Casework, 50*:75-82, 1969.
2. Orcutt, B. A.: Casework intervention and the problems of the poor. *Social Casework, 54*:85-95, 1973.
3. Mostwin, D.: Multidimensional model of working with the family. *Social Casework, 55*:209-215, 1974.
4. Ishisaka, H. A.: *Alternative to Foster Care: Evaluation Report.* Seattle, Seattle Indian Center, 1975.
5. Cohn, M. and Ewalt, P. L.: An intensive program for severely disturbed children. *Social Casework, 56*:337-342, 1975.
6. The National Research Council: *Toward a National Policy for Children and Families.* Washington, National Academy of Sciences, 1976.
7. Reynolds, M. K. and Crymes, J. T.: A Survey of the use of family therapy by caseworkers. *Social Casework, 51*:76-81, 1970.
8. Wells, R. A.; Dilkes, T. C.; and Trivelli, N.: The results of family therapy: a critical review of the literature. *Family Process, 11*:189-207, 1972.
9. Bell, J. E.: Family context therapy: a model for family change. *J Marriage Family Counseling, 4*:111-126, 1978.
10. Davis, T. S. et al.: *Recovery for the Alcoholic Mother and Family Through Home-Based Intervention.* Washington, Am Psychol, 1976.
11. Umbarger, C.: The paraprofessional and family therapy. *Family Process, 11*:147-162, 1972.
12. Epstein, N. and Shainline, A.: Paraprofessional parent-aides and disadvantaged families. *Social Casework, 55*:230-236, 1974.
13. Curtis, J. H. and Miller, M. E.: An argument for the use of

paraprofessional counselors in premarital and marital counseling. *Family Coordinator, 25*:47-50, 1976.

14. Meyerstein, I.: Family therapy training for paraprofessionals in a community mental health center. *Family Process, 16*:477-494, 1977.

15. Nelsen, J. C.: Dealing with resistance in social work practice. *Social Casework, 56*:587-592, 1975.

16. Fizdale, R.: Peer group supervision. *Social Casework, 39*:443-450, 1958.

17. Cohen, M. W.; Gross, S. J.; and Turner, M. B.: A note on a developmental model for training family therapists through group supervision. *J Marriage and Family Counseling, 2*:48, 1976.

18. Haley, J.: *Strategies of Psychotherapy*. New York, Grune, 1963.

19. Selig, A. L.: The myth of the multiproblem family. *Am J of Orthopsychiatry, 46*:526-532, 1976.

20. Minuchin, S.: *Families and Family Therapy*. Cambridge, Harvard U Pr, 1974.

21. Aponte, H. J.: Underorganization in the poor family. In Guerin, P. (Ed.): *Family Therapy: Theory and Practice*. New York, Gardner, 1976.

22. Hoover, C. F.: The embroiled family: a blueprint for schizophrenia. *Family Process, 4*:291-310, 1965.

23. Hoffman, L. and Long, L.: A systems dilemma. *Family Process, 8*:212-234, 1969.

24. Auerswald, E. H.: Families, change and the ecological perspective. In Ferber, A.; Mendelsohn, M.; and Napier, A. (Eds.): *The Book of Family Therapy*. New York, Aronson, 1972.

25. Mannino, F. V. and Shore, M. L.: Ecologically oriented family intervention. *Family Process, 11*:499-504, 1972.

26. King, C.: Family therapy with the deprived family. *Social Casework, 48*:203-208, 1967.

27. Johnson, J. T.: A truancy program: the child welfare agency and the school. *Child Welfare, 55*:573-580, 1976.

28. Speck, R. and Rueveni, V.: Network therapy: a developing concept. *Family Process, 8*:182-191, 1969.

29. Kerr, M. E.: The importance of the extended family. In Andres, F. O. and Lorio, J. P. (Eds.): *Georgetown Family Symposium: A Collection of Papers*. Washington, Georgetown U Pr, 1972.

30. Collins, A. H. and Pancoast, D. L.: *Natural Helping Networks: A Strategy for Prevention*. Washington, Nat Assn Soc Wkrs, 1976.

31. Tolsdorf, C. C.: Social networks, support, and coping: an exploratory study. *Family Process, 15*:407-418, 1976.

32. Rueveni, V.: Family network intervention: mobilizing support for families in crisis. *Int J Family Counseling, 5*:77-83, 1977.

33. Minuchin, S.; Montalvo, B.; Guerney, B. G.; Rosman, B. L.; and Schumer, F.: *Families of the Slums: An Exploration of Their Structure and Treatment*. New York, Basic, 1967.

34. Camp, H.: Structural family therapy: an outsider's perspective. *Family*

Process, 12:269-277, 1973.
35. Foley, V. D.: Alcoholism and couple counseling. In Stahmann, R. F. and Hiebert, W. J.: *Klemer's Counseling in Marital and Sexual Problems,* 2nd ed. Baltimore, Williams & Wilkins, 1977.
36. McAdoo, J. L.: *Family Therapy in the Black Community.* Washington, Am Orthopsychiatric Assn, 1976.
37. Lance, E. A.: Intensive work with a deprived family. *Social Casework, 50*:454-460, 1969.
38. Moynihan, S. K.: Home visits for family treatment. *Social Casework, 55*:612-617, 1974.
39. Cassert, H. P.: Homemaker service as a component of casework. *Social Casework, 51*:533-543, 1970.
40. Barnes, G. B.: Chabon, R. S.; and Hertzberg, L. J.: Team treatment for abusive families. *Social Casework, 55*:600-611, 1974.
41. Avery, N. C.: Viewing child abuse and neglect as symptoms of family dysfunctioning. In Abeling, N. B. and Hills, D. A. (Eds.): *Child Abuse: Intervention and Treatment.* Acton, Publishing Sci, 1975.
42. Justice, B., and Justice, R.: *The Abusing Family.* New York, Human Sci Pr, 1976.

Chapter 26

HOME-BASED SERVICES TO PROTECTIVE SERVICE FAMILIES

Ann Tuszynski and James Dowd

Introduction

DURING the past ten years there has been an increasing awareness regarding the scope, nature, and dynamics of child maltreatment, and a greater demand to define more accurately the components of the maltreated child syndrome. Historically, a dichotomy has existed in the theory proposed to explain the etiology of child maltreatment. Definitions of this maltreatment have attempted to separate abuse from neglect in terms of both parent and child personalities, and economic and social class. Polansky attempts to define the distinctions between abuse and neglect, and feels that "Identification and proof . . . (of child abuse and neglect) . . . demand quite different criteria."[1] He further states that neglectful parents do not willfully hurt their children nor keep them isolated from the greater society. Polansky summarizes by hypothesizing that abusive and neglectful parents have differing personality structures. In her classic study, Leontine Young reported on marked differences between the abusive and neglectful parents. Her research led her to state that maltreated children for the most part are either abused or neglected: "The two (abuse and neglect) do not generally go together."[2] Testimony before the Subcommittee on Children and Youth in 1973 which preceded the Child Abuse Prevention and Treatment Act focused in part on the difficulties inherent in such a dichotomous approach: "The concept of abuse is subject to varying interpretations, ranging from serious, intentional, physical damage of the child by the parent to parental inability to provide basic care and protection for the child. This confusion is reflected in the definitions of

296

child abuse which appear in the statutes which have been enacted in all 50 states."[3] Perhaps the New York City Mayor's Task Force on Child Abuse and Neglect summarized the difficulties best through their statement: "The line dividing abuse and neglect is a precarious one at best."[3]

In moving towards a more functional treatment it is more productive to suggest a continuum, a spectrum of child maltreatment. Fontana states: "Any treatment by which a child's potential development is retarded or completely suppressed, by mental, emotional or physical suffering, is maltreatment, whether it is negative (as in deprivation of emotional or material needs) or positive (as in verbal abuse or battering)."[4] The Family Life Center's treatment program is based on the notion that child maltreatment is a continuum, and that personality types of parents who mistreat their children are similar and do not in practice lend themselves to exacting definitions. By structuring a treatment modality that does not attempt such definitive labeling an atmosphere is created where the focus is on the family system.

Scope

Fontana estimates that 1.5 million children are maltreated annually with 50,000 expected to die as a result. A 1975 report by the American Humane Association in a survey of twenty-nine states estimates a total of 290,000 reported cases of maltreatment involving 304,000 children.[5] Using various actual and estimated figures, between 19,000 and 24,000 children are subjected to maltreatment in New Jersey annually.[6] These statistics reveal the inconsistencies apparent in the various reporting systems. These numbers, however, indicate a problem of massive and growing dimensions: "The problem (of child maltreatment) has often been compared to an iceberg; reported cases account for the visible tip, but estimates suggest a problem of staggering proportions yet to be revealed.[3]

Present Management

Presently, the case management of child maltreatment consists of varying services: homemaker services, public health nurses, day care, referral to private mental health facilities, hospital emergency rooms; and as a base, supervision through an overloaded public agency caseload. Where multidisciplinary teams exist, they often lack alternative resources indicated for the enormity and complexity of the problem. This approach is all too frequently scattered, and often the emphasis in treatment is on only certain individual family members. Perhaps the most damaging aspect of such an approach is the deemphasis of family life. The importance of the strengths and supports of the family unit tend to be overlooked; individual pathology is emphasized with little attention focused on intrafamilial pathology.

> Child . . . (maltreatment) . . . requires a systems approach for several reasons: . . . the entire family is involved, not just a mother, father or some other caretaker who deliberately injures a child. The father, mother, child and the environment — all play a part. The interlocking symbiosis that develops between spouses and child can be understood and broken up only through a systems approach.[7]

The family is assigned the major responsibility for inculcating values, mores, and roles, as well as providing nurturance, structuring personality, and transmitting essential adaptive techniques.[8] The protective service family tends to encounter difficulty with these functions. One of the primary factors preventing protective service families from performing these vital functions is their emotional and social isolation from a supportive family network.[9] As Polansky has detailed, a desire to be helped, some notion of the kind of help wanted, an ability to express oneself, and some willingness to form a dependent relationship all are prerequisites in the traditional service approach.[1] A frequently encountered difficulty with protective service families is their inability to establish a therapeutic relationship necessary to effect change.

The Family Life Center was established to provide treatment approaches that would focus on maintaining the family unit and to share the responsibility of seeking help.

History

The basic concepts of the Family Life Center treatment program grew out of experiences in a public child welfare agency, the New Jersey Division of Youth and Family Services. An experimental group was established in an attempt to provide a modality that would be free of the problems previously mentioned. The impetus for establishing this experimental group was the attempt to better utilize the worker's time and to closely examine the feasibility of group work treatment. An additional concern was that protective service children under the age of five were not receiving adequate therapeutic treatment through referral to day care centers. These centers were not equipped to meet the special needs of maltreated children. In addition, no special mental health programs existed for preschool maltreated children. The lack of these needed services and the uncoordinated approach resulted in the intrafamilial and interfamilial pathology being untreated.

Based on these considerations, the local district office of the New Jersey Division of Youth and Family Services established a group of six mothers and their preschool children which met in the basement of a local church once a week. This experience provided several different results from those expected. Observation revealed that more regular and intensive treatment was required since the children displayed both marked developmental delays and severe emotional problems. Group therapy with protective service parents seemed to be an integral part of successful treatment but here also more involvement was required. The experience indicated the need for a more holistic environment which could provide an array of unfragmented services to the family as a unit.

A proposal for such an approach was submitted and favorably reviewed by the state central office; however, the funds necessary to implement a project of this scope were not available within the local office system. It was suggested that an alliance be made with private social service providers who would be eligible for Title XX funds. Serendipitously, contact was made with Family Service Association of Atlantic County. Family Services was interested in expanding its services to include a clientele that at that time was not being served. A unique partnership developed between the Division of Youth and Family Services and Family Service Association, which combined varied talents and expertise in the final and successful proposal for the Family Life Center. Historically, there did not exist any great degree of cooperation between the public and private arena within this county. Only through compromise, cooperation, and the willingness not to battle over *turf*, this needed and nontraditional program developed.

Funding for the Center during the initial year was 250 thousand dollars, a combination of Title XX monies, local Board of Freeholders match, New Jersey Social Service incentive monies, and State Bureau of Day Care funds. Due to these funding patterns the Center's fiscal and service responsibilities were split between two major state bureaus which caused major administrative problems. Each bureau was essentially autonomous, with its own legal mandates, guidelines, and policies. Policies at many times contradicted each other. The uniqueness of the treatment approach encouraged these bureaus to be more flexible than usual, and in several instances they made exceptions to their own policies. Much time was spent in education and sensitization of individuals within the state's bureaucracy to the special needs of these protective service families. After the first year it became apparent that splitting the funding between two bureaus was not administratively feasible.

Present funding is a combination of Title XX monies, administered through the State's Purchase of Service Unit; Child Nutrition monies from the Department of Education; New Jersey Social Service Incentive monies; and local Atlantic County government match monies. These funds provide a total operating budget of 165 thousand dollars per year, and the accompanying program proposal must be renegotiated annually. Alternative funding mechanisms which would provide more long term stability, flexibility, and research are continually being investigated.

Program

The purpose of the Family Life Center is to develop and strengthen family life of protective service families. The overall goal is to offer rehabilitative and preventive services to parents while caring for and promoting the development of their children so that the family unit can be maintained. The program attempts to help parents learn about child development and growth and gain parenting skills through educational and therapeutic experiences in order to change their parenting behavior. The Center offers services to the parent to develop his or her own self-concept and interpersonal skills, to increase the capacity to cope and adjust to environmental and family pressures, and to learn to use community resources and institutions. Underlying each activity and objective is the more general goal of maintaining the family unit, through the prevention of removal of the child.

The structure of the Center's program is based on a notion that one of the primary determinants in child maltreatment is the inability of the isolated parent to establish a supportive network of relationships. This dysfunctional pattern of relating is not only damaging to the children within the system, it also appears to be cyclical in nature: the child continues the destructive pattern in the next generation. Young makes the point that protective service families do not effectively support each member, especially during times of crisis:[10]

> The effects of this lack of support are demonstrated most vividly during times of family stress, i.e., birth of a child, death of a parent or close relative, major illness, unemployment, or the termination of a relationship. During these life crises neglectful and/or abusive parents become immobilized, then frustrated, which often leads to violent behavior with the child being the easiest target for misplaced feelings.[9]

Fontana described relationship problems as stemming from the parent being untrusting, immature, and isolated which results in the parent having enormous difficulties relating to other significant adults, as well as to their children. Justice and

Justice found that the majority of the protective service parents have very little positive contact with their immediate family. In order to change this dysfunctional pattern the Center confronts this method of relating, while simultaneously aiding in the establishment of a nonisolating supportive network. This is a very difficult task since it means changing ingrained behavioral patterns.

The initial confrontation of the isolation is accomplished through the Center's transportation system. To ensure program participation as well as aiding the client in the helping process, the Center maintains two vehicles with trained staff who go directly to the home to pick up the families and assist in preparing the children. Many authors in this area, including Steele, Alexander, Justice, Bean, and Polansky, point out that protective service parents are distrustful, suspicious, emotionally needy, and impulsive, with very little ability to delay gratification. Because of these factors clients rarely successfully use agency services: *reaching out* must be an integral component of the agency's services. The Center's transportation system is the first step in this effort of asking for help.

The Family Life Center is housed in one building and is designed to offer services to thirty families with thirty-five preschool children. The children from six weeks to five years of age are placed in three classrooms based on their ages. A staff ratio of one adult to four children is maintained in each classroom. In most situations the children attend the Center five days a week, six hours a day (the parents are required to attend twelve hours weekly and children thirty hours a week), while a milieu is established in which the family is exposed to alternative methods of relating, positive role models, and a different type of support system. The Center operates on an open system which fosters much formal and informal interaction between staff and families, between families and families, and between parents and children. The focus on openness and interacting confronts the dysfunctional patterns of behavior. The strength of this approach is that treatment is not confined to formal sessions.

Formal treatment for the parents consists of group therapy, parenting training classes, socialization therapy, basic education, and home management classes. All treatment is provided in groups with the underlying goal of promoting a positive social network, establishing guidelines for appropriate social behavior, and also confronting intrapsychic pathology. The parenting training class is directed by a psychiatric nurse who provides a classroom forum for the discussion of child development and particular childhood behavior problems that a parent may have encountered. This class provides the parent with the opportunity to discuss problems that commonly occur in raising children. Emphasis in this class as well as others is placed on the parent expressing him or herself on a feeling level, as well as strengthening individual egos. The socialization therapy is conducted by an experienced social worker who encourages the parents to express themselves in concrete, socially acceptable ways. The emphasis within this group is on completing tasks, working together, and experiencing the enjoyment of success through guided group interaction. The formal group therapy sessions are focused on confronting the strong denial system that most clients utilize as a defense mechanism and are led by the Center director and assistant director, both social workers.

The primary emphasis in these sessions is on supporting the client, while at the same time producing a level of anxiety which is necessary for change. This process is facilitated through the use of male and female cotherapists. A nonviolent relationship between the male and female therapists establishes an empathic relationship as a possible alternative, exhibits positive role models, and also provides an outlet for transference of unresolved emotional issues. This at times places the therapists in the roles of father or mother, and the strong accompanying feelings associated with these figures are allowed to be expressed.

The treatment program is geared to be flexible around the client's needs and includes couples therapy, family therapy, and individual play therapy for very disturbed children. Such special needs are diagnosed during the initial evaluation session which is conducted by the Center's team. The team completes an evaluation consisting of social history, psychiatric evaluation, psychological testing, and developmental scaling for the child or the Learning Accomplishment Profile. The team provides training and support to other staff members, including a certified early childhood education teacher, seven teacher aides, a cook, a bus driver, and a secretary. The director and assistant director are responsible for the administration of the Center as well as coleading group therapy.

While the parent is involved in treatment, the Center plays an important role in the child's growth and development. The children's program, housed in the same building as the adult program, is a fulltime therapeutic day care center. The children tend to show behavior which is very withdrawn or overactive. They may be distrustful of their new environment and many times are violent in their responses to both staff and other children. Besides requiring protection, these children are in need of stimulation, affection, limit setting, structure, self-expression, and perhaps most importantly, the freedom to just be children.

The program is structured to correct some of the developmental lags and inappropriate social functioning by exposing the children to adult direction and interaction that is different from that experienced in their homes. A gentle, supportive, and firm adult can help a child learn to deal with life's situations, to develop a positive self-image, and to accept limits set by staff and later by parents. Sometime during the treatment process, usually in the seventh month, the parent is placed in the classroom to work alongside staff. A prescription is completed by the child therapist on the Center's team detailing the child's needs and prescribing specific joint activities of parent and child. The head teacher continues the prescriptions daily when the parent is not in the classroom. This approach allows the parent an opportunity to observe and experiment with different modes of parent-child interaction. These sessions are generally quite intense for parents because the atmosphere fostered in the classroom usually is in direct contrast to, and in conflict with, their own methods of discipline and basic attitudes about children. Following this half day in integrated classroom experience, the parents are involved in group therapy. These sessions provide a structured outlet for discussion and ventilation of feelings and experiences of the morning activities.

In addition to the therapeutic specialized day care setting, the Center also provides a number of auxiliary services. The head teacher schedules weekly visits to the pediatrician, which focus on teaching the parents the importance of regular health care, while at the same time helping the parent ask pertinent questions of the pediatrician. The head teacher acts as a role model in the doctor's office, and also insures that the child receives medical care. Particularly disturbed children are closely evaluated by the team's child therapist and an appropriate schedule of play therapy is begun by the therapists and continued by classroom personnel. A number of children have speech problems: under the head teacher's guidance, the parent and child are accompanied to a speech therapy clinic for evaluation and treatment. As with the medical program described above, the parent is supported throughout the process and encouraged to question the treatment. Following the team's initial evaluation, a small percentage of children are referred for complete medical and neurological evaluations to rule out any organic impairment. No attempt was made to provide these auxiliary services in the Center; although it is more time-consuming to accompany parents to these services, the parent learns how to utilize local community resources. By learning to deal effectively with these service systems the parents gain confidence in their own abilities while receiving much needed services for their children.

Summary

By creating a setting that is predictable and dependable, the Center offers the child and parent a feeling of security through availability and consistency of staff. We have observed personal growth in both the parents and the children. This growth is more apparent with the children, who quickly respond to the warmth and gentleness of the staff. The change in parental behavior is more difficult to gauge and at times is nonexistent. Most parents, however, do eventually accept the need for change. This change does not imply achievement of the middle class notion of the "good" parent. Life does become more safe for the children and overt child maltreatment ceases.

The first two years of operation of the Center have demonstrated that this type of program meets needs that traditional approaches do not. These comprehensive services offered to protective service families are an alternative to the destructive and damaging effects of child removal, and emphasize the maintenance of the family unit within the home.

REFERENCES

1. Polansky, Norman; DeSaix, Christine; and Sharlin, Shlomo: *Child Neglect: Understanding and Reaching the Parent.* New York, Child Welfare, 1972.
2. U. S. Senate, Committee on Labor and Public Welfare, Subcommittee on Children and Youth: *Child Abuse Prevention Act, 1973. Hearings.* Washington, Govt Print Office, 1973.
3. U. S. Department of Health, Education and Welfare, Office of Child Development, Children's Bureau/National Center on Child Abuse and Neglect: *Child Abuse and Neglect: The Problem and Its Management.* Washington, Govt Print Office, 1975.
4. Fontana, Vincent: *Somewhere A Child Is Crying.* New York, Macmillan, 1974.
5. U. S. Department of Health, Education and Welfare, Office of Child Development, Children's Bureau/National Center on Child Abuse and Neglect: *Child Abuse and Neglect Reports.* Washington, Govt Print Office, 1977.
6. New Jersey, Department of Human Services, Division of Youth and Family Services, Bureau of Research: *Child Abuse and Neglect in New Jersey.* Trenton, State Print Office, 1977.
7. Justice, Blair and Justice, Rita: *The Abusing Family.* New York, Human Sci Pr, 1976.
8. Lidz, Theodore: *The Person.* New York, Basic, 1968.
9. Tuszynski, Ann and Dowd, James: An alternative approach to the treatment of protective service families. *Social Casework,*

59:175-179, 1978.
10. Young, Leontine: An interim report on an experimental program of protective service. *Child Welfare, 45*:373-374, 1966.

SECTION IV
Research

Chapter 27

RESEARCH OBJECTIVES OF IN-HOME INTERVENTION

Patricia Cautley

THE purpose of the research to be described here is to permit a systematic examination of a specific kind of work with families in an attempt to determine its value, both in terms of the human beings involved and also in terms of understanding of the process. Do the findings, or hypotheses, or hunches based on the work add to understanding of work with children and families? Are they helpful in pointing the way to more fruitful approaches with highly dysfunctional families? These and many other questions may appropriately be raised. Finally, if found to have positive value, are these methods replicable?

Description of Project

Project OPT, a shorthand title for "Facilitating Long Term Optional Planning for Children," is one of eleven projects supported by a grant (90-C-996) from the National Center for Child Advocacy, Children's Bureau, Department of Health, Education and Welfare, to the Wisconsin Department of Health and Social Services for two years, ending in September 1978. These projects are focused on the importance of permanent planning for children because of the national concern for the number of children *in limbo* in foster care, a focus receiving particular impetus from the Oregon Project, "Freeing Children for Permanent Placement," in which it was found possible to make permanent plans for about three-fourths of some 500 children adrift in foster care.[1]

Our project is one of two concentrating on problems at one

311

end of the continuum; that is, on keeping children in their own homes whenever possible, rather than risking the problems created by removal to substitute care. At the same time, however, the goal of maintaining the natural family intact is regarded as appropriate only if this family is able to provide an adequate environment for the health, growth, and development of the child. The goal of our work, then, could be stated as working to provide a permanent plan for each child, in the natural family if possible. If not, serious consideration is given to cooperating with the agency involved to work toward other permanent plans.

Families meeting the following criteria may be referred by a helping professional:

1. There are problems in parent-child interaction such that eventual removal of the child(ren) is judged likely if no changes are made.
2. The child, or the oldest of a group of siblings involved, should be no older than twelve years, and preferably younger. Occasional exceptions are made, but the problems of teenagers per se are regarded as beyond the scope of this project.

The first stage of work involves a contract, in which the family agrees to be interviewed with every member present, and to permit project staff to observe interaction in the home three times, each lasting for about an hour and a half.[2] This information comprises the *baseline data*. It is studied carefully and summarized in a report to be presented to and discussed with the family in a feedback session. Included are statements of the family's strengths, of the areas needing change, and of specific goals or treatment. The format, amount of detail, and degree of specificity presented to the family may vary. An agreement is worked out with the family as to the time and frequency of contacts. Except when court-ordered, participation is voluntary.

All work is done in the home, with an average of three contacts a week for an hour and a half each, generally at a time when the parents and children are present. It is made clear to the family at the beginning that our involvement, excluding

Table 27-I

OBJECTIVES OF BASELINE DATA AND SOURCES OF INFORMATION

Source	Objectives
Parent(s)	Parenting each has experienced in terms of: Discipline / Willingness of parent to explain reasons to child / Praise / Affection
	Current relationship with parents (if living) and with siblings
	Perceptions of self and of each other member of family in terms of: What is especially liked / What is disturbing or of concern
Parent(s) and Child(ren)	Perceptions of main problems of family in terms of: When they began / What seemed to account for their beginning / What has been tried, reasons for effectiveness or lack of effectiveness
	Others outside the family each likes to spend time with, can depend on in a crisis
	Observed interaction in terms of: Written descriptions, in 5 or 10 minute segments, in which the behavior of one family member is the focus. Precise counts, for 5 or 10 minute segments, of specified behavior of parent(s) interacting with one child, and of specified behavior of child (Fahl, 1978)
Child(ren)	Report of expression of feelings in the family; do family members show when they are angry, sad, happy?
Agency records	History of family's contact with agency; past experiences of members of family related to present status and problems; other resources with which family has had experience
Agency records and parents	Demographic data including education level, work history, changes in family composition

the baseline data collection period, will be limited to a period of eight to twelve weeks. from these characteristics the description of our method is derived: Intensive In-Home Intervention. This time limit was initially necessitated by the length of the grant, just one year, with no expectation of renewal. With the extension to a second year, however, there was merit in continuing to test the effectiveness of such short-term intervention. There is no doubt that it places pressure on the staff, and often the client, to work hard.

A team of two staff members works with a family in most instances. This has many advantages, not the least of which are the benefits of two differing perspectives, points of view, ways of relating, and sets of skills.

The model developed for intervention has drawn very heavily on that used by the Home and Community Treatment staff at Mendota Mental Health Institute because of its emphasis on the total setting in which the child is living and functioning.[2] Project OPT also uses a systems approach, with emphasis on examining the interactions among all members of the family unit and with significant persons outside the unit. The focus of training depends upon the needs of the particular family and the problems they perceive, as well as on the staff's evaluation of the interaction. There is a strong behavioral component, that is, examining the behavior of the child in terms of the antecedents and the consequences and introducing change by altering one of these components. Specific parenting methods are taught. The goal of treatment is an attempt to reverse the negative relationships between parent(s) and child(ren) and help parents develop more positive and constructive feelings and attitudes toward their children. Learning to play with each other and to enjoy this is often one of the goals. Methods of family therapy and counseling are used when appropriate, and in addition, the staff perform many facilitative functions. One of the most important has been to bring together all of the agencies involved with a given family so that there is a clearer understanding of the role of each and closer cooperation and consistency in treatment. Contact is maintained with the worker having primary responsibility for the family so that this person will be in a position at the end of treatment to help maintain the progress made.

When treatment ends, the family is again interviewed, by a staff member not on the treatment team, and three observations are again made. More will be said later about the several kinds of evaluations obtained at this time. Contacts with the family are tapered off and do not end suddenly. Occasional contacts may continue for several months.

Research Goals and Methods

A basic question to be answered is whether our intervention has facilitated or maximized the possibility of permanent plans for the children involved. This is the question of the *outcome*, the *effects* of our intervention, or the assessment of the *dependent variable*. In such a complex matter as parent-child interaction, it may seem foolhardy to attempt such an answer, and we do not claim confidence in accomplishing this. However, various kinds of evidence related to the following questions are being collected. When taken together, they may be expected to provide a general assessment of the outcome.

1. Did the family continue in treatment for the specified period? Out of the first eighteen families served, five dropped out before treatment was expected to end. In every instance, this appears to have occurred because of their unwillingness to change, which occasionally was openly verbalized, but more often was covertly revealed by behavior such as failure to keep appointments. In two of these instances, termination of parental rights seemed to the staff to be an appropriate course of action, with the record of our attempted work providing one kind of evidence useful to the agency. If pursued, this could be considered as a significant step toward permanent planning for the child.

2. Of the families which continued treatment for the expected period of time, what evidence is there that permanent plans were facilitated? This could mean either preservation of the intact family or resort to termination of parental rights. Clearly this is a question which requires longitudinal study.

Assessment at the End of Treatment

The following indications of outcome or responsiveness to treatment are being obtained:

1. *Systematic observations of interaction within the family.* These data will be compared with those obtained initially — the descriptive data compared qualitatively in terms of positive and negative aspects of interaction and the objective data, consisting of counts of specific behaviors on the part of the parent interacting with each child, will be analyzed by an analysis of variance to see if there is a statistically significant difference between the initial and final observations.[3]

2. *Comparison of ratings made by the treatment team at the beginning and end of treatment on a Family Rating Scale.* The two members of the team independently complete this scale, then discuss their ratings if not in perfect agreement and agree on a joint rating. The following characteristics are assessed on five-point scales, each point described verbally:

   a. Life maintenance of physical nurturance — maximum rating given to the family judged not deficient in providing enough food, clothing, shelter, and hygiene or health care to sustain life at a healthy level.

   b. Emotional nurturance of the children by the parents — extent to which the parents have warm positive interaction with each child and demonstrate recognition of the child's separateness and worth.

   c. Cognitive development of children — extent to which a positive and stimulating environment is provided by the family for each child.

   d. Socialization of children — extent to which an environment is provided for socializing the children at appropriate levels for age and development, rated on a four-point scale.

   e. If more than one adult in the family, extent to which adults in the family support each other emotionally.

   Each child is rated individually. Changes in the ratings will be examined qualitatively, and an analysis of variance used to determine whether a statistically significant difference occurs between the two sets of ratings.

3. *Written responses by the treatment team,* which are part of a lengthy questionnaire regarding the status of the family at the end of treatment, regarding each of the treatment goals, the direction and extent of change, and judgment as to the likelihood that positive changes will be maintained. These goals are those stated at the beginning of treatment, reviewed after the first four weeks of treatment and amended or added to at that time. The limitations of analyzing such verbal statements, which may range from highly specific behavioral, operationally stated goals to more general statements, is recognized, but the complexity of the situation with which we are working would seem likely to be lost if structured checklists were depended upon. The overall judgment of the team, shown in Table 27-II, made independently of the evaluation of the specific goals, shows a high level of agreement thus far with a composite summary of changes indicated.

4. *Responses by the parents and children to a structured interview at the end of treatment* (conducted by a staff member not on the treatment team), including questions about the current strengths of the family, current problems, changes in the family during the period OPT staff was involved, changes made by individual members, and attitudes toward the treatment team members and the ways in which they tried to work with the family. The primary comparison will be made between the changes enumerated by the family with the goals of treatment listed by the staff; the closer the agreement, the more convincing the evidence of change.

5. A questionnaire, developed in the second year of the project, is now being sent to the ongoing professional involved with the family following their involvement with OPT to obtain the following information:

   a. Ratings on five-point scales comparing the family's current overall functioning, and also the environment they are currently providing for the healthy growth and development of the children with that which existed before treatment began.

Table 27-II

REASONS FOR REFERRAL RELATED TO OUTCOME OF TREATMENT

Reasons for Referral	Number of Cases	Treatment				
		Completed			Not Completed	
		Success*	Partial†	Not Successful	Dropped Out	In Process
Child(ren) uncontrollable or difficult	7	3	2			2
Child allegedly has been abused	3			1	1‡	1
Child shows delayed development	3	2			1	
Child evidences emotional disturbance	1		1			
Social worker concerned regarding signs of inadequate parenting	5			1‡	3§	1
Self-referral by parent aware of problems in interacting with child(ren)	3	2				1
Social worker concerned over extremely inadequate physical care	1		1			
Social worker concerned over mother's own problems and anticipated return of daughter from foster care	1					1
Totals	24	7 (10)‖	4	2	5	6

* Made significant changes in parenting behavior during treatment; expected to maintain these.
† Made significant changes in parenting behavior during treatment but staff not confident these will be maintained.
‡ Project data will be used in these two instances by agency to push for termination of parental rights.
§ Project data have been submitted as evidence for TPR but agency is not proceeding.
‖ Work toward permanent plans for this number of children has been judged effective.

b. A listing of the problems of the family, identified at the time of referral, and judgment on a seven-point scale as to whether any change, positive or negative, occurred during OPT's involvement, and, if so, the extent of change.

c. A listing of any other significant changes that occurred during OPT's involvement with the family, along with a rating of the direction and extent of change on a seven-point scale, and a statement of factors contributing to the changes.

d. An evaluation of other aspects of OPT's work judged helpful and not helpful.

Again, the extent of agreement between this information and that provided by the treatment team will be examined, and the overall direction of change summarized from the information given.

In the analysis of verbal statements, careful attention will be given to developing well-defined coding procedures with demonstrable reliability; that is, showing a high degree of agreement between two persons doing the analysis.

Follow-up at Six Month Intervals

We propose to follow each family at six-month intervals for eighteen months after the end of treatment, seeking other support to permit this after the project itself ends. The primary purpose is to determine the composition of the family at these points in time; that is, to learn whether any member has been removed to substitute care at any time and if so, for how long. This is the most *objective criterion* available. However, it is not necessarily adequate in itself, as removal could be in the best interests of the child, or the lack of removal could represent an absence of appropriate action. Therefore, other information will also be requested:

1. The family will be asked for an interview when six months have elapsed. In addition to questions about any changes, even temporary, in the composition of the family and the reasons therefore, they will be asked about the status of each

member and how they are getting along with each other, what they remember about OPT's working with them, an appraisal of whether it is regarded as helpful or not helpful, whether they are behaving any differently when problems come up than they did before OPT began, and whether special help has been requested from anyone. The family's evaluation of its status will be carefully compared with that provided by the ongoing professional, as well as with the earlier statement of goals and change.

2. The ongoing professional involved will be asked to make four ratings on five-point scales, comparing the family's current overall level of functioning, as well as the current environment provided for the healthy growth and development of the children, with the levels existing prior to the time treatment began, and at the time treatment ended. Comments are invited. The worker is also asked whether any aspects of OPTs work appear to be helpful or not helpful at the present time.

The same questionnaire will be sent to the ongoing professional involved with the family twelve and eighteen months after OPT treatment has elapsed. The principal difficulty anticipated with this kind of data collection involves changes in worker, as a worker unfamiliar with the family at the time of treatment could not make the comparative ratings.

Although the analysis of the detailed data in the interviews and questionnaires is not yet in process, an example can be provided of one way in which the outcome of treatment may be examined (Table 27-II)

Factors Related to Outcome — The Independent Variables

Although the outcome of treatment may at first appear to be the most important research question, it quickly becomes apparent that unless something is learned about the variables related to different outcomes, the work will not have advanced understanding of either the families or the method, nor will replicability be encouraged. These variables fall into two general groups, the characteristics of the families involved and the characteristics of the treatment team and methods used in treatment.

The Characteristics of the Families

Information regarding the families is obtained primarily from the interview and from the records of the referring professional. The sources of information and the kinds of dimensions examined are summarized in Table 27-I. An underlying assumption is that the individual's primary learning about parenting is from his or her experience as a child of specific parents, and that it is essential to obtain some understanding of the experiences each of the parents we are working with have had. Ten out of the first eighteen mothers we have worked with have come from broken homes; a few spent part of their growing-up years in foster care.

A detail which has been particularly helpful in making treatment plans has been the answer given by each member to the question of what is especially liked about each member of the family, including the respondent himself. An indication of self-confidence or self-esteem, or the lack of it, may occur. Clues as to some of the values of the family may be given, such as emphasis on material goods or on personal relationships.

The demographic section of the interview provides the educational status and employment status of each individual. However, the lack of educational achievement of a parent gives only a rough indication of the level of ability of the person. There is some evidence that ability level may be a significant variable. Three of the mothers who dropped out of treatment appeared limited in ability, although only one had attended special classes in school. It is possible that emotional factors also contribute to the lack of adequate functioning, but we do not have adequate measures of this dimension.

The Characteristics of Treatment

Analyzing the characteristics and the process of treatment is without question the most challenging and difficult aspect of data analysis, as we do not know what are the significant dimensions of treatment nor how they may interact with the characteristics of the families.

A detailed description of every treatment session is written. This information can be analyzed in terms of the methods of teaching used: didactic training, including the provision of reading materials and exercises to be completed between sessions, modeling of desired behavior, coaching the parent, role-playing by treatment team or by family members, preparing charts for use by the family to record certain behaviors of parent or child or both, developing specific reward programs for either parent or child or both, and the like. The kinds of interaction encouraged by the team are noted, such as playing games. The number and length of treatment sessions is recorded. It seems quite possible, however, that there may be other important, perhaps very subtle, variables accounting for the relative effectiveness of treatment, such as the following:

1. whether participation was court-ordered or voluntary.
2. the kind of relationship developed between the treatment team, or one member, with family members. Although all members of the staff experienced the same training, there are doubtless differences in the personal characteristics and working styles of individuals on the staff.
3. the degree of confidence conveyed by the staff in the family's ability to change, evidenced in the effort put into treatment, the encouragement expressed, and the consistent working toward certain goals. For highly dysfunctional families, this may contrast markedly with the relative lack of confidence shown by some of the professionals with which they worked.

These are just some of the variables which we do not have appropriate techniques to measure or evaluate, although there may be some clues to be found in the detailed record of treatment, which hopefully may lead to the development of specific hypotheses.

Assessment of the Time-Limited Approach

Since a time-limited approach of eight to twelve weeks of intensive work is used with all families, there will be no evidence comparing its value with that of a longer period of work. However, this aspect is covered in the evaluation completed by the treatment team at the end of treatment; they are asked to make a judgment as to the appropriateness of the time period used. The current opinion of the staff is that the advantages of the time-limited approach could be retained if a family were informed at the beginning of treatment that the team will plan to work with them for eight to twelve weeks, and, if progress is continuing at that time, will continue working with them for additional periods of time if the family desires to do so and continues to make progress.

Value of Random Assignment of Cases

The most appropriate way of determining whether a given method is effective in treatment is to assign cases at random to a treatment and a control group. It is then possible to compare the status of the two groups, using whatever variables are appropriate to the particular goal of treatment, after certain intervals of time to see if the treatment group differs significantly from the control group. Our project began with such a design; all families referred were to be studied initially and baseline data collected for all, but only those designated for treatment were to receive feedback and intensive interaction. However, when referrals dropped to nearly zero for over a month, and we were forced to inquire as to the reasons, we found workers were reluctant to refer families in case they might be assigned to the control group. They did not want their families to miss treatment. Although it seemed possible to present the project to a family in such a way that they would be willing to participate and contribute to the understanding of similar families, we recognized that this experience, especially if added to other attempts to refer the family which had ended with no help being received, could be very undesirable for families. Since our need for referrals was paramount, and it seemed unlikely that an adequate number of referrals would be made if the control-treatment design were kept, this design was dropped. All families referred to the project are offered treatment.

Summary

In this research and demonstration project, the goal is not only to provide intensive in-home intervention to families referred because of problems in parent-child interaction but also to collect data to permit understanding and evaluation of both the process and outcome of such treatment. The methods of assessing the independent variables, the characteristics of the families and of the treatment, and the dependent variable of outcome of treatment have been described.

1. Emlen, Arthur et al.: *Overcoming Barriers to Planning for Children in Foster Care.* Portland, Regional Research Institute for Human Services, 1977.
2. Fahl, Mary Ann: Home-Community Treatment: The Mendota Model. Paper read at First National Symposium on Home-Based Services for Children and Their Families, Iowa City, Iowa, 24-26 April 1978.
3. Hayes, W.: *Statistics for Psychologists.* New York, H R & W, 1963.

Chapter 28

HOME-BASED CARE TO CHILDREN: HARMONIZING THE APPROACHES OF RESEARCH AND PRACTICE

LUDWIG GEISMAR

THE starting point of this chapter is a research project that fell short of expectations. Upon its completion, both the agency that sponsored the project and the researchers who were doing it felt disappointed, although the emotion had different reference points and led to different decisions with regard to publicizing findings. As a case study, this project represents a valuable learning experience, because the problems presented are fairly typical of such endeavors and invite thinking aimed at their solution.

The story of the study, summarized briefly, is as follows: This writer and a research colleague at Rutgers University Social Work Research Center were approached by a child care agency in the mid-Atlantic region to study the effectiveness of a new program in which children with a variety of social and emotional problems were treated in their homes. The agency, which had been using group and foster homes as the primary means of caring for children, was interested in the effectiveness of the alternative program that provided service to the children and their families.

The study sample was composed of ninety-seven children in fifty-seven families who had received between one and two years of service. About one-half the children and their families were in the home treatment group; the remainder were divided between a foster care (roughly one-third) and residence care (one-fifth) programs.

Measurement of the social functioning of the children by a specially devised instrument for role analysis, and of their families by the St. Paul Scale of Family Functioning, were obtained at intake and twenty-four months later, or at the point of termination if it occurred earlier. The change in scores for the three programs were then calculated and related to the type of program, as well as to some service variables.

The study revealed that few changes in social functioning by role or area of functioning reached statistical significance, though most leaned in a positive direction. Home treatment cases did show a change pattern comparable to cases in placement. The cost of home care was estimated at about 20 percent of that of the foster home service, but only 8 percent of the cost of the residential care program.[1]

The mixed reaction to this study on the part of the sponsoring agency and the Research Center flowed from essentially different sets of expectations. Both reveal orientations which are inherent in the task requirements of the respective organizations. The author can merely infer a point of view based on extensive collaboration and lengthy debate, in speech and writing, about the meaning of the study following its completion and cannot speak for the sponsoring agency. Both perspectives will be summarized and subsequently some of the major problems and possible solutions in this type of research will be analyzed.

The Agency Perspective

The agency is a reputable child care service with high professional standards. Its director and service supervisors are research oriented and have engaged in a number of collaborative research endeavors. Their request for an evaluation study of the in-home care program was based on a genuine desire to subject all their programs to an objective test of performance.

The agency was unsympathetic to an early research proposal that assignments to programs utilize one of several possible experimental designs which would assure comparability of subsamples. The objection rested on the contention that such a procedure would interfere with professional practice which bases assignment to one program or another on professional judgment. The agency believed an experimental approach would also delay the study and adversely affect funding.

Professional staff members and volunteers who took part in the study became readily attuned to the research procedures, which included abstracting and coding case record information, interviewing service personnel, and computer processing of data.

In like manner, the research findings themselves evoked a strong reaction from the organization. Both the director and senior associates felt that the findings did not properly reflect the good work that was being done. A request to check selected success cases against their respective quantitative data was carried out by the researchers and no discrepancies were found. That did not put to rest the agency's mistrust about the validity of the data. Questions were then raised about the competence of coders who were volunteers, but additional funds were not available for recoding all the data.

The agency was most distressed over the study's failure to show significant gains in any of the three programs. This result, they contended, cast doubts on the validity of the study, and they argued forcefully against publication of results.

The Researchers' Perspective

The researchers believed that their inability to use a true experimental design put limitations on the research project. They expressed hope that statistical controls would at least in part compensate for the absence of such preferred alternatives as case matching and/or random assignment to programs. They thought that the use of a control group would have strengthened the study immeasurably, but for budgetary reasons this alternative was never seriously considered.

The research team's reaction to the findings varied substantially with the agency's reaction. The researchers believed that overall findings were not out of line with those of similar studies,[2,3] and that in the absence of a control group, no conclusions could be drawn regarding the effectiveness of agency programs. The outcome was felt to be cause for neither pessimism nor optimism, but called for a variety of research approaches utilizing both experimental and field research models to determine the effectiveness of intervention. Similarity of results between the placement and home care programs impressed the researchers as a finding with important practice implications, because treatment in the home is widely held to be the preferred method of intervention and is also known to be much less costly than child placement.

Critique of the Study and Implications

Research on home-based services to children is handicapped by the lack of theory. Although a theoretical framework is not a necessary condition for pursuing systematic inquiries, its absence leaves the researcher without a firm base for postulating hypotheses within a broader context of knowledge building and for interpreting study findings.

Different modes of child care are favored by different societies because of ideological appropriateness rather than evidence of efficacy. Researchers take the method of care that is rooted in national or subcultural values as the focal point for their research and study that method itself or in relation to other methods viewed as less desirable. Research on child intervention programs, unlike child development research, has not been supported by psychological and sociological theories but has taken a more pragmatic approach rooted in the prevalent practice modalities. There are objective reasons for less emphasis on theory in practice research: practice has to confront problems as they arise, its academic roots are not as firm as those of child development, and its sponsors tend to take a guarded view of theory. There is little question but that this situation accounts for the ad hoc quality that characterizes the practice enterprise.

Granted that the lack of theory-based research is often a function of the training and subsequent orientation of those who design the study, equally important are those circumstances under which studies are formulated. Agencies and their collaborators, both academic and nonacademic, are generally thrust into the situation where the research mandate grows out of a program in process. This situation, and the attendant conditions of funding, impose deadlines which severely restrict the possibilities of drawing on the best scholarly resources for the study. To remedy this, long-range planning with professional programming guided by a careful review and analysis of the theoretical frameworks of the agency's treatment modalities is needed.

A second handicap of this study, as well as others reported in the literature, is the lack of fit between research problem and research design. Practice researchers are generally recruited from those academic disciplines which favor textbook approaches whose preferred mode of operation are experimental models of one sort or another. These models are generally poorly suited to the conditions of field research encountered in practical studies.

This is not to say that practice research has to reject experimental designs. The foregoing project could have been strengthened greatly by random assignment of children to the three treatment settings. Except in cases of extreme need or special pathology, the argument that any mode other than professional judgment of placing clients is injurious must be modified. Practice generally does not have enough valid knowledge about the effect of various types of placement to justify dogmatic adherence to "professional judgment." Beyond that, the moral issue revolving around the use of a pure control, nontreatment group does not arise in a comparative design such as was employed in our child care study which precluded denial of treatment to any child or family.

Undoubtedly, field conditions rarely provide suitable settings for pure experimental design models. This recognition, neither new nor original, calls for alternative modes of practice research. There are a number of ways in which valid results can be obtained in the absence of laboratory-like conditions and experimental control over variables.

The most obvious alternative is a large study distributed among a variety of service patterns, but few social agencies have a large enough clientele to make this possible. A coordinated approach within a national organization, such as the research under Family Service Association of America auspices by Beck and Jones on services to families,[4] or among independent regional agencies can afford the opportunity to pool samples and integrate research design, measurement, and data analysis. Large samples provide the opportunity to study a range of interventive patterns, which invariably include cases of minimal intervention tantamount to a control group. Such studies also provide an opportunity to apply sophisticated statistical controls which can compensate for the lack of experimental groups.

Research and development models borrowed from the field of engineering, which has long been faced with the need to adapt research methods of the pure sciences, holds promise for studies such as those dealing with home-based services to children. The research and demonstration approach represents a careful blending of process and outcome which is more closely geared to the requirement of evaluating programs of intervention, especially new ones still undergoing development, than are the more classical experimental designs. Research and development research makes close involvement of practice personnel in the research process absolutely necessary. A fully integrated research process would alleviate the problems that arose in the aforementioned study as the result of converging but diverse sets of orientations on the part of researchers and practitioners.

One of the most important requirements for the development of knowledge in practice areas such as home-based services to children is replication and/or cross-validation, which refers to the retesting of hypotheses with different types of populations. The slavish adherence to the 5 percent confidence level in single evaluation studies in and of itself provides little guidance to the policy maker. More important than this statistical significance is the attainment of substantial correlations which explain a good portion of the variance in the same direction in a series of replication and cross-validation studies. Collaboration among several agencies, as suggested above, is the major means for doing replication research.

A third handicap facing this study and other research on home-based services to children is the inability or difficulty in confronting undesirable results. Practitioners have no premium on this type of reaction pattern, but the two groups vary in the specific coping mechanisms they employ. Researchers are more prone to be critical of the research setting and the degree and kind of collaboration extended by practitioners. Desertion of the whole enterprise is not uncommon, nor is flight to greener research pastures. The practitioner, by contrast, has too much invested in the undertaking to abandon it altogether. His or her typical response to undesirable results is denial or criticism of the research philosophy or the method. Such reactions may provide psychological relief, but they do not contribute to the growth of professional knowledge.

A basic reorientation toward the role and function of research is very much needed. Agencies, by virtue of their service mandate, will find it more difficult than research bodies to accept the basic proposition that practice theory is the result of the cumulation of findings within a framework of testable hypotheses. This is a slow process that requires a critical analysis of results and a tolerance of outcome that contradicts study hypotheses.

Disappointment or disagreement with findings is more likely when the study proceeds without a theoretical framework with which to compare results and the parties who joined in the project put all their stakes in successful outcome. Adherence to a theoretical perspective makes it possible to broaden one's view of the enterprise to include not only the attainment of desired results but also the goal of knowledge building which transcends any single research project.

The comparative child care study described at the beginning of this paper was launched without such an explicit theoretical formulation. Given more time to plan the study, it might have been possible to study the three child care programs not only in relation to the methods of service but also within a framework of child socialization or family development. Such an approach, requiring case assignment to facilitate the control of these factors, would have examined the effects of each type of service within the context of other known significant influences.

Research on home-based care to children thus needs a concerted approach by the fields of practice and research. Practice will bring to the undertaking a commitment, generally found in treatment and community organization agencies, to improve services. Research can furnish the skill for objective inquiry and orientation to theory development essential for knowledge building. Home-based services to children and other patterns of child care in our society can scarcely expect to acquire a scientific footing or gain professional recognition as long as they remain outside the mainstream of significant scholarship being generated by such related disciplines as child development and family study.

REFERENCES

1. Wolock, I.; Geismar, L.; Fink, H.; and Dazzo, B.: Unpublished data, 1977.
2. Sherman, Elizabeth et al.: *Service to Children in Their Own Homes*. New York, Child Welfare, 1973.
3. Jones, Mary; Neuman, R.; and Shyne, Ann: *A Second Chance for Families*. New York, Child Welfare, 1976.
4. Beck, Dorothy and Jones, Mary: *Progress on Family Problems*. New York, Family Serv, 1973.

Chapter 29

HOME START WITHIN HEAD START*

ANN O'KEEFE

Introduction

THE Administration for Children, Youth, and Families, formerly the Office of Child Development, bears responsibility for many programs designed to benefit young children. Principal among these programs is Head Start.

In 1972, Home Start was funded as a Head Start demonstration program. Although Head Start has always emphasized the importance of the role of parents in the development of their own children, this emphasis was highlighted in the Home Start program. Based to a large extent upon the prior research and experience of a number of earlier parent-focused child development programs, Home Start was specifically designed to enhance the quality of children's lives by building upon existing family strengths and by emphasizing the role of parents as the first and most important influence in the growth and development of their children. Like Head Start, Home Start primarily served three- to five-year-old children from income-eligible families and had the same basic program components: education, social services, parent involvement, and health services which included physical, dental, and mental health, and nutrition.

Concurrently with the initiation of the Home Start demonstration, the High/Scope Educational Research Foundation of Ypsilanti, Michigan, and Abt Associates of Cambridge, Massachusetts, were contracted to conduct a major Home Start evaluation project running parallel with the demonstration project.

---

*Excerpted from reports of Home Start evaluations, 1972-1976.

The research design, developed by Dr. Esther Kresh, Home Start Evaluation Project Officer for the Administration for Children, Youth, and Families, focused on the effects of Home Start on children and parents. Through overrecruitment it was possible to randomly select families for Home Start and for a non-Home Start control group at each of six research sites. Random selection is vital to the clear interpretation of outcome differences, but it is seldom used in large evaluations of this kind because it is so difficult to carry out.

In addition to outcome data (program effects), the design required collection of data on the home visits (program process), the local project staff and families (inputs), and project budgets.

In general, the evaluation study provided clear evidence of the positive effects of the Home Start experience. Gains of Home Start children on the evaluation measures generally exceeded those of the randomly assigned control group children and were about the same as those of children in the comparison center-based Head Start programs.

This chapter describes the Home Start demonstration program and details some of the specific evaluation findings, during the 1972 to 1975 period. In June 1975, the demonstration entered its dissemination phase, and by 1976 nearly 300 Head Start programs had incorporated the Home Start concept in part or all of their overall program.

1972 to 1975 Home Start Demonstration Project

Home Start is a program for low-income preschool children and their families. It is funded by the Administration for Children, Youth, and Families, Office of Human Development Services, Department of Health, Education and Welfare. Home Start provides Head Start-type comprehensive services in education, social services, parent involvement, and health to low-income families with three- to five-year-old children. This home-based program provides services in the family's home rather than in a center setting.

A unique feature of Home Start is that it builds upon existing family strengths and assists parents in their role as the

first and most important educators of their own children. The
Home Start demonstration has four major objectives, as stated
in the national *Guidelines* of December 1971:

1. to involve parents directly in the educational development
   of their children.
2. to help strengthen parents' capacity for facilitating the
   general development of their own children.
3. to demonstrate methods of delivering comprehensive Head
   Start-type services to children and parents for whom a
   center-based program is not feasible.
4. to determine the relative costs and benefits of center- and
   home-based comprehensive early childhood development
   programs, especially in areas where both types of programs are feasible.

Sixteen programs were funded as part of the Home Start
demonstration study. Each program received approximately
100,000 dollars with which to serve about eighty families for
twelve months. Participating families came from a wide variety
of locales and represented many different ethnic, cultural, and
language backgrounds including white, black, urban, rural,
Appalachian, Eskimo, Native American, migrant, Spanish-
speaking, and Oriental.

The Home Start demonstration staff consisted primarily of
home visitors who visited the homes of enrolled families for
about one hour several times each month. Most programs
planned weekly visits, but cancellations due to illness, weather,
and change in families' or visitors' schedules resulted in an
average rate of visits twice a month. Programs with more frequent visits tended to elicit greater gains in children's development. In addition to working with parents on matters of child
development, the home visitors also addressed social service
needs of the family, as well as a wide range of health needs.
When appropriate, home visitors or other program staff referred families to community agencies for specialized services.

Families enrolled in Home Start also participated in group
activities or meetings on specific topics such as parent effectiveness or health. Each program had a policy-making

council, which included Home Start parents as members.

Home Start Evaluation Overview

The national Home Start evaluation incorporated three distinct components: the formative evaluation, the summative evaluation, and the information system. All three were complementary ways of viewing the effects of Home Start. While all sites participated in the formative evaluation and information system, only six, selected as being representative of the rest of the programs, were involved in the summative evaluation.

The formative evaluation provided basic descriptive information about key aspects of individual Home Start projects. This information was used to give feedback about project implementation and to establish a context for the statistical and analytical findings. Elements of the formative evaluation included project-by-project case studies, observations of home visits, analysis of staff time-use patterns, and development of cost models. Trained interviewers gathered formative data by visiting each of the sixteen projects to interview staff and to review project records. They visited the six summative sites each fall and spring, and visited the remaining ten sites each spring.

The summative evaluation was conducted at six sites and provided information about Home Start's overall effectiveness by measuring changes in parents, primarily mothers, and children. Three features characterized this kind of evaluation in the Home Start program. First, there were before-and-after measurements of parents and child performance along criteria provided in the Home Start *Guidelines*. Measures included the Preschool Inventory; Denver Developmental Screening Test (DDST); Schaefer Behavior Inventory; High/Scope Home Environment Scale; 8 Block Sort Task, which includes a Child Talk Score; a parent interview, child food intake questionnaire; height and weight measures; Pupil Observation Checklist; and Mother Behavior Observation Scale.

Second, there was a randomly assigned, delayed-entry control group who did not enter the Home Start program until after they participated in one complete cycle of fall and spring testing. Outcomes for these control families, who had not yet experienced Home Start, were compared to outcomes for Home Start families who had received full benefits. Control families, who of course volunteered their participation, received a full year of the Home Start program after their control year was completed.

Third, during the 1973-1974 program year, selected comparison data were gathered from children and families enrolled in center-based Head Start programs at four sites. During 1974 to 1975, Head Start programs in the two other summative sites were added to the Head Start center-based comparison group. Thus, comparison could be made involving samples of Home Start, control, and Head Start children, and an examination could be made of the dual hypotheses that Home Start could stimulate gains in children comparable to gains made by children in center-based Head Start programs and that children participating in either Home Start or Head Start would achieve at a higher level than control children who had not been enrolled in a preschool intervention program.

Before-and-after measurements were collected from the six summative sites each October and May, beginning in 1973. Thus, data were obtained at four time points to assess program impact: pretest in fall 1973; in spring 1974 or seven months later; in fall 1974 or one year later; and spring 1975, or twenty months after the pretest. The final phase of the evaluation in 1974-1975 included a comparison of program impact after one or two years of program involvement, as well as a replication study of the seven-month findings.

An information system, designed to gather basic statistics about each of the sixteen programs, formed the third component of the national evaluation. Information was gathered quarterly on family and staff characteristics, services provided to families, and program financial expenditures. These statistics were needed to help local and national staff make better administrative decisions, to assist in the interpretation of summative evaluation outcomes, and to serve as input to the cost-effectiveness analysis of the Home Start program. The necessary information was gathered by local program staff members as part of their routine recording; then the information was summarized into quarterly reports which were sent to national staff.

Highlights of Findings

In general, Home Start evaluation findings provided convincing evidence of the effectiveness of a parent-focused, home-based child development program. Test results of Home Start children were often statistically significantly better than those of the control children and were, for the most part, comparable to the results for Head Start center-based children. Further, there were some favorable parent effects, which contributed to the evaluators' conclusion that Home Start was effective for parents as well as children. For example, in the area of parent-child relationships, the findings showed that Home Start mothers were more likely than control group mothers to encourage their children to help with household tasks. Home Start parents taught more prereading and prewriting skills to their children, provided more books and playthings, and had more positive interactions with their children than did the control group parents.

Compared across groups, costs for a home-based program were about the same as costs for a like number of children in a Head Start center-based program.

At any given time during the three-year demonstration, there were approximately 1,100 families enrolled in the sixteen Home Start projects. Naturally, enrollment varied from time to time, but a typical enrollment picture can be drawn from the October 1974 data of 1,150 families with 1,443 children from age three to five. The average income of the Home Start family was less than 6,000 dollars a year.

At the close of the demonstration there were 195 staff members, 107 of whom were home visitors. The typical Home Start project had a staff of twelve, including seven home visitors; a director; three specialists, including a nurse, a social service or parent involvement coordinator, and either a home visitor supervisor or an educational or child development specialist; and a secretary. The typical home visitor was a thirty-four-year-old woman who had a family of her own. She had completed high school, spent some time in college, and before joining Home Start was employed in a job which in some way related to her work as a home visitor. Each visitor provided services to ten or eleven families.

Based on data from sixteen sites gathered during the three-year period, the cost of Home Start to the federal government was about 1,400 dollars per family per year, or roughly comparable to the cost of center-based programs. About 75 percent of Home Start program budgets were expended on personnel costs, including consultants. Of the remaining 25 percent, typically about 6 percent went to travel, 8 percent to consumables, and 11 percent to space and equipment.

The effectiveness or program outcome assessment comparing Home Start with the randomly selected control group was based largely on a seven-month period from fall 1973 to spring 1974; the control group had begun their Home Start involvement by the time fall 1974 testing and interviewing had begun.

In school readiness, after seven months, the Home Start children had gained significantly more than the control children on three of the four school readiness measures, including the Preschool Inventory which measures children's achievement in skill areas that are commonly regarded as necessary for success in school; the DDST Language Scale which measures children's ability to understand spoken language and to respond verbally; the 8 Block Child Talk Score, measuring how many task-related comments children make while mothers teach them to sort four kinds of blocks; and gains in ability to acquire abstract concepts taught by the mother.

After one year, the Preschool Inventory was the only single school readiness measure to differentiate the groups, but when all four outcomes were analyzed simultaneously using multivariate analysis, a significant difference was found favoring the Home Start children.

With regard to mother-child relationships, the seven-month findings indicated that Home Start mothers when compared with controls were more likely to allow their children to help with household tasks, reported teaching more reading and writing skills to the children, provided more books and playthings, and read stories to the children more often. Home Start mothers were more likely to employ a teaching style involving thought-provoking questions, to engage in a higher rate of verbal interaction in that situation, and to focus their talk around the dimensions of the task.

The findings also showed that Home Start parents reported more involvement in community organizations such as parent-teacher groups, Scouts, and church organizations than control parents. When asked about their use of community resources such as housing authority, job training programs, etc., Home Start mothers reported greater usage of only one out of ten.

After one year of involvement in the program, some of the differences between Home Start and control families diminished. In most cases where the findings changed, it was due to improved performance on the part of the control group since, as noted above, they had entered the Home Start program by fall 1974 testing.

In social and emotional development after seven months, there were no statistically significant differences between Home Start and control children, except on a Task Orientation Scale, which is part of the Schaefer Behavior Inventory. The Task Orientation Scale measures the child's ability to become involved in tasks for extended periods of time. Results favored the Home Start children in this task. However, after a year, Home Start children were rated by their mothers as having greater tolerance as well as higher levels of task orientation, and the tester continued to rate Home Start children as superior to the controls in task orientation.

In physical development, Home Start children had gained statistically more weight after seven months than control children; while this indicated change, it did not indicate improvement in eating patterns. By one year, the differences between Home Start and control children in weight had disappeared, but Home Start children were statistically significantly taller than control children.

For medical care, significant improvements were observed for Home Start children in comparison with control children both after seven months and one year. More Home Start children had seen a physician more recently for preventive reasons, and 89 percent had seen a dentist, compared to only 17 percent of control children. However, there was no difference after either seven or twelve months in the number of basic immunizations children in both groups received; about 10 percent had not yet received all their essential immunizations.

In nutrition, after seven months there was no improvement in total nutrition scores among Home Start children compared to control children. Children's diets appeared to be deficient in calcium, vitamin A, riboflavin, and vitamin C. After one year, the overall quality of diets for both groups continued to be comparable and low in relation to levels commonly recommended by nutritionists. However, intake of citrus fruits was greater among Home Start children.

At the end of the first seven month period, the major differences between the Head Start and Home Start groups were in the areas of nutrition, immunizations, day care, and parental teaching. With regard to the first three, Head Start children fared significantly better on the nutrition food intake measure (due in large part to the fact that center-based children were receiving food daily), had more immunizations, and received day care services (which are usually not necessary for Home Start families). However, Home Start mothers did more "teaching" to their children than did Head Start mothers.

Evaluators' Conclusion

Because so few differences were found between the effects of Home Start and Head Start programs on children or their parents, the evaluators concluded that the two programs can be virtually equally effective.

High/Scope and Abt Associates are conducting a follow-up evaluation of a sample of Home Start children into their early school years. This should be completed in late 1978 and available through the ERIC system.

Recognizing the great need to promote understanding of and quality in home-based programs, six Home Start Training Centers were funded in 1975. In addition to these Centers the Home Start office has developed a wide array of resource materials to assist programs in making decisions about, and planning and implementing home-based programs. This dissemination effort is particularly important in light of the continuing growth of interest in the home-based concept.

BIBLIOGRAPHY

O'Keefe, Ruth Ann: Home Start: Partnership with parents. *Children Today,* 2:12-16, 1973.

U. S. Department of Health, Education and Welfare. Office of Child Development. *Bibliography: Home-Based Child Development Program Resources.* Washington, Gov Print Office, 1973.

U. S. Department of Health, Education and Welfare. Office of Child Development, Office of Human Development. *Directory of Training Programs for Family-Focused Home-Based Child Development Programs.* Washington, Children (1st) First, 1977.

U. S. Department of Health, Education and Welfare. Office of Child Development, Office of Human Development. *Status of the Home-Based Effort Within Head Start.* Washington, Children (1st) First, 1977.

U. S. Department of Health, Education and Welfare. Office of Child Development, Office of Human Development, Early Childhood Research and Evaluation Branch. *National Home Start Evaluation: Final Report. Findings and Implications.* By John Love, Marret Nanta, Craig Coelan, Kathryn Hewett, and Richard Ruopp. Ypsilanti, High/Scope and Cambridge, Abt Associates, 1976.

U. S. Department of Health, Education and Welfare. Office of Human Development Services, Administration for Children, Youth, and Families. Head Start Bureau. *A Guide for Planning and Operating Home-Based Development Programs.* Washington, Gov Print Office, 1974.

Chapter 30

WARM BODIES AND COLD CASH: ESSENTIAL INGREDIENTS FOR HOME-BASED RESEARCH

WILLIAM THEISEN

THIS chapter discusses factors involved in designing research activities for home-based care. Attention is given to the more general problems in trying to include research activities in a service-based setting rather than the technical problems of research design.

A well-designed research project is a commitment to knowledge about our profession; it is an expression of man's intent to improve our social world; it is an opportunity for academic fame and fortune. But as most of us know, research in practice or service-based projects is bedeviled by many obstacles, including theoretical paucity, lack of testable hypotheses, insufficient funding, inadequate staffing, and inappropriate administrative structures.

It seems appropriate to note here that two strong traditions dominate the literature published about research. The first tradition is primarily concerned with how researchers go about building knowledge, a tradition we have come to know as the scientific method. This tradition pays great attention to how we know what we know, and consequently pays attention to the technical aspects of research design.

While most of the reported research in the social sciences is not laboratory-conducted, authors who publish in this tradition typically ignore reporting any of the administrative problems which might have interfered with the project operations. The reader of the research is then left with the impression that if the research design accounts for all of the technical problems of instrumentation, sampling, data analysis, and so on, there will be minimal problems with research during project operations.

Nothing could be further from the truth.[1,2,3] The technical problems and issues in research design, although an important factor in good research and in evaluation, are only a small part of the research process which occurs in a practice-based setting. Researchers confront the same management and supervisory problems as other professionals, and too little research has paid attention to administrative problems of budgeting, staffing, equipment, and facilities.

The second tradition in research literature concerns the measurement of organizational activities and organizational output. Since the late 1960s, social work administrators and practitioners have been under pressure to document, with empirical data, both program efficiency and program effectiveness. Part of the reason for this pressure was the hostility of the Nixon administration toward social welfare programs. Another reason was the inability of social workers to document, with any reliable data, what they were doing or the effects of their activities.

The demand for monitoring, evaluation, and accountability has created the situation where agencies, like it or not, are having to include research activities in their ongoing operations. Specifically, those agencies that rely on federal, state, or local grants to fund operations must have research. While it is not always clear how rigorous the methodology of a research or an evaluation component should be, federal guidelines for evaluation seem to be shifting from the requirement that agencies submit a simple descriptive program narrative to the demand for relatively sophisticated evaluations of agency operations and interventive outcomes.

It is at this juncture that agency or project administrators find themselves in a dilemma. The knowledge-building tradition will have limited value to the agency in assessing short-range operations, particularly in terms of agency plans to request refunding or seek funding increases. At the same time, there is no generally accepted model for evaluating the quantitative or qualitative effects of overall project operations. Thus, administrators need to be exceedingly careful and thoughtful about the type of researcher they employ, and which of the two traditions is most likely to produce a useful report. While the following discussion will not resolve this dilemma, the chapter presents guidelines administrators might find helpful when considering research activities in their setting.

Timeliness

Once the decision is made to include research as part of project operations, one of the first problems or issues an administrator confronts is when to bring a researcher on the staff. In most projects, this is a critical decision. Typically, agency administrators try to raise the money needed to fund the project before worrying about a researcher. If seed money is being used to plan the project and to apply for funds, as well as to underwrite application expenses, there may not be enough money to hire a researcher as part of the initial project staff. If sponsors are not sure they will be funded, they may be especially reluctant to cover expenses for a researcher on a project which may never do more than submit a grant application.

Thus, even with the best of intentions, there is some question from the beginning in most projects about just where and how research will fit into project activities. It is during the early phases, particularly during the grant application process, that service activities are planned. If a researcher is not readily available during the planning of service activities, certain commitments to project structure, service activities, and administrative operations will be made without researcher input. These decisions may later conflict with research goals affecting the research or evaluation process, and even with the conclusions which can be drawn about service operations.

The consequence is that researchers often become involved with the project only after decisions about intake procedures, caseload size, administrative structure, referral sources, and working arrangements with other agencies are already negotiated and complete. Even if a researcher is brought into the project as soon as funding is assured, the lead time for most grants is so short, usually six to eight weeks, that the appearance of the researcher with questions about case assignments, sampling, control groups, and instruments typically leads to project turmoil.

The administrative and service decisions made earlier in the grant application process now need to be reviewed and perhaps revised and, horror of horrors, may even need to be resubmitted to the funding agency for approval of any changes. It is hardly surprising that many practitioners regard proposed interaction with researchers with a certain amount of dismay.

Project Variables

The decision to analyze a service project presents certain methodological problems with those variables which will measure treatment methods, as well as those variables which will measure project operations. The two are not always conceptually or methodologically differentiated, but the issue is critical in terms of what is to be measured.

What is to be measured in a service project is not always clear. We noted earlier that social welfare organizations are being increasingly challenged to document their efficient and effective use of their resources. Traditionally, effectiveness has been defined as the extent to which an organization or program realizes its predetermined goals and objectives. Empirically, however, organizations have been shown to have a multiplicity of goals and objectives — goals and objectives which are responsive to internal and environmental pressures of the moment.[4-7] At the same time, there has been little empirical attention focused on how organizations control who benefits, and who is excluded from organizational services and activities.[8-11] Most programs have limited resources and cannot provide service to every eligible person in the community.[12-18] Although service programs may draw clientele from the general population, the caseloads of these agencies generally comprise only a small segment of the total population.

Another problem measuring project variables is that the program staff tend to take the concept of *client* as a given; that is, it is often assumed that everyone in and out of the agency knows and agrees on the definitions used for the population at risk and the client population.[10,11,19] As noted above, research by social workers and sociologists in suicide prevention, public assistance, medical assistance, and child welfare programs have demonstrated that assumptions about who an agency is serving are indeed risky.

Administrators, practitioners, and researchers need a clear sense of what goals and objectives the project is trying to accomplish, who its project services are aimed at, and which variables are most appropriate for measuring project activities.

Treatment Variables

During the early phases of a service-research project, considerable work needs to be done in selecting appropriate treatment variables for measurement. One of the key problems in treatment research is trying to specify in sufficiently measurable terms the relevant outcomes of a treatment intervention. Treatment literature must be reviewed. Hypotheses, or propositions, need to be formulated. Instruments to measure the selected variables need to be developed, or acquired from other researchers. Sampling and measurement protocols need to be established. These are complex and time-consuming activities and are not always completed before service operations begin.

Reviewing the literature presents special problems, and this section will be limited primarily to the literature and research on in-home care, ignoring the larger body of literature having to do with foster care, residential treatment, and institutional placement. Journals and books are full of material about marriage counseling, marriage therapy, family therapy, conjoint family therapy, behavior therapy, communication therapy, etc. Some of this literature is based on instruments developed by researchers, but other literature is based only on what seems to be a reasonable theory. A typical problem with this literature is the difficulty in establishing which specific interventive treatments will result in specific changes in a client's condition.

A Lagey and Ayres survey in 1963 found that at least 143

communities with a population over 100,000 were delivering some type of service to multiproblem families and their children. The survey also cited some 300 studies on multiproblem families to date, and it seems likely that many hundreds more projects and studies have since been initiated. Yet, as we know, the problem of selecting and measuring relevant treatment and outcome variables remains. It is, of course, highly desirable that the research be designed to provide reasonable empirical documentation that the treatment intervention was responsible for any change in the client's condition. The researcher, then, is responsible for designing the research to eliminate as much as possible alternative hypotheses or explanations of client changes.

Evidence seems to indicate that in-home treatment may be both quantitatively cheaper and a qualitatively superior alternative to institutional treatment. Perhaps the most relevant feature of research on in-home care, or any other type of child care, is to determine the mode or process by which children enter a child welfare system. What kind of children are in the system? What problems do they bring with them? On what basis do social workers decide to refer children for treatment? What are social workers doing which leads to positive or negative effects of treatment?

Three themes in the literature seem most relevant to research on in-home care: the first theme is literature on parental adequacy and care; the second is on parental and family communication patterns; and the third theme is literature on the specific behavior of the "problem" child. While there is some overlap in the content of these themes, each theme has its own theoretical base as well as preferred research methodologies.[20,21]

The parental adequacy and care theme probably is best exemplified in the well-known St. Paul Study.[22] This study used the criteria of "children in clear and present danger," defined as a situation in which the immediate welfare of the child(ren) is so threatened that the community has a clear responsibility to intervene.[23-25] The theme of treating children through family communication patterns is more recent, and the best known work is probably by Virginia Satir in her books, *Conjoint*

Family Therapy[26] and *Peoplemaking.*[27] The emphasis here is on the process changes in the family system in which the child is located. The theoretical expectation which comes out of this theme is that as family communication patterns change and improve, the child's behavior will also change and improve.[28-30]

The third theme is the literature which is primarily concerned with treating the "problem" child.[31-33] The problem child literature can be further subclassified into the categories of disturbed child, delinquent child, and dependent child. The category dependent child is used here to include handicapped children, including those with minimal brain dysfunction, autism, retardation, and physical handicaps.

Researchers, practitioners, and administrators need to remember that no one theme is better than the other, but that the assumptions and research methodologies which flow from these themes are quite different. Thus, we are not suggesting that one theme is preferable to another, but that staff needs to be clear about which theme is being used by the project, so that appropriate variables and their indicators can be selected and measured.

Research Administration

A final issue addressed in this chapter is the problem of administering a research project. Most researchers will encounter the same management and supervisory problems on their projects as other practitioners, including the usual problems concerned with facilities, equipment, budgeting, and personnel. Most researchers, like practitioners, are trained in an academic setting which emphasizes developing the technical skills of research design, sampling, instrumentation, data collection, and report writing. They are not typically trained in management and supervisory skills.

Most research projects have start-up problems with regard to hiring personnel. As noted in a paper by Shyne,[34] it is easier to staff a research project on paper than it is to obtain the "warm bodies." Research projects tend to be time-limited, particularly for funding, and while the sense of excitement and adventure is useful in recruiting the warm bodies, there is a notable lack of job and economic security.

Staffing needs for a research project tend to vary over the life of the project. Certain skills are needed only at certain times to perform specific tasks. For example, specific skills are needed to review the literature and to develop or select appropriate instruments to measure the selected variables. Another set of skills is needed to collect the data. Data organization and analysis may require complex computer operations to store and statistically analyze the data, as well as produce intelligible output. Most of these activities require people who have specialized skills, and it is often difficult to recruit or even train people who can function in two or more activities during different phases of the project.

At the same time, most research projects have some carry-over functions. That is, there may be a need to continue research activity after service operations have ceased, and there is the question of which staff to retain to continue activities such as follow-up client evaluations, data processing, statistical analysis, and report writing. Another question is how long will facilities, equipment, and secretarial staff be needed to complete the final report.

A final caveat needs to address the university-project relationship. Projects which include research are often closely tied to a university. There are many good reasons for this relationship. Personnel, particularly part-time or consultative personnel, are often readily available. Computer facilities and programs are accessible. University professors and students are usually familiar with the research and theoretical literature and may be already involved in their own research.

There is a risk, however, for both parties. Research can be time-consuming, and to the extent that project administrators and university staff ignore the amount of time needed for project activities when negotiating their agreements, they may later encounter severe time problems. While recruiting faculty and students, project administrators need to remember that university schedules may not necessarily match or fit project needs and schedules. Universities have spring breaks, Christmas breaks, and summer schedules, as well as semester exams. Students graduate and professors change jobs. Consequently, a long-term project may find personnel turnover a problem, and the people at the end of a project may know very little about a project's origins. There is a valid and legitimate base for developing university-project relationships, but in an era which emphasizes service accountability and evaluation, these relationships may need to be much more contractual to ensure that a project can meet its research commitments.

REFERENCES

1. Hammond, Philip: *Sociologists at Work*. New York, Basic, 1964.
2. Kuhn, Thomas: *The Structure of Scientific Revolutions*. Chicago, U of Chicago, 1962.
3. Watson, James: *The Double Helix: A Personal Account of the Discovery of DNA*. New York, Atheneum, 1968.
4. Barnard, Chester: *The Functions of the Executive*. Cambridge, Harvard, U Pr, 1938.
5. Braeger, George: Commitment and conflict in a normative organization. *Am Sociol Rev, 34*:482-492, 1969.
6. Perrow, Charles: Analysis of goals in complex organizations. *American Sociol Rev, 26*:854-865, 1961.
7. Yuchtman, E. and Seashore, S. E.: A system resource approach to organizational effectiveness. *Am Sociol Rev, 32*:891-902, 1967.
8. Blau, P. and Scott, W.: *Formal Organizations*. San Francisco, Chandler Pub, 1962.
9. Gouldner, Alvin: The secrets of organizations. In Kramer, R. M. and Specht, H. (Eds.): *Readings in Community Organization Practice*, 2nd ed. Englewood Cliffs, P-H, 1975.
10. Maris, Ronald: The sociology of suicide prevention: Policy implications of differences between suicidal patients and completed suicides. *Social Problems, 17*:132-149, 1969.
11. Purvine, Margaret: *Into and Out of a Child Welfare Network*. Unpublished doctoral dissertation. New York, Columbia University, 1966.
12. Rein, Martin: The social service crisis: The dilemma — Success for the agency or service to the needy. In Gold, H. and Scarpetti, F. R. (Eds.): *Combatting Social Problems*. New York, H R & W, 1967.
13. Piliaven, Irving: Restructuring the provision of social services. *Social Work, 13*:34-41, 1968.
14. Billingsley, Andrew: Bureaucratic and professional orientation patterns in social casework. *Soc Serv Rev, 38*:400-407, 1964.

15. Marris, P. and Rein, M.: *Dilemmas of Social Reform: Poverty and Community Action in the United States.* Chicago, Aldine, 1973.
16. Blau, Peter: Orientation towards clients in a public welfare agency. *Administrative Sci Q, 5*:341-361, 1960.
17. Francis, R. and Stone, R.: *Service and Procedure in Bureaucracy.* Minneapolis, U of Minnesota Pr, 1956.
18. Maniha, J. and Perrow, C.: The reluctant organization and the aggressive environment. *Administrative Sci Q, 10*:238-257, 1965.
19. Lerman, Paul: Evaluative studies of institutions for delinquents: Implications for research and social policy. *Social Work, 13*:55-64, 1968.
20. Hawes, Joseph: *Children in Urban Society: Juvenile Delinquency in 19th Century America.* Fair Lawn, Oxford U Pr, 1971.
21. Geiser, Robert: *The Illusion of Caring: Children in Foster Care.* Boston, Beacon Pr, 1973.
22. Geismar, Ludwig and Ayres, Barbara: *Patterns of Change in Problem Families: A Study of the Social Functioning and Movement of 150 Families Served by the Family Centered Project.* St. Paul, Family Centered Project, 1959.
23. Giovannoni, Jeanne and Billingsley, Andrew: Child neglect among the poor: A study of parental adequacy in families of 3 ethnic groups. *Child Welfare, 49*:196-204, 1970.
24. Goldstein, J.; Freud, Anna; and Solnit, A.: *Beyond the Best Interests of the Child.* Riverside, Free Pr, 1973.
25. Polansky, Norman: Myth and manner in treating the disorganized family. *Children, 15*:201-202, 1968.
26. Satir, Virginia: *Conjoint Family Therapy.* Palo Alto, Sci & Behavior, 1972.
27. Satir, Virginia. *Peoplemaking.* Palo Alto, Sci & Behavior, 1972.
28. Barten, Harvey and Barten, Sybil (Eds.): *Children and Their Parents in Brief Therapy.* New York, Behavioral Pub, 1973.
29. Broderick, Carlfred: Beyond the five conceptual frameworks: A decade of development in family therapy. *J Marriage and the Family, 33*:139-159, 1971.
30. Murrell, Stanley: Family interaction variables and adjustment of non-clinic boys. *Child Dev, 42*:1485-1494, 1971.
31. Johnson, Claudia and Katz, Roger: Using parents as change agents for their children: A review. *J Child Psychol Psychiatry, 14*:181-200, 1973.
32. Mazza, J. and Pumroy, D.: A review of evaluation of behavior modification programs. *Psychol Record, 25*:111-121, 1975.
33. O'Leary, K. and Wilson, G.: *Behavior Therapy: Application and Outcome.* Englewood Cliffs, P H, 1975.
34. Shyne, Ann: Warm bodies and lively minds: Recruiting and retaining research staff. *Social Work, 14*:107-113, 1969.

INDEX

A

Advocacy, family, 84
  home training services, 172
  program description, 177-185
Aid to Families with Dependent Children, 56
American Association of Mental Deficiency, Wisconsin chapter, 168
Assessment
  as intervention, 122
  developmental, 128
  family, 170, 229-230, 289-290, 325-326
  infant, 200-203
  parenting potential, 188-189
  Portage Project, 128-129
  program (see Evaluation)
Association for Jewish Children of Philadelphia, 237-247
  as extended family, 238-239
  population served, 238
  volunteers, 239-247
Attachment, 187, 189, 197

B

Bachelor degree workers, 268, 285
Baseline data, 129, 312-314
Behavior modification, 164, 227, 314
  (see also Social learning theory)
Brainstorming, 258
Burn-out, prevention of, 150, 234

C

Caretaker service, emergency, 108
Case assignment, random, 323-324, 327, 334
Case load
  FIND, 199
  Home and Community Treatment, 234

homebuilders, 248
youth service, 264
Child abuse and neglect, 106, 177-179, 182, 191, 296-297
  management of, 297-298
  personality of abusers, 296
Child care, 46, 47, 53, 56, 58, 59
  techniques, 82
  variations, 328
  (see also Family day care, Family Life Center)
Child care workers, 86, 158
Child Welfare League of America, 14
Childrearing practices, 183, 197
Children at-risk for developmental disabilities, 198, 201-203
Client role, 83, 346-347
Comprehensive Emergency Services (CES), 19, 103-111
  coordination of services, 107
  cost, 111
  description, 107-110
  development, 104-107
  evaluation, 106, 110-111
  philosophy, 105-106
  scope, 103-104
Consultation
  family day care networks, 94-102
  on-site, 103
Continuum of services, 79, 81
Contracts, 222-223, 230, 312
Coordination of services, 105-107, 195-196, 202, 212-214, 222, 287
Cost of service
  comparative, 262, 326
  FIND, 205
  foster care, 16, 224
  home-based service, 15
  Home Start, 339
  Iowa Children's and Family Service, 292
  Lower East Side Family Union, 224

residential, 15, 16, 18
Youth Service, 267
Crisis, definition, 106

D

Day care, 8, 58-59
definition, 91
for protective service families, 304-305
Death
family-centered approach to, 136-144
importance of communication about,
138, 140-142, 143
management of, 136
naturalness of, 136-137
Development (*see* Social policy)
Developmental perspective on child development, 117, 120, 140
Developmental Principle, 64
Developmentally disabled, 64-76, 157-164
case-finding, 197
definition, 157
effects of, 147
parental expectations of, 196-197
prevention, 197-204
programs, home training, 165-174
support services, 69-71, 164
(*see also* FACT; FIND; Home training
services)
Dignity of Risk, 64, 66
Divorce
as changing family form, 51
centers for, 57

E

Early childhood education, 17
(*see also* High/Scope; Home Start; Portage Project; Saturday School)
Economics, 41-43, 47, 55
Education
community-based, 116
public, 43
Educational service, home-based, 133
Emergency services, 108-109, 110
(*see* Family crisis)
Environment
antecedent of pediatric social illness,
178, 179, 183, 184
changes in, 71-72

effects on children, 198
helping potential of, 227
reintegration to, 74, 226
single-parent family, 55
Evaluation
child's progress, 130-131
Family Rating Scale, use of, 316-317
indicators in, 316-319
interviews in, 317
program
Comprehensive Emergency Services,
110-111
FIND, 203-205, 206
High/Scope, 122-123
Home Start, 336-341
Homebuilders, 248
Portage Project, 131-132
Project OPT, 315-324
Saturday School, 151-152, 153
Youth Service, 266-267
random assignment in, 323-324, 329
rating scales, 290-291, 316-317
systematic observation, 316
time orientation of, 313-314, 323
treatment, 322
variables in, 320-322
written reports, use of, 317
(*see also* Research)
Executive Review Committee, 33
Exit criteria, 75

F

FACT (*see* Family and Child Training
program), 157-164
Failure to thrive, 177, 178
FAMILIES, 15, 272-282
community-based approach, 277
description, 275
family relevance in
initiative, 274, 280
involvement, 274
therapists, 278
home as location of treatment, advantages of, 275-277
parenting techniques, use of, 279-280
staff roles, 280-281
team approach of, 277-278
Family

changing needs of, 56-57
definition, 29, 52, 292
disengaged, 286-287
ecological perspective on, 137, 144, 288-289
enmeshed, 287
extended, 93, 159
 agency as, 160, 238
functions of, 5, 136, 186, 298
high-risk, 177, 286-287
importance of in school success, 56, 146
in crisis, 250
in urban society, 212
mental health of, research on, 32
multiproblem, 238, 262-263
nuclear, 53
protective service, 296, 298-299, 301-302
relevance in treatment, 272-282
supports, 216
Family as
center of learning, 21, 137, 143
colleagues in therapy, 254, 278
institution of, 19, 23, 24, 186
unit of service, 20-22, 273, 275, 283, 293, 298
Family Advocacy, 177-185
advocate as facilitator, 180
characteristics of users, 182-183
definition, 179
description of, 179-182
process orientation of, 181
program description, 177-185
time orientation, 179
Family and Child Training program (FACT), 157-164
description of, 158-159, 162
philosophy, 157-158
recreational therapy in, 158, 164
support services, 160-161
Family care worker, 264
Family crisis, 23, 104, 106, 250
Family day care, 91-102
consultants in, 94-102
day care neighbors, 92-102
definition of, 92
development of, 92-93
networks, 92-102
 establishment of, 100-101
 location of, 96-99

partnership with agencies, 94, 98, 102
preventive role, 93
Family forms, 51-52, 56, 60
Family life, as growth, 281
Family Life Center, 296-307
day care in, 304-305
description, 302-305
development of, 299-300
funding, 299-300
isolation of families, 301-302
parenting training, 303, 304-305
purpose, 301
staff as liaison for families, 305
treatment, 303-305
Family policy, 6, 22, 24-25, 32, 56-58
Family programs, federal, 9-10, 30-31, 103, 126, 333
Family resource centers, 59
Family Service Association, 300, 329
Family shelters, 109
Family system, 16, 21, 349
approach, 288, 314
theory, 283
Family therapy, 21, 348-349
definition, 283
home-based, 283-284
process, 272-279
FIND (Follow-Up Intervention for Normal Development), 194-208
case load, 199
costs, 205
counselors, 199-200, 201, 202
description, 196-199
development of, 194-196
evaluation, 203-205, 206
funding, 196, 205
Finer Report, 55-56, 57, 59
Follow-through, 110
Follow-up
evaluation of, 319
services, 194-195
Follow-Up Intervention for Normal Development (see FIND)
Foster care, emergency, 109
Funding, 10, 16
community, 116
FACT, 159
Family Life Center, 299-300
FIND, 205

Home Start, 333, 341
home training services, 172
Homebuilders, 248
Iowa Children's and Family Service, 284-285
Lower East Side Family Union, 213
Portage Project, 126
Project OPT, 311
Saturday School, 147

G

Group care
continuum of, 81
definition of, 81
ecological approach to, 81
family intervention, 82
supportive family service, 79-82
(*see also* Residential services)

H

Handicapped, 10, 64-76, 165
(*see also* Developmentally disabled)
HCT (*see* Home and Community Treatment)
Head Start, 9, 333
Health programs, maternal and child, 22, 31-32
Health visitors, 23
(*see also* Lay health visitors)
High/Scope Parent-to-Parent Model, 115-124
description of, 117, 121-122
home visiting, 121
model, 116
philosophy of, 116
staff, 118-120
training, 118-119, 120-121
Home and Community Treatment (HCT), 225-236, 279
assessment, 229-230
case load, 234
description, 229-232
development of model, 226-229
dissemination, 229, 235-236
parental involvement in, 230-232
parenting course, 228, 235-236
prevention of burn-out, 234

teams, 228, 233-235
time orientation, 230
treatment, 230-232
use of by OPT, 314
Home and Community Treatment (manual), 277
Home-based services
advantages of, 21-22, 250, 328, 348
assumptions, 260-261
costs, 15
definition, 19
differences, 162
educational, 133
effectiveness, 198, 325
family focus of, 272
federal support, 9-10
liaison function, 164, 166, 170, 172, 193
literature of, 348-349
Home-helps, 23
Home Start, 333-342
center-based, comparisons to, 337, 338
control groups, 336-337
cost, 335, 338, 339
description, 335-336
development, 333-334
evaluation, 336-341
home visitors in, 335, 338-339
objectives, 335
Home teacher, 129-130, 132
Home teaching, 148-150
Home training services, 165-174
as advocates, 172
consultants, 166-173
development, 167-169
funding, 172
Home visitor
educational, 119-123, 129-132, 147-153, 158, 161-163, 170-171, 335, 338-339
health, 179-180, 187-191, 201-202
Homebuilders, 15, 248-259
coordination of services, 250
evaluation, 248-249
funding, 248
staff, 250-254
training, 251-258
Homemaker service, 7-8, 19, 59
emergency, 108-109
Lower East Side Family Union, 221

I

Income, adequate, 44-45, 46-47, 54-55
Infancy Early Childhood Program (IEC), 194, 199
In-Home Family Support Service (*see* Iowa Children's and FAMILY Service)
In-home services, 5
(*see* Home-based services)
Infant stimulation, 169, 197
Initial Review Committee, 35
Initial Review Groups, 33-34
Inland Counties Developmental Disabilities Service, 194-195, 198-200, 202-205
Institutional care, 10, 15, 18
cost, 15
(*see also* Residential services)
Institutions
egalitarian, 44
ideology-shaping, 41
political, 40-50
social control of, 13-14
social, economic, 42, 43
Intake, emergency, 108
Intervention
definition, 201
effects of early, 171
group care as, 82
parental involvement in, 198
preschool handicapped, 125
Investigators, principal, 33, 37
Iowa Children's and Family Services, 15, 283-295
bachelor degree workers, 285
client population, 286-287
costs, 292
description of service, 289-290
development of, 284-285
ecological family systems approach, 288-289
evaluation, 290-292
family assessment, 289-290
treatment, 289-290
Isolation
single-parent family, 57, 59
social, 85, 178, 184, 238, 263, 301-302

L

Lay Health Visitor Program, 186-193
assessment, 188-189
coordination of services, 190
description, 188-191
evaluation, 191
home visitors, 189
liaison role, 193
prevention, 193
Learning disabilities, 151
(*see* Developmentally disabled)
Least Restrictive Alternative, principle of, 71-75
Life cycle, in teaching about death, 138-139
Lower East Side Family Union, 211-224
advocate role of, 215
contracts, use of, 222
coordination of services, 214-215
cost, 224
evaluation, 223-224
homemakers, 221
model, 212, 217-223
philosophy, 218
teams, 217-218
training, 222-223

M

Maternal sensitive period, 186
Mental health funding, family, 32
Mentally retarded
definitions, 68
environmental causes, 126
(*see also* Developmentally disabled)
Minority communities, 35, 212, 217-218
Minority scholars, 33, 37
Modeling, 22, 148, 171, 230, 232, 250, 254, 264, 277, 302, 304
Motivation
crisis, role in, 250
family, 85-86
parental, use of, 151
treatment, 272-273
volunteers, 244-245

N

National Advisory Mental Health Council, 34
National Clearinghouse for Home-Based

Services, ix, xi, 5, 12, 77
National Institute of Mental Health (NIMH), 32-38
Natural network central figures (day care neighbors), 92-93, 94-102
Networks, 79, 84, 91-102, 288, 301
  preventive, 93, 102
  recognition, 93
Normalization, 65-66, 164

O

Out-of-home service, 77, 78
  (*see also* Residential service)
Outreach, 110, 169, 187

P

Parent-Child Early Education Program (*see* Saturday School)
Parent-child interactions, 188-189
Parent education
  impact, 198
  in residential service, 85-86
Parent-infant curriculum, 117
Parent training, 158, 303-305
Parental involvement, effect on learning, 127-128
Parenting, abnormal, 187
Parenting skills, 126, 263, 301
Parents as
  coparticipants in life space, 86-87
  equals in services, 116, 118, 123
  partners, 83, 150
  teachers, 126, 130, 133-134, 146, 148-149, 159, 304-305, 334-335
Parents' wages, 45-50
Pediatric social illness, 178-179, 182
Peer review, 33-34
Petition, of neglect, 104, 110, 214
Placement (*see* Residential service)
Policy, social (*see* Social policy)
Politics, definition, 29
Portage Project, 125-135
  assessment, 128-131
  description, 129-130
  evaluation, 131-132
  funding, 126
  parental involvement, 127-128, 132-134

Poverty, 48, 211-212
Prevention, 9
  primary, 20, 177
  use of networks in, 93, 102
Project OPT, 311-324
  baseline data, 312-314
  contracts, use of, 312
  description, 311-315
  evaluation, 315
  family system approach, 314
  teams, 314
Protective services, 104, 107
  families, 298, 301

R

Recreation therapy, 158, 164
Reforms
  reformist, 42, 50
  revolutionary, 42, 46, 49
Replication studies, 130, 330
Research
  administration of, 33, 343-346, 349-351
  agency perspective on, 326-328, 331, 344
  approaches to home-based, 348-349
  control groups in, 327, 329, 334
  Executive Review Committee, 33
  expectations of, 326
  experimental, 326-327, 329
  family, definition of, 29
  funding, 30-38, 344-345
  home-based care, 343-352
  objectives, 347
  peer review, 33-34
  planning for, 345
  principal investigators, role of, 33, 37
  problems of, 328-330, 343-346
  professional judgement in, 329
  reactions to, 331
  replication, 133
  research and demonstration approach to, 330
  researchers' perspective, 327-328, 331
  theoretical framework, 331
  timeliness, 345-346
  value of, 311
  variables, 315, 320-322, 346-349
Residential Assumption, 67-68, 76
Residential services, 68, 72, 76-87, 260-262

costs, 18, 213, 292
descriptions, 68-69
emphasis on, 213
family and community involvement in, 80-81, 83
parent education in, 85-86
prevention of placement, 213, 237, 248-249, 301
problems with, 72-75, 225-226, 261-276
rate of placement, 15
Respite care, 82, 264
Rutgers University Social Work Research Center, 325

S

Saturday School, 145-153
description of program, 147-150
development of, 145-147
evaluation, 151-152
funding, 145
philosophy, 146
Self-help, 57, 212
Separation, 9, 14, 17-18
avoidance, 105-106
distress, 57
Services, support, 19, 58-59, 69-71, 79-82, 84-85, 105-106, 146, 150, 157-159, 205-206, 216, 238, 301
availability of, 188-189
community-based, 116
Shelter, emergency, 109
Single-parent family, 51-60
employment, 53-55, 58
isolation of, 55, 57, 59
provider role in, 54-56, 58
public image of, 51-52, 55, 60
variant perspective on, 58
women as single parents, 51, 54-58
Social change
in family structure, 51
through collective action, 42
Social learning theory, 227, 230-232, 279
Social policy, 177
conventional
history, 40-43
solutions to, 43
egalitarian, 42
initial steps toward, 44-45

parents' wages as a step towards, 45-47
revolutionary, 42, 49-50
work under, 47-48
family, 22, 24, 51
Stress
family, 78, 263
impact, 178-179, 184, 301
Substitute care
decrease in, 110
industry, 78
Support group, parent, 84, 85
Systems approach, 137, 218, 314
Systems Unlimited, 157

T

Taxation, 45
Team approach, 150, 172, 180, 217-218, 228, 277, 314
Time orientation
program, 179, 202-203, 230, 248, 312, 314, 323
research, 349-351
Title I, 168
Title III, 147
Title XX, 10, 16, 153, 159, 248
Training, staff, 119-121, 222-223, 233-234, 246, 251-258, 285-286

U

Unemployment, 43-48
Unraveling Social Policy (book), 47

V

Values, social, 40, 258, 270
Values clarification, 255
Volunteers, 19
in home-based services, 239-247
motivation of, 244-245
need for, 241-242
recruitment, 243-245
training, 246-247

W

Welfare state, 41, 44
White House Conference on Children and

Youth (1909), 14
White House Conference on Families (1979), 5
Wisconsin Association of Home Training Consultants in Developmental Disabilities, 169, 173
Women as single parents, 51, 55, 58
Work
 redefinition of, 47-48
 single-parent families, 54-55, 56, 58

Y

Youth Service, Inc., 260-271

assumptions, 261-262
caseload, 264
characteristics of families, 262-263
cost, 267
description, 263-265
evaluation, 266-267
family care workers, 264
model, 270-271
staffing, 268-269
Title XX, restrictions of in funding, 269
values of, 270